HISTORY OF THE MARATHAS

R.S. CHAURASIA

ATLANTIC
PUBLISHERS & DISTRIBUTORS (P) LTD

Published by

ATLANTIC

PUBLISHERS & DISTRIBUTORS (P) LTD

7/22, Ansari Road, Darya Ganj, New Delhi-110002
Phones : +91-11-40775252, 40775214, 23273880, 23275880
Fax: +91-11-23285873
Web: www.atlanticbooks.com
E-mail: orders@atlanticbooks.com

Printed & bound in India by Atlantic Print Services

FOREWORD

The book, *History of the Marathas* (with special reference to Daulat Rao Sindhia A.D. 1794 to 1827), has a characteristic title and satisfies all the requirements of a good outline of History of the Marathas from 1794 to 1827. The author Dr. R.S. Chaurasia is an experienced teacher of History of long standing. This book is in the series of studies on Indian History dealing with the History of the Marathas for establishing their respective supremacy in India. It is intended to meet the growing demand of research students and general readers interested in the subject.

There is dearth of good books on the last phase of History of the Marathas. Most of the books have been written with a subjective approach and represents only the British point of view.

The approach of this book is objective and is based on the latest researches and the recent advances in the methodology of historical writings. Due emphasis is laid on cultural, religious, social and economic developments and the interaction of the forces generated by these are shown in a balanced manner. This book will give a clear understanding of the various aspects of the subject.

The subject matter of the book is novel and original. In view of the qualities of the book, it is hoped that it will be received with enthusiastic welcome by the students, research scholars as well as general readers.

AMBA PRASAD
Ex. Professor of History,
University of Delhi.

PREFACE

The book, *History of the Marathas*, deals with the crucial period 1794 to 1827, as this period of history paved the way for the ultimate downfall of Maratha Power in India against the British Power.

The rise of the Marathas gave a death blow to the tottering Mughal Empire but the Marathas failed in their bid for supremacy in India against the British Power. The failure of the Maratha Power was the failure of a divided nation and this fact is amply borne out by the ensuing study.

A good deal of research work has been done on history of the Marathas but Daulat Rao Sindhia, who led the Marathas during this period, seems to have escaped the critical eye of serious researchers. His description has been given in detail.

The book covers the last phase of Anglo-Maratha contest for supremacy, touching the history of India for thirty-three years. A brief survey of economic, social and cultural conditions of the period in question has been provided. Military and administrative set up as well as the causes of the downfall of the Maratha Confederacy have been dealt with in a simple and lucid style.

Indian system of Justice, on which Maratha system of Justice was based, has been beautifully compared with the modern judicial set up of India which was based on distorted form of British Judicial system.

I feel highly obliged to late Prof. K.S. Bhatnagar and Dr. B.D. Shukla of Kanpur, who constantly illumined my path and without their help this book might not have seen the light of the day.

I thank all those who have provided me with their rare records and valuable comments. I am specially thankful to Dr. Amba Prasad who is kind enough to write the Foreword to the book.

If this book helps in some measure to "broaden the stream" of our country's history, my labour will be amply rewarded.

R.S. CHAURASIA

Contents

INTRODUCTION

This book deals with the latter phase of Anglo-Maratha struggle for establishing their supremacy in India. Shivaji and Peshwa Baji Rao challenged the supremacy of the Mughal Empire in India, and the Marathas during the regime of Peshwa Balaji Baji Rao succeeded in reaching upto Attock and in imposing some kind of Maratha hegemony or influence over the whole of India. The Marathas were clever diplomats, so they tried to keep the fiction of theoretical traditional supremacy of the Mughal Emperor alive (but to keep real power in their own hands) so as not to antagonize the Muslim masses, but the Third Battle of Panipat gave a severe blow to their designs.

After the Third Battle of Panipat, the British power entered the arena to contend for supremacy in India. By defeating Shuja-uddula, the ruler of Oudh and nominal Wazir of the Empire and Emperor Shah Alam in the battle of Buxar, fought in 1765, the Britishers not only gained control of Bengal and Bihar but also succeeded in making Emperor Shah Alam their prisoner and the Nawab of Oudh a subordinate ally of theirs.

On the other hand, the Marathas recovered very quickly and were able to defeat the Rajputs as well as the Nizam and Haider Ali. After gaining victories over such formidable adversaries, the Marathas directed their attention to North Indian affairs. It was too much for them to tolerate the Mughal Emperor being under British control, so they manoeuvred to bring the Mughal Emperor Shah Alam to Delhi and kept him under the tutelage to utilize his political prestige and theoretical supremacy for their own advantage. The Maratha diplomats guided by Peshwa Madho Rao and later on by Nana Phadnavis and Mahadji, not only succeeded in bringing Shah Alam to Delhi, but, also thwarted the British designs to fish in the troubled waters of Maratha politics.

The Britishers kept mum when the Maratha forces installed Shah Alam on the throne of Delhi, but tried to intervene in

Maratha's domestic troubles, caused by the murder of Peshwa Narain Rao. However, they met with rebuff when a formidable confederacy was formed by Maratha diplomats during the First Maratha War. After it, both the powers prepared themselves for the final contest to gain supremacy in Indian politics. The Britishers increased their prestige and power by defeating Tippu Sultan and the Marathas by getting the control of Delhi and of Mughal Emperor Shah Alam. To utilise the fiction of Mughal Emperor's supremacy and to exercise all real power in the name and under the pretext of Mughal Emperor was a long converted ambition of Maratha diplomats. They succeeded in achieving their aim, when the Peshwa was made Vakil-i-Mutlak and Mahadji Sindhia was made Deputy Vakil-i-Mutlak and the real control of Delhi passed into the hands of Mahadji Sindhia, but he died in 1794.

Many books have been written on Mahadji Sindhia, Nana Phadnavis and the diplomacy of that period. V.V. Joshi's 'Clash of Three Empires', Dr. S.P. Verma's 'A Study in Maratha Diplomacy', Sen's 'Anglo-Maratha Relations' are excellent books of this period. A number of books in English, Hindi and Marathi about this period as well as on different personalities are available but no book on Daulat Rao Sindhia or dealing with the last phase of Anglo-Maratha relations is available. P.C. Gupta has dealt with Baji Rao II and the East India Company, Dr. S.K. Kanungo has dealt with Jaswant Rao Holkar, and Dr. Choksey with the Raja of Satara and with the British diplomacy in the court of the Peshwas. Most of the Marathi writers have confined themselves to the Marathi records and papers available in the Peshwa's Daftar or at Satara, Kohlapur and other places in Maharashtra. The monumental book of Grant Duff, Kincaid and Parasnis and of G.S. Sardesai dealt with the expansion of Maratha empire in detail, but paid little attention to the critical phase of Anglo-Maratha struggle for establishing their supremacy in India, though it was a clash of two social systems, opposite methods of warfare, administrative set up and diplomacy. The Britishers were able to crush the power of the Maratha's in 1818 and succeeded in establishing their unchallenged sovereignty. Perceival Spear says, "The year 1818 marks the beginning of a new phase in the history of British India. The period of internal wars and struggles for supremacy is over."[1] His statement has been contested by others. Historians dealing with the Sikh history point out that Ranjit Singh remained independent and Sikh States continued upto 1848. G.S. Sardesai also ends his 'New History of the Marathas' with the extinction of Satara State in 1848. "When I submitted my *Thesis* the main controversial point was whether the Gwalior State became a fully protected state in 1817 or in 1843? I succeeded in establishing my point that the Sindhian State of Gwalior became a fully protected state only in 1843", and as P.E. Robert states "Gwalior was now (1843) definitely made a protected state.[2]

This view has been corroborated by Dr. R.C. Majumdar and others, the learned authors of *Advanced History of India* on p. 766, and as stated in the *Thesis*. Other, controversial points were the episode of Krishna Kumari and the diplomatic role of the historian Col. Tod who having worked at the court of Sindhia, became aware of inner secrets of Maratha diplomacy, and successfully thwarted the Sindhian conciliatory policy to gain the support of Rajput states. The diplomacy of Col. Tod not only thwarted Maratha designs but also succeeded in making Rajputs states subordinate allies of the East India Company, and in making them accept British suzerainty without a murmur. No Maratha diplomat was able to match the diplomacy of either Col. Tod, Metcalfe or, Malcolm or Elphinstone. Not only that, great historians like Sir Jadu Nath Sarkar, Dr. Raghubir and even G.S. Sardesai relied on the writings of Col. Tod and believed in the concocted stories of Col. Tod of Maratha atrocities and loot. Recently with the discovery of Jaipur treasure it has been established that the Marathas were not able to get even a fragment of the fabulous wealth, which they coveted and the stories of Maratha loot may be considered merely the hyperbolic pictures painted by Col. Tod. Raids of the Marathas on Rajasthan not only brought a bad name to them, but proved a drain on their resources both in men and money. To antagonize, Rajputs against the Marathas and to make them subordinate allies of British Govt., without any opposition, was a great feat of British diplomacy Recently lots of books have been written dealing

1. *Oxford History of India,* edition 1958, p. 574.
2. P.E. Roberts — *History of British India,* p. 331.

with Anglo-Rajput and Maratha-Rajput relations of different states, but they have relied either on records of Rajput states or on British records and ignored the Maratha point of view. Even most of the Marathi writers confined themselves to the records available to them in Maharashtra, and extolled the feats of the pioneers of Maratha expansion upto Mahadji Sindhia and Nana Phadnavis, but did not pay much attention to the last phase of Maratha confederacy in the North, and consequently have not gone deep to bring into light Sikh-Maratha relations or Maratha-Nepal relation or relations of Mughal Emperor Shah Alam and Daulat Rao Sindhia. Maratha relations with Jat States, with Oudh and other states were too minor affairs in eyes of the Maratha historians residing in Maharashtra, to divert them to a serious study. Actually these relations counted much, when Baiza Bai hatched a plot and Nana Sahib, Tantia Tope, Rani Laxmi Bai of Jhansi and the Nawab of Banda, descendants of Peshwa Baji Rao revolted in their last bid to challenge the British supremacy in alliance with Bahadur Shah Zafar, Begum of Oudh and others and got shelter in such a manner that the Britishers, were not able to trace either Nana Sahib or Begum of Oudh. The last diplomatic flicker of chitpawan genius came to meet British diplomacy, when Tilak, Gokhale and others rose to oppose the mighty sway of British imperialism, and a greater personality of Mahatma Gandhi, who was well versed both in British and Maratha diplomacy forced Britishers to quit India. Thus, the Anglo-Maratha contest for supremacy was a continuous struggle, which ended, when Mahatma Gandhi come on the forefront and succeeded in gaining mass support against British Imperialism. To deal with all this is beyond the scope of this book, and as my *Thesis* was confined to a limited period of 1794 to 1827 *i.e.*, the period of Daulat Rao Sindhia, I have touched upon these in the introduction to pave the way for new researchers on these aspects.

There is a controversy or difference of opinion among the historians as to whether any period of Indian history can be called the period of Maratha Paramountcy. This controversy is due to the fact that while most of the Empires in India began with a single conquering head, the Maratha Power began with the Maratha Peshwa, the agent of the leader, who became the effective ruler, and revolution proceeded even to the point of division. British historians are of the opinion that no period of Indian history can be called as a period of Maratha Paramountcy. The same view has been propounded by Sir Jadu Nath Sarkar. He states "By the treaty of Sarji Arjungoan, the Padshah of Delhi became a British subject. It is not true that this treaty merely transferred to the British Government is a general status of Sindhia in the political framework of the Mughal Empire.[3] He concludes: "Thus the treaty of Sarji Arjungoan, (30th Dec. 1803) marks 'the true end' of the Mughal empire as a political institution." He forgets that the Mughal emperor Shah Alam was under Maratha control. Practically all his authority was exercised by Sindhias, who utilised the fiction of Mughal Emperor's, superiority, as it was advantageous to do so and this fiction was continued upto the time the Britishers felt strong enough to do away with the fiction. Tradition dies hard and even Britishers had to face Mutiny in 1857, when it came to knowledge of the general public that the Britishers desired to wipe out that fiction. Both the Mughal Emperor and the Peshwa rose in revolt and the Britishers were able to establish their unchallenged supremacy and paramountcy only when they were able to crush the mutiny of 1857.

Thus, a plausible conclusion can be drawn that after the death of Aurangzeb, his successors retained nominal sovereignty. In the first phase, his Nobles like Zulfikar Ali Khan, Sayyid brothers, Khan Dauran and Safdar Zang wielded authority with the support of the Marathas and later on Marathas themselves began to exercise this authority. The Nobles of the Mughal court and rulers like Najibuddulla realized that with the supremacy of the Marathas in the Mughal court, their own power was at stake, and called Ahmad Shah Abdali to halt this process. Ahmad Shah Abdali with the support of Shujauddulla and Najibuddulla and Bangash Nawabs of Farrukhabad, and others was able to defeat the Maratha forces in 1761, but he failed to stop the process. The Marathas were able to establish their authority again at Delhi by bringing back the Mughal Emperor Shah Alam to Delhi from Allahabad, where he was living as a British Pensioner. After many ups and downs and

3. J.N. Sarkar : *Fall of the Mughal Empire*, Vol. 4, p. 335.

after a short eclipse, Mahadji Sindhia succeeded in gaining not only control of Delhi but began to demand and realise tributes in the name of the Mughal Emperor. This state of affairs continued even during the time of his successor, Daulat Rao Sindhia upto 1802. Lord Lake defeated the Sindhian forces at Delhi as well as at Laswari and the control of Delhi passed to the Britishers. Thus Sir Jadu Nath Sarkar considers 1802, as the date of extinction of Mughal sovereignty and its replacement by British paramountcy. Sir Jadu Nath Sarkar ignores the Maratha supremacy, and accepts 1802 as the year of establishment of British Paramountcy while Percival Spear and most other historians push it to 1818, *i.e.*, when Peshwa Baji Rao and the forces of Bhonsle and Holkar were defeated. Others argue that the date can be pushed to 1843, *i.e.*, when Gwalior was reduced to the status of a protected state, while others push it to 1848 *i.e.* when the State of Satara was confiscated.

The most controversial point is whether any period of Indian History can be considered as the period of Maratha Paramountcy in the sense, we consider the period of Mauryas or of Guptas or of Mughals or of Britishers. My contention is that the Marathas were never able to achieve that distinction, but those who argue that there was no period of Maratha Paramountcy forget that the Maratha Empire was far larger than the Empire of Harsha, or of Iltutamish or of Balban or of Babar or of Humayun, but in Indian history we call period of 1206 to 1526 as the Sultan Period, though probably except Allauddin Khalji, nobody was able to exercise such extensive authority as the Marathas were able to exercise. Even in Mughal Empire unchallenged authority was exercised only by Akbar, Jahangir and Shah Jahan. Both Muhamad Tughlaq and Aurangzeb had to face continual revolts, challenging their sway. Even Britishers were able to exercise undisputed paramountcy only from 1857 to 1947, *i.e.,* only for 90 years but British historians begin the British period from 1740. The same procedure has been followed by Maratha historians who begin Maratha history from Shahji Bhonsale and end it with the extinction of Satara State in 1848, but, period means when a power may be the dominating power and in that sense Marathas were dominating power from 1707 to 1818, and this period may be considered as the period of Maratha paramountcy, though some historians argue the period of Maratha paramountcy can be considered to have begun with the advent of Shivaji and end with the extinction of Satara state, which represented the last symbol of Maratha paramountcy. This is the view of the extremist school of thought, representing the ideas of those who confine themselves only to the history of the Maratha. P. Spear states, "The Marathas rather than the Persians or Afghans were the successors of the Mughals as the holder of Imperial powers.... They controlled the larger part of India than anyone else."[4] The same view has been supported by the Editors of *Vidya Bhawan* series in the book : Maratha Paramountcy, so the period of 1707 to 1818 may be considered as the period of Maratha Paramountcy.

Sources

Before we proceed with the actual study of our subject, it is necessary to analyse the various sources in order to assess their comparative merit as the basis of our study :

1. Principal general books : For the history of the Marathas, there is the monumental work of Grant Duff's, *History of the Marathas*, which gives a bird's eye view of general survey of the Marathas, but the author has confined himself only to political history. However for primary knowledge the book is very useful.

2. Another book which deals with the general history of the Marathas is *History of the Maratha People*, written by Kincaid and Parasnis, which also gives a broad picture of the activities of the Marathas.

3. *New History of the Marathas* written by G.S. Sardesai, represents the Maratha point of view about the general happenings connected with the Marathas, but the writer has confined himself to political history and has paid more attention to the affairs of the South than to North Indian affairs.

All the above mentioned books are important for the student of general history of the Marathas, but for a researcher dealing with North Indian affairs and with Socio-Economic details, these histories are inadequate thus he has to depend on principal contemporary chronicles.

---

4. P. Spear & Others : *Oxford History of India*, p. 492, ed. 1958.

So for as the principal contemporary sources in Marathi, Persian and French are concerned, I have given a brief details about them in the Bibliography, but I may throw light on the principal contemporary chronicles available in English and Hindi.

1. After the first Anglo-Maratha War, *i.e.*, after 1782, Residents were appointed by the British Government in the courts of the Peshwas, Sindhias, Bhonsles, Gaikwars and others. These Residents were shrewd observers and their letters supply not only the minutest details but also inside picture as well as secret consultations and motives of the British actions. These papers are very useful for researchers and excel contemporary Marathi and Persian records in every respect. The Poona Residency Correspondence has been edited mainly by Sir J.N. Sarkar and G.S. Sardesai, but some volumes have been edited by Prof. N.B. Roy and Dr. Raghubir Singh and others. Most of the important papers have been published in these volumes, but a researcher must consult also unpublished letters connected with his research.

2. Malcolm was a contemporary British Officer who himself played a very important part during the period with which this *Thesis* is concerned. As an Ambassador at Sindhia's court, he succeeded in injecting Munshi Kamal Nain, through whom he diverted the crisis which would have been caused, if all the Marathas had faced the Britishers unitedly. He made the treaty with Baji Rao also. In January 1818, he was given military and political charge of Central India. During this period he prepared the record about the general conditions of Central India, dealing with all the states of Central India, including Malwa. This record was published under the title *A Memoir of Central India including Malwa* in two volumes. This record gives a fairly good picture of socio-economic conditions and of general conditions in detail. He also wrote political History. Both the books written by him as well as Kaye's *Life of Malcolm* and B.G. Sharma's unpublished Thesis on Malcolm, available in Agra University, are very useful for the researchers of this period.

3. Broughton's book *Letters written from a Maratha Camp* available with illustrations provides a fascinating picture of Daulat Rao Sindhia's camp and of his private life. The author has described all happenings in detail, and even translated the

songs sung in the camp and the festivals celebrated there. The book is fascinating and interesting, and has been relied upon by many writers, as Broughton was an eye-witness to all the happenings, but he presents a partial view and paints Daulat Rao Sindhia in the blackest colour, which is supported neither by contemporary Marathi nor by Persian records, nor by the observations of other British contemporary officers. This book is a kind of satire on Daulat Rao Sindhia and his court, so it should be utilized by a researcher with caution, so far as description of political happenings and opinions about leading court personalities are concerned.

4. Col. Tod is considered as a great historian and he is considered as an Authority on Rajput History. He is a contemporary figure as he worked at Sindhia's court under many Residents, and succeeded in gaining the secrets of Maratha diplomacy, by which they used to control Rajput states. On account of his expert knowledge, he was transferred as a Resident to deal with the Rajput states. His mission was to win over the Rajputs to the British side, as during the Second Maratha War, there was apprehension that a Rajput, Maratha, Jat and Sikh combination may thwart British expansion. The Maratha diplomats spread a rumour that the Marathas were satisfied with the tributes, but the Britishers might bring about complete extinction of Rajput states. Rajput Rajas did not take part in the Second Maratha war, but the Britishers were defeated in the Jat territory of Bharatpur and Col. Monson was defeated at Mukund Dara pass in the Rajput territory. Jaswant Rao Holkar even approached Ranjit Singh to gain Sikh alliance. But due to efforts of Malcolm, plans of united opposition by the Marathas and on account of Metcalfe, plans of Marathas-Sikh alliance were frustrated. But to cause a breach between the Rajputs and the Marathas was a hard nut to crack. This task was entrusted to Col. Tod. In order to achieve this, he showered praise on Rajputs and concocted stories of Maratha atrocities.

Sunk in luxury and living in ivory towers, the Rajput Rajas fell an easy prey to Col. Tod's diplomacy, and accepted British paramountcy without a murmur. The stories of Maratha atrocites concocted by Col. Tod are corroborated neither by Marathi records nor by contemporary persian records, and even British diplomats did not rely on them. About the episode of Krishna

Kumari, C.T. Metcalfe gave a conflicting report to Governor General Minto which in spite of the deceptive lyricism of Col. Tod, seemed to me more reliable.[5] Similarly, Malcolm states the "Bheels from their mountains and the Rajputs and others from their strongholds (which were multiplied by fortifying villages) not only resisted but retaliated upon the Marathas by laying waste their lands."[6] He further states "Ambaji Ingaliah...was kind and considerate to the inhabitants."[7] After the Second Maratha War, under the terms of treaty of Sarji Arjan-Gaon, Daulat Rao had to give up his rights of tribute from Rajputs, but the British diplomacy of that time did not succeed in enticing the Rajputs, so they gave back the rights to the Marathas. It was a great diplomatic feat of Col. Tod to entangle Rajputs in the British diplomatic net, and for this he painted a hyperbolic picture of Maratha atrocities. Col. Tod's literary presentation, his vivid lyricism enticed our historians to put reliance on Col. Tod, without taking care to ascertain the truth by examining Marathi records, such as Gulgule Daftar, etc. or Persian records, or even the records of contemporary British diplomats. Hence I discarded the views of eminent historians based on the works of Col. Tod, and drew my own conclusions.

Selections from the works of G.W. Forrest, Martin Montgomery, Gurwood, Charles Ross and S.J. Owen give a reliable picture of the period and are very useful to a serious researcher. Private Diary of Hastings, 'Memoirs of Lord Teignmoth' and of James Skinner, 'Memoirs of Amir Khan' are very useful. For general history, Warring's 'History of the Marathas', Hope J.'s 'House of Sindhia', Tone's 'illustration of some institutions of the Maratha people' are also useful, for general outlook Mill's *History of British India* in 15 Vols., Thornton's *History of British India* in 5 Vols. and Wilks' *History of Mysore*, Crompton's *European Adventurers in Hindustan*, Keene and Prinsep's *History*, also present a fairly good picture from the British point of view.

But I have relied more on secret Foreign Political Papers and other Papers at National Archives, Delhi, and on the records

---

5. E.R.C., XIV, No. 30 Letter dt. 10-8-1810. Metcalfe to Minto, F.N. p. 153.
6. C.I.I., pp. 126-27, ed. 1970.
7. *Ibid.*, F.N. p. 129.

of Gwalior and Poona, etc., which helped me to solve many doubtful problems. I also consulted unpublished theses of Dr. B.N. Mehta's 'Sir George Barlow in India', Dr. E.G. Sharma's 'Sir John Malcolm in Madhya Bharat', Dr. P.C. Mehta's 'Relations between Mewar and the Marathas' preserved at Agra University Library, and found them very useful.

It will be a tedious task to mention all the writers and the Persian, Hindi and Marathi records, which were available to me in abundance. I may state, therefore, that I tried to make use of all the records listed in the Bibliography. I also made use of recent publications and reflected on their views.

As a researcher, I had to face the greatest difficulty in drawing a socio-economic picture of the period and saying something about the dynasties, which became extinct without leaving historical records. Therefore, I had to rely on the books and records locally available to me at Chanderi, Shivpuri, Gwalior and other places, dealing with the incorporation of minor states into Sindhia's dominions.

Sen's book, dealing with the administrative system of the Marathas and the Military system of the Marathas, are excellent studies, but they confined themselves to Poona Government, without dealing in detail with the north. P.R.C., Malcom's political history, selections from S.J. Owen and Gurwood, etc. helped me a lot. French sources had to be consulted as De Boigne, De Perron and Bourounquin were the generals, who commanded Sindhia's forces. Marathi records are scattered about different Maratha Generals and I had to face great hardship in utilising them.

I had to face a lot of hardship in depicting the socio-economic conditions as Marathi records did not describe them in historical perspective, but Malcolm, Broughton, Court poets' poems and records preserved by the houses of some Jagirdars helped me a lot in my work.

Judicial system of the Marathas has been praised by Tone, Coolbrooke, Kincaid, Parasnis and Grant Duff, etc. Grant Duff states : "We preserved the Panchayat system of the Marathas, as there can be no better judicial system which can be introduced in Maharashtra." The Maratha system of justice was quick and cheap and the peasantry did obtain a fair medium of justice through that system. Many books on the judicial system of the Marathas are available but from the research point of view these are inadequate. So far as the economic side is concerned, I have to say while the Britishers utilized their resources for development of trade, industry and other capitalistic enterprises, and for scientific development, the Maratha states used to utilise their resources for giving feasts to Brahmins and for holding ceremonies. Consequently, the Maratha states were no match for the East India Company, either in economic stability or in capitalistic enterprise or in scientific advancement, and this inferiority paved the way for their downfall.

For Sikh-Maratha relations I had to rely on Dr. Hari Ram Gupta, Cunnigham and other writers; and for Sindhia-Nepal manoeuvres, on P.R.C. and the books and articles written about them. About Shah Alam I consulted Persian, Marathi and English records, but I had to give only glimpse in my book, as space, scope, and purpose of my thesis were limited.

Achievements of the Marathas

1. The greatest achievement of the Marathas was that they gave a death blow to the tottering Mughal Empire, and utilized the fiction of Mughal Emperor's supremacy to establish their own rule, in such a manner that the Delhi kingdom to a great extent became a Maratha province.

2. The Marathas succeeded in controlling a larger part of India for a longer period than any one else, after the fall of the Mughal Empire and before the establishment of British Paramountcy.

3. The Marathas perfected the art of guerilla warfare and succeeded in utilizing it when Mughal power was at its zenith. The art of guerilla warfare was successfully utilized by Arthur Wellesley (who later on became the Duke of Wellington) against Napoleon Bonaparte in the Spanish War. Probably during the French rule over Indo-China, the Vietnamese also became aware of it and utilized it against U.S.A. Thus, the Maratha art of guerilla warfare made its impact all over the world.

4. The Marathas produced a glaxy of women rulers who have been rarely surpassed in the annals of mankind, and that too in India and at a period, when social prejudice against the fair sex was at its height. The Maratha History begins with

women, *e.g.*, with Jija Bai and ends with Laxmi Bai, the Rani of Jhansi.

Tarabai, Ahayla Bai, Baija Bai and Laxmi Bai are some of the prominent figures that adorn annals of the Marathas. Of lesser importance are Tulsi Bai Holkar, Maina Bai, Rajas Bai, Gopika Bai and Mastani.

5. Lastly, these were the Marathas who had tried to halt the march of British imperialism and continued their struggle in spite of many ups and downs for a long time. It is true that they failed against the British power; but they failed only when the British power was at its zenith and even Napoleon failed against the British might. Moreover, in my opinion the failure of the Marathas was the failure of a divided nation and of a society which failed to adjust itself to changing times.

Most of the conclusions that have arrived at in this book have not been changed, as both Prof. K.S. Bhatnagar and Dr. B.D. Shukla, who helped me in writing this book, have passed away. I refrained from changing the conclusions arrived after much discussion with them. To draw the conclusions, I tried to consult as many books as could be made available to me, and I tried to be objective and impartial. Sometimes, it happens that an author unconsciously draws subjective conclusions, as he is influenced by his own environment. The same might have happened in my case also, but I have tried to be as objective and impartial in my approaches as was humanly possible for me.

1

EARLY LIFE OF DAULAT RAO SINDHIA

Rise of the Marathas

The Maratha country and its people have enjoyed a fairly clear identity in India's history at least since the sixth century A.D., when Varamihira, the great astronomer of the Gupta age, first mentioned "Maharashtra" as the name of the region occupied by the "Marathas" since corrupted into 'Maharathas' or 'Marathas'. Yuan-Chwang visited Pulkesin II's court about that time and wrote about Maharashtra and its people. "The inhabitants are proud-spirited and warlike, grateful for favours and revengeful for wrongs, self-sacrificing towards suppliants in distress and sanguinary to death with any who treated them insultingly."

India fell progressively under Muslim rule from the end of the 12th century. When it reached the South, the Vijaynagar Empire was established to halt its extension to the peninsula and Maharashtra was a part of that empire. Even after its downfall in 1565, many indigenous chiefships survived in the region as semi-independent principalities, owing allegiance to the local Muslim Kingdoms. During the reign of Aurangzeb, however, after much of the region had passed under Mughal rule, the burden of the alien yoke became unbearable to the Marathas, as it threatened the annihilation of Hindu religion and culture.

The teachings of Gyaneshwar and Namdev in the 13th and the 14th centuries, and Ekanath and Tukaram in the 15th and 16th centuries, supplied the spiritual inspiration for a Maratha revival, the political aim of which was to unite the Marathas into a militant nation.[1] They soon became a dominating factor in Indian History with the advent of Shivaji. He gave a political

1. Ranade, *Rise of the Maratha Power.*

shape and form to the hitherto unorganised movement for freedom from Muslim rule. Even Shambhaji, his unworthy and incompetent successor, chose a martyr's death rather than compromise national independence. Raja Ram, the second son of Shivaji, and after his death, his widow, Tarabai, faced heavy odds, but emerged successful against the mighty Mughal Empire.

Rise of the Peshwas

When the Marathas could not be subdued by force of arms, the Mughal tried to create factions among them, and to achieve their purpose they released Sahu, the grandson of Shivaji and son of Shambhaji. This fomented internal disturbance but, in the end, Sahu emerged triumphant. However, owing to his love of ease, and sloth, power passed to Balaji Vishwanath, his Peshwa, and the latter's lieutenants — the Sindhias, the Holkars and the Bhonsles of later history.[2] Balaji Vishwanath's son, Baji Rao I, who followed the maxim : 'Strike at the trunk, and the branches must fall of themselves,' proved himself a worthy military heir to Shivaji by his tact, energy, and generalship, he extended the Maratha Empire from the South to the North. Had he remained alive for a few years more, the course of Maratha history would have been different, but he died in 1740 at an early age, exhausted by military exertions and family discords. In Maratha history, he stands next to Shivaji.

His son Balaji Baji Rao did not prove equally competent, but during his regime the Maratha Empire reached the zenith of its glory. The Third Battle of Panipat, however, gave a shattering blow to the Maratha Empire and the centripetal force, that had so far kept the Maratha Confederacy together under the Peshwas, weakened considerably. The Sindhia, the Holkar, the Bhonsle, and the Gaikwar families, now became more independent of the Peshwas and came to the forefront in Maratha affairs.

Rise of Sindhia and Holkar

Bajirao I himself had contributed greatly to the prominence of the Sindhia and the Holkar families. The founder of the Sindhia family was Ranoji Sindhia, Patel or Headman of the village of Kuneirkher.[3] It is said that he begin his career as a

2. Sardesai, *New History of the Marathas,* Vol. I, II, III and H.N. Sinha, *Rise of the Peshwas and Dighe : Baji Rao I.*

3. Grant Duff, *History of the Marathas,* Vol. I, p. 212.

slipper bearer of the Peshwa, Baji Rao I,[4] who later conferred on him the Jagir of Ujjain in Malwa. After his death, his youngest son, Mahadji Sindhia, succeeded him, and in course of time came to dominate the history of North India in the last quarter of the eighteenth century.

The Holkar was also originally a family of shepherd's belonging to the village of Hole or Hull about 20 Kms from Poona.[5] One, Malhar Rao Holkar, entered the service of Baji Rao I[6], and by dint of his tact and ability succeeded in forging to the forefront and establishing his power on a firm footing. He died in 1766, and since there were no surviving male heirs, his son Khande Rao's widow, Ahalyabai, became regent of the Holkar state and ruled with conspicuous wisdom at Indore. She adopted Tukoji, a faithful and brave soldier, as her successor. During the regime of Mahadji Sindhia, a clash occurred between him and Tukoji in which the latter's force were routed at Lakheri on 1st June 1793.[7] In spite of this defeat, however, Holkar maintained his rank as next only to Sindhia in power and influence among the Maratha chiefs. Rule of Ahlya Bai is still praised.

The Bhonsles of Nagpur and the Gaikwads of Baroda

Two other chiefs — the Bhonsles of Nagpur and the Gaikwads of Baroda — originally shared the leadership of the Maratha Confederacy with the Peshwas. The Bhonsles were near relations of Shahu, who first raised them to riches and power. They overran Bengal and Bihar in Alivardi Khan's time, but played no part in the battle of Panipat nor in the First Anglo-Maratha War, and so they gradually sank to a secondary position in the Maratha Confederacy. The *Gaikawads of Baroda,* originally dependents of the Pant Pratinidhi, Dabhade, in Shahu's time, and unpopular at the Peshwa's court owing to Dabhade's quarrel with Baji Rao I, had since overrun nearly the whole of Gujarat. They entered into a treaty with the East India Company during

4. Maratha Manuscripts and Sir John Malcolm's Report on Malwa quoted by Duff *Ibid.* footnote : *C.I. Memoir* 1, p. 116.
5. Grant Duff, *History of the Marathas,* Vol. I, p. 212.
6. Malcolm's *Memoirs of Central India,* Vol. I, p. 143, 3rd. ed. 1832.
7. Sarkar, *Fall of the Mughal Empire,* Vol. IV, pp. 92-96. Holkarkaif, 64 No. (ii) 241, Sardesai. N.H.M. (iii), pp. 243-49.

the First Anglo-Maratha War and remained loyal to it ever since, thereby, confining themselves, so to speak to the backwaters of Maratha politics thereafter.

Other States

Two Rajput States, Dhar and Dewas, established by the Pawars and included within the framework of the Maratha power; played no significant role in Maratha History.[8] There was also the satellite Muslim family of Banda, where the grandson of Baji Rao I by Mastani, named Ali Bahadur, ruled. At Jhansi and Sagar, officers appointed by the Peshwa ruled and collected tributes from the petty Rajas of Bundelkhand, in their respective spheres.

Rise of the Sindhias

The power and prestige of the Sindhia family, with which this *Thesis* is concerned, was based upon the part played in Maratha affairs mainly by Mahadji's political and military exploits. Mahadji made good his succession to the gaddi despite the opposition of the Peshwa down to December 1767, and the troubles created for him by the members of his own family. In May, 1766, Malhar Rao Holkar died and his death paved the way for a further increase in the power of Mahadji. By December, 1767, he was secure in his saddle, as Madho Rao I, the Peshwa was kind to him. After that one success followed another and within a few years, Mahadji became the most powerful Maratha chief. He persuaded the Mughal Emperor Shah Alam II, then living as a client of the East India Company at Allahabad, to accompany him to be proclaimed Emperor at Delhi. On 6th January, 1772, the Emperor's forces defeated Zabita Khan, the Rohilla leader, with the aid of Sindhia, who was now rewarded with the position of Deputy (Deputy Vicegerent) of the Emperor, which Sadashiva Rao Bhau had lost by the disaster of Panipat.

On November 18, 1772, Peshwa Madho Rao I, the greatest and ablest of the later Peshwas, died and his death proved no less fatal to the Marathas than the disaster of Panipat.[9] Narain

---

8. Malcolm, *Political History of India,* C.I. Vol. 1, 3rd ed. 1832 Ch. IV, pp. 97-115.
9. Grant Duff, *History of the Marathas,* Vol. I, p. 352 (The Plains of Panipat were not more fatal to the Maratha Empire than the early end of this excellent prince).

Rao became the next Peshwa, but he was soon murdered by the Guards at the instigation of his uncle Raghunath Rao.[10] Raghunath Rao was not proclaimed Peshwa, but soon Ganga Bai the widow of Narain Rao, gave birth to a posthumous child and the Maratha nobles proclaimed the child Peshwa. Being foiled in his evil designs, Raghunath Rao entered into an alliance with the East India Company to get the Peshwaship and took arms against his own countrymen.

The First Anglo-Maratha war followed, as this domestic quarrel among the Marathas gave a chance to the diplomats of the East India Company to sow the seeds of discord in the Maratha confederacy. The Gaikwar separated himself from the Maratha confederacy and the Bonsle was bribed[11] by the East India Company to stand aside. However, the treaty of Salbai, which ended the War, recognised Mahadji Sindhia as an independent ruler, and a mediator between the East India Company and Mysore.

The First Maratha War was proved fatal to the Marathas, as it exposed the weakness of the loose Maratha Confederacy, heralded the advent of the East India Company in the internal politics of the Marathas and lastly led to the appointment of British Residents at the courts of the Sindhia and the Peshwa, who, by their diplomacy, wove a spider's web of intrigue at these courts and ultimately brought out the downfall of the Maratha empire.

Lastly, Mahadji Sindhia fell under the spell of Western military organisation and pinned his faith to the adoption of western methods of warfare which, as many critics aver, being foreign to the military genius of the Marathas, became a serious handicap to them in their wars against the Company.

Meanwhile, the prestige acquired by Mahadji at Salbai was further enhanced by his strengthening his position at the Emperor's court at Delhi against local intrigues. He occupied

---

10. Basu, *Rise of the Christian Power in Indian States* [it is said that he wrote an order for 'Dhuru' (catch) but his wife Anandi Bai changed the word to Marvo-(kill)].

11. R.D. Banerji, *History of Orissa*, Vol. II. *Cambridge History of India*, Vol. V, pp. 263-69 ed. 1929, Forest Selections from the State papers in the Foreign Deptt. II, p. 707.

Agra and Mathura in 1785 and practically added these places to his own dominions. The Rajput Chiefs combined and defeated him at Lalsot in 1787, and his Governor at Delhi was driven out of the Imperial capital shortly after. But three years later he defeated the Rajas of Jaipur and Jodhpur separately and captured Ajmer. Next year, he negotiated an agreement with Afghanistan under which the Sutlej was recognised as the boundary between the Afghan and Maratha spheres of influence. In 1793, he defeated the Holkar at Lakheri. Having securely entrenched himself in the North, he proceeded to Poona to secure a similar position of eminence at the Peshwas' Court but unfortunately died in 1794, before he could accomplish his object.

"He was the nominal slave but the rigid master of the unfortunate Emperor Shah Alam; the pretended friend but designing rival of the house of the Holkar; the professed inferior in all matters of form but the real superior and oppressor of the Rajput provinces of Central India; and proclaimed soldier but actual plunderer of the family of the Peshwa."[12] According to Sir J.N. Sarkar, "In the ashes of his funeral pyre outside Poona, perished also the hope of a Maratha Empire in Hindustan, but the grouping of powers on the political chess board in Europe and India concealed this fact for ten years."[13] In the words of Sardesai, "He towers over Maratha history in solitary grandeur as a ruler of India, without an ally, without a party."[14] Keen says, "He was an Indian ruler of successful capacity in times of exceptional difficulty."[15] He was the most successful of Maratha leaders.[16] Kincaid and Parasnis write, "that Mahadji Sindhia was a great man, none can deny,"[17] In his life, he had two main objects : one to found a kingdom, the other to prepare for the contest with the English.[18] The one man who could keep

12. Malcolm, A *Memoir of Central India*, Vol. 1, p. 122, 3rd Ed. 1832, Peter-Auber, *Rise and Progress of the British Power in India*, Vol. II, p. 275.
13. Sarkar, *Fall of the Mughal Empire*, Vol. IV, p. 132.
14. Sardesai, *New History of the Marathas*, Vol. Ill, p. 269.
15. Keene, *Mahadji Sindhia*, p. 192.
16. Malcolm, *A Memoir of Central India*, Vol. I, p. 125.
17. Kincaid & Parasnis, *A History of the Maratha People*, Vol. III, Ed. 1925, p. 168.
18. Malleson, *The Native States of India*, p. 145.

order in Hindustan was now dead.[19] The only man capable of restoring order was Sindhia.[20]

In spite of these tributes, we must not forget that Mahadji's reign, like that of Shahjahan, was the afternoon of the Maratha Empire, bright in splendeour but bearing also the message of the advance of the evening also. According to R.D. Banerji and Dr. Sen, his employment of foreign adventurers in his army without any secure lever on their loyalty was a blunder and his successor had to pay the price. The loss of national character by the Maratha Army proved suicidal. His introduction of more north Indian soldiers in it was also a mistake. His levying of chauth on and Rajas and with the Rajputs gave a death blow to the already half-dead idea of a Hindu Pad-Padshahi.[21]

According to Kincaid and Parasnis Mahadji's "conduct after the peace of Salbai was not in the interest of the Poona Government. He had no desires save for his own advancement."[22] In the words of Dr. S.P. Verma, "Mahadji never seems to have understood the danger to the home provinces fully.... Mahadji took a long time, and Nana still longer, to realise the magnitude of the English designs and the assiduity by which they were to push them on."[23]

His policy of appeasement of the East India Company and agreement to have residents at his court proved fatal to the Maratha Empire. He was over-ambitious and cared for his own advantage only and thereby weakened the Maratha Confederacy.

He did not establish any administrative system which might give permanency to his rule and prosperity to his kingdom. He failed to make his kingdom compact and left semi-independent feudal chiefs like the Khichy Raja of Ragho Garh, the Raja of Narwar and Raja of Chanderi and others as potential centres of intrigue in his kingdom.

---

19. Feasting, 175, quoted by Dr. H.R. Gupta, *History of the Sikhs*, p. 247, ed. 1944.
20. Keene's *Hindustan Under Free Lances*, 42.
21. R.D. Banerji, *History of Orissa*, Vol. II, p. 265 and Dr. Sen, *Administrative System of the Maratha*, also *Military System of the Maratha* for detail.
22. Kincaid & Parasnis, Vol. III, p. 168.
23. Dr. S.P. Verma, *Anglo-Maratha Relations 1772-1783*, p. 406.

He spun a masterly spider's web of policy by his alliance with the Mughal Emperor, by declaring himself the Deputy Vakil Mutlaq to the Peshwa, by adopting a policy of non-intervention with the British Power, by imposing tributes on Rajput Rulers, by creating internal feuds among Marathas and by tolerating the existence of semi-independent Sardars. It required a master-mind like Bismarck to handle the situation, but no man of his calibre appeared on the scene after his death to keep his power intact and to place an effective curb on the rising British power.

He never changed his capital from Ujjain though it was far off from the Punjab. However, it is to be remembered that he did not get any breathing time to consolidate his rule owing to constant wars. Yet in Maratha history, he ranks amongst the stalwarts like Shivaji, Baji Rao I and Madhav Rao, and had no equal amongst his contemporaries. If he had succeeded in his objective at Poona, "One Maratha would have had in his hands all the power from the Ganga and Indus to the frontiers of the Carnatic and Mysore : touching the complete (British) frontier on the whole line, and possessing the means of attacking it, where he should think proper."[24] Malcolm concurs by writing that he wielded "greater, if not consolidated, power than any prince had attained since the death of Aurangzeb."[25]

State of the Maratha Confederacy in 1794

Daulat Rao Sindhia inherited all the powers and realms of Mahadji Sindhia without any dispute, after the latter's death in 1794, but being a lad of 14 years, he did not naturally command the prestige that Mahadji had enjoyed either in Maratha politics or in wider diplomacy. Ahalyabai was still the ruler of the Holkar State, and her forces were under the command of Tukoji Holkar. Sawai Madho Rao Narain II was the Peshwa and head of the Maratha confederacy but all the affairs were conducted by his Minister Nana Phadnavis, who was practically the ruler at Poona. Raghoji Bhonsle II was the ruler of Nagpur and his sway extended from Berar to Orissa, but, as stated earlier, he was no participant in the main stream of Maratha affairs. The

---

24. Owen, *Selections from Wells's Despatches Wide his Introduction*, pp. 20-21. India Under Wellesley by P.E. Roberts, pp. 32, ed. 1961.
25. Malcolm, *Political History of India*, Vol. I, p. 127.

Gaikwads of Baroda professed nominal allegiance to the Peshwa, but always helped the East India Company against the Marathas. The Raja of Satara was still called Chhatrapati, but his power was insignificant.

Daulat Rao Sindhia's Heritage

Mahadji Sindhia bequeathed a splendid legacy to his grandnephew and successor, Daulat Rao Sindhia. Two-thirds of the province of Malwa and some of the finest districts of the Deccan were directly ruled by him, while he exercised virtual sovereignty over the country from the Sutlej to Agra, holding the Mughal Emperor, Shah Alam, in tutelage. Towards the close of his life, he was about to gain control over Poona also. This was the heritage that came to Daulat Rao Sindhia when he was only fourteen years of age.[26] This splendid domain was, however, not a bed of roses but a thicket of thorns. Daulat Rao had to exercise the authority of the Mughal Emperor as the individual Vakil-a-Mutlak's Deputy (*i.e.,* the Peshwa) and of Baji Rao II, by making him his puppet. He had to face formidable opponents. Like Akbar, however, he was not fortunate enough to have a single servant as faithful as Bairam Khan, who might steer the ship of state through these troubled waters. He had to face single-handed Nana Phadnavis, who has been called the Chitpawan Machiavelli, and a cunning person like Baji Rao II.

On the battle-field, he had to face Wellington, who later on defeated Napoleon, Lord Wellesley, one of the greatest English rulers of India, and administrators and diplomats like Malcolm, Close, Palmar, Tod, Munroo, Elphinstone, Matcalfe, Malet and the like, Lord Lake, a veteran who possessed wide experience of war, and Jaswant Rao Holkar, the greatest Indian General of his age and master of guerilla warfare. The Rajputs and the Sikhs, the foremost martial races of India, were hostile to him. Bhonsle, Shah Alam, Begum Samru, and his own generals like De Perron, Lakhwa, Dada, Ambaji Ingale, Munshi Kamal Nain, nay, more than this, his own adoptive mothers worked against him. It would have needed a man of superhuman will power and ability to overcome all these difficulties successfully.

---

26. N.B. Roy : Introduction to *Poona Residency Correspondence,* Vol. II, *Daulat Rao Sindhia and his North-Indian Affairs.*

The legacy that Daulat Rao Sindhia received included the distracted Empire of Delhi, unsatisfied Rajput tributaries internal feuds among the Marathas themselves, semi-independent chiefs like Ambaji Ingale and Lakhwa Dada, treacherous generals like De Boigne and De Perron, discontented and ambitious Bais. There was no compact and orderly government even in Malwa. Near the capital of Mahadji, the Rajas of Khichi, Chanderi and Narwar were semi-independent and the Jat ruler of Gohad was still half-crushed.

Geographically, Daulat Rao Sindhia inherited an Empire from the Gulf of Cambay to the Sutlej and from the Kumaon Hills to the Ganga, including the Suba of Delhi, Ajmer, part of Allahabad, Broach, Ahmednagar, the strong fort of Asirgarh and some of the finest portions of Gujarat and of the Peshwas dominion, bringing a revenue of 4 or 5 crores. He had 70 battalions of sepoys.

According to Sardesai Vol. III, p. 273, he inherited the Emperor's Estates and

Ghulam Qadir's		2 crores 25	lakhs
Rana of Gohad's territory worth		42	lakhs
Bhadawar, Kachwah and Bhunder		18	lakhs
	Total	2 crores 85	lakhs
Cash in rupees and Jewellery etc. from Rana of Gohad		32	lakhs
Mirza Shafi Khan		33	lakhs
Afrasab Khan		40	lakhs
Jhangir Khan		4	lakhs
Naryandas		3	lakhs
Mohamed Beg Handani		6	lakhs
Sikh Admn. Th. Ranjit Singh Jat		12	lakhs
Raja of Jaynagar twice		85	lakhs
Administration of Patiala		6	lakhs
Datia and Bhadawar		8	lakhs
Imperial Lands		3	lakhs
Pratap Singh of Machedi		4	lakhs
Ghulam Qadir Khan		60	lakhs
	Total	296	lakhs

Relations with the East India Company and Other States

Apparently, Mahadji's relations with the East India Company were cordial as Warren Hastings trusted him, but actually the position was far from satisfactory. Mahadji demanded tribute from the East India Company that had been promised to the Mughal Emperor by the treaty of Allahabad, but Macpherson, who was the Governor-General at that time, bluntly refused to pay amount[27], as we shall see later on. Similarly, Sir John Shore was hostile to Mahadji. He wrote on the latter's death to Resident Malet : "In Sindhia's character, the ruling principle was ambition[28]...the Company has little reason to regret his death."[29] The power of Mahadji Sindhia made the East India Company jealous, since he became an eye sore to the British Government. By the treaty of Salbai, Mahadji was recognised as an arbitrator between the English and the Marathas and thus his independent status was implicitly acknowledged by the British Government.[30] A British Resident was appointed by the East India Company to represent it at his court. The ambiguous language of the treaty of Salbai however gave rise to confusion later on. On the occasion of the Second Maratha War, the main argument on behalf of Daulat Rao Sindhia was that, according to the treaty of Salbai, he ought to have been consulted first before the Company entered into any dealings with the Peshwa.

Relations with the Other Maratha States

No love was lost between Mahadji Sindhia and Nana Phadnavis. It goes to the credit of Daulat Rao Sindhia that he immediately appeased the Peshwa Madho Rao Narain by his courtesy and tactful behaviour. But hereditary mutual suspicions could not be removed at one stroke and only a temporary reconciliation could be effected. The members of Daulat Rao Sindhia's family were against Nana Phadnavis and the widows of Mahadji brought about the downfall of Aba Chitnis, the supporter of the Nana at Sindhia's Court, and the succession

---

27. *Cambridge History of India*, Vol. V, p. 364 ed. 1929 and Malcolm, C.I., *A Memoir of Central India*, Vol. I, pp. 89-91.
28. *Poona Residency Correspondence*, Vol. VII, p. 269 later dated 7-4-1794.
29. *Ibid.*, I, pp. 399-400 No. 289.
30. Treaty and Malcolm, *Central India Memoir*, Vol. I, ed. III, p. 192.

of Balloba Pagnis as minister. The policy of Balloba Pagnis accentuated the smouldering enmity between the Sindhia and Nana Phadnavis, and during the regime of Daulat Rao Sindhia, it reached its climax.

The *Gaikwar* also coveted the possessions of Sindhia in Gujarat, and so the Sindhias and the Gaikwar's were at daggers drawn. The relations of the Sindhia family with the Bhonsles of Nagpur were not satisfactory in the beginning, but Daulat Rao Sindhia contrived to improve them later on, and they both fought against the East India Company during the Second Maratha War.

Relations with the Muslim Powers

The Mughal Emperor, Shah Alam II, was the nominal ruler of the whole of India, but he was really a puppet in the hands of Mahadji Sindhia and remained as such upto 1802, during the regime of Daulat Rao Sindhia also.

Relations between the Nizam and the Maratha powers as a whole were not satisfactory, particularly with the Sindhia family. Tipu and the Maratha powers never acted in co-operation, but relations between the Sindhia family and Tipu were not so bad. Lord Wellesley always dreaded Daulat Rao Sindhia's co-operation with Tipu.[31]

Oudh was under the domination of the East India Company. Sir John Shore had appointed Saadat Ali Khan as Nawab of Oudh, setting aside the real successor Wazir Ali, who was the son of Nawab Asaf Udaulla. Daulat Rao Sindhia's relations with Wazir Ali had been cordial and accordingly officers of the East India Company accused him of intriguing with Wazir Ali through Ambaji.[32] His relations with Bhopal State were good and the rulers of Bhopal used to get robes of honour from the Sindhia regularly.

Relations with the Rajputs

The Rajput states of Rajasthan were subservient to the Marathas. Mahadji Sindhia realised tributes from the

31. *History of Mysore* by Walks, Vol. II, p. 324.
32. *Journal of Indian History*, Vol. XLIII, Part I, April, 1965 p. 287 Article by Dr. Nandlal Chatterji, Wazir Ali's Plans against the Company's Power, pp. 285 to 291.

leading states of Rajasthan such as Jaipur, Jodhpur, Udaipur, Kotah, Boondi, Rupnagar, Jaisalmer and Bikaner. In the words of Dr. H.R. Gupta, "most of these states were under Maratha domination; and they were looking for an opportunity to throw off their yoke."[33]

Relations with the Jats and the Sikhs

The State of Bharatpur was an apple of discord as a balancing factor between Sindhia, Holkar and the East India Company, but relations of Daulat Rao Sindhia with the Bharatpur state were satisfactory.[34]

The Ruler of Gohad was an enemy of Sindhia family because Gwalior was conquered by Mahadji Sindhia from the Ruler of Gohad.

Relations of Mahadji Sindhia with the Jat ruler of Mursan and Hathras were cordial and remained so during the regime of Daulat Rao Sindhia.

Mahadji Sindhia ruled the Punjab on behalf of the Emperor and the Sikh Sardars and Rajas of the Cis-Sutlej region paid tributes to him, because he had been Deputy Vakil-i-Mutlak of the Emperor since 1785.[35]

Problems facing Daulat Rao Sindhia

Thus, the position of Daulat Rao Sindhia on his accession to Mahadji's gaddi was far from enviable. He had inherited a weak and invertebrate empire. His position was comparable to that of a man standing on a volcano apparently extinct but smouldering internally. Daulat Rao, if he wanted to survive, had to check the expansion of the British Empire in India, to secure the Maratha Empire by checking internal feuds within the Maratha Confederacy, to reconcile the turbulent chiefs, and to conciliate or crush the feudatory nobles and semi-independent states. He had to conserve his financial resources and to place the empire on a sound and stable basis. Good Government and administration called for his immediate attention. But he

---

33. Dr. H.R. Gupta, *History of the Sikhs*, p. 9 ed. 1944 and for details : *Annals and Antiquities of Rajasthan*, Ojha, Rajasthan and Dr. Raghubir Singh, Rajasthan.
34. Dr. H.R. Gupta, *History of the Sikhs*, ed. 1944, p. 9.
35. Dr. H.R. Gupta, p. 170.

was still an immature youth, surrounded by astute Maratha and British diplomats. The widows of Mahadji Sindhia were opposed to his installation. Thus, shackled tight by heavy odds he addressed himself to the task ahead.

EARLY LIFE OF DAULAT RAO SINDHIA

He was born in 1780, the year in which his contemporary Ranjit Singh was born. Ranoji, the founder of the greatness of the Sindhia family, had two sons by a Rajput lady, named Chimabai, Mahadji and Tukoji. Daulat Rao was the grandson of Tukoji and son of Anand Rao and Maina Bai daughter of Yesaji Angria of Kolaba.[36] Anand Rao was the favourite nephew of Mahadji, who, out of affection for him, adopted the former's son, Daulat Rao, as his heir. There is some controversy about the age at which Daulat Rao succeeded to the gaddi. According to Grant Duff, he was only 15 years old at the time of his accession.[37] *The Imperial Gazetteer* accepts Grant Duff's view, but Marshman and Malcolm speak of him as a lad of 13 at his accession.

Broughton in his book *Letters Witten in a Maratha Camp* has written: "He is turned of 30" in 1809.[38] N.B. Roy states "that he was yet only 15 at the time of his accession."[39] According to Major Basu, "he was in the 15th year when he became master of the vast territory of Mahadji."[40] According to Sunderlal, he was 23 years old in 1803 *i.e.* during the Second Maratha War.[41] Peter Auber speaks of him as fourteen years of age.[42] The British Resident at Poona wrote that "Daulat Rao Sindhia, 14 years of age, was to arrive from Tuljapur."[43] S.M. Edwardes writes, a thirteen-year old nephew, Daulat Rao, succeeded to the possessions of Mahadji." Sardesai also states that he was

36. M.M., I, p. 131 & Sardesai, *New History of the Marathas*, III, p. 264.
37. Duff, *History of the Marathas*, 1, p. 505.
38. Broughton Thomas D., *Letters Written in a Maratha Camp*, p. 38 ed. 1813.
39. N.B. Roy, Introduction to Vol. II of *Poona Residency Correspondence*.
40. Basu, *Rise of the Christian Power in India*. p. 286.
41. Sunder Lal, *Bharat Men Angrezi Rajya*, p. 663 ed. 1938 and p. 445 ed. July 1960.
42. On p. 140 and of 13 years on p. 281.
43. *Poona Residency Correspondence* , Vol. I, No. 287, p. 398 Mallet from Poona to Shore.

born in 1780.[44] Resident Malet also states : "I apprehended Daulat Rao to be about 14 years of age, of a short stature but ingenuous countenance and discreet department with a general character of prudence beyond his years, nor does he seem wanting in that degree of bodily health and vigour requisite to an active life." It is not possible to give the exact date of the birth of Daulat Rao Sindhia, as we have no authentic supporting records. On the basis of available information, we can therefore conclude that he was between 13 and 15 years of age at the time of his accession in 1794.

His Childhood

Daulat Rao Sindhia passed his childhood in luxury and was taught horsemanship, swordsmanship and hunting. He gave proofs of intelligence even during his childhood. Mahadji, a shrewd judge of men was so impressed by the behaviour of this promising boy that on several occasions before his death, he declared that he would make Daulat Rao his successor.[45] Grant Duff however, writes that "the ceremony of adoption had not actually taken place, but Mahadji had repeatedly declared Daulat Rao his heir, although Laxmi Bai opposed Daulat Rao's succession. Her objections were overruled, as even Nana Phadnavis approved of it. Tukoji Holkar was one of the first to acknowledge Daulat Rao.[46]

During his childhood, he came in contact with Muslim Officers, Rajput Chieftains, and foreign generals. He came under the spell more of Muslim culture than of Maratha culture. Amir Mohammad son of Shah Nizam Uddin, became his constant companion and played a notable part in moulding his character. "If evil company ever ruined a man, it did young Sindhia."[47] Malcolm concurs that these were "the counsellors who betrayed and corrupted his youth...(he) is personally of a good disposition."[48] Undesirable contacts early developed certain evil habits in him, such as spending his time in vain pursuits.

44. Cambridge V, p. 367 ed. 1929.

45. Sardesai, *New History of the Marathas*, III, p. 264.

46. Duff, *History of the Marathas*, Vol. I, p. 595.

47. Choksey, *A History of British Diplomacy at the Court of the Peshwas*. p. 129.

48. Malcolm, *Political History of India*. C.I., *A Memoir of Central India*. Vol. I, p. 141.

He was fond of personal ornaments and even when he grew old, he used to wear a necklace of pearls and so came to be called "Moti Wala." His mother, Maina Bai, generally used to live at Ujjain, the capital of Mahadji Sindhia but sometimes she used to accompany her husband Anand Rao with his son Daulat Rao on the former's tours. In this way Daulat Rao also became accustomed to camp life from the very beginning.

Among the members of his family, Mahadji showed the greatest affection for Daulat Rao and his influence on the young boy was profound though the latter was too young to learn anything of his great uncle's wisdom and political sagacity. The impact of the Muslim and Rajput companions, with whom he passed the most impressionable years of his life, however, was supreme. Born and educated far from the Deccan, he cared more for show than for the reality and was unable to cloak his designs under a diplomatic cover. Instead of calling himself a mere 'Patel' as Mahadji did, he assumed the grandiloquent title of Ali Jah Bahadur, Daulat Rao Sindhia.

Living generally in the north, he became addicted to luxury and indolence. The luxurious habits of Muslim nobles had already gained a firm foothold among Maratha princes ever since the days of Shambhaji and they profoundly affected Daulat Rao also. He learnt kite-flying and such other frivolous past-times in his early childhood and even when he came of age, he did not give up such past-times. He used to celebrate Moharrum with great enthusiasm. "On the celebration of the Shabe-Burrat Sindhia directed Rs. 5000 to be distributed among the *pagas*."[49] All these things show that the impact of Islam on Daulat Rao Sindhia was considerable. The bitterest critic of the

49. Broughton has given a very fascinating description of the festival of Moharrum. "The Maharaja himself even goes into the ridiculous custom; he is a future during the whole of he Moharram." He further says: "At the Darbar, the other day, he was dressed entirely in green, the mourning of the Musliman, with no other ornament, then eight or nine strings of beautiful emeralds round his neck on this garb, accompanied by a few of his confidential servants, he roams about at nigh and visits Tazias through the camp. In a similar manner Broughton speaks, of his kite-flying" The season for flying paper-kites being now come in, the Maharaj is to be seen every evening attended by large bodies of cavalry employed to keep the ground, partaking of this princely diversion, pp. 60, 70 and 140.

Marathas. Dr. Choksey, writes about Daulat Rao : "A tiger or a pretty face, an elephant fight or even a supply of paper-kites has each sufficient attraction to divert his charging and restore him to his wanted thoughtlessness and good humour." He further writes "Virgin charms were diligently sought for and almost daily sacrificed at the alter of his lust; woman and low company were his bane and appear to have quite corrupted a heart and mind originally meant for better things." This was Daulat Rao, successor to the proud achievements of Mahadji Sindhia.[50] Dr. Choksey goes even a step further and states, "If character is density, nowhere was the truth brought home more forcibly than in case of Baji Rao and Daulat Rao Sindhia."[51]

After the death of Mahadji Sindhia, his widows Laxmi Bai, Yamuna Bai, Bhagirathi Bai and above all Kesra Bai, a morganatic wife of Mahadji, who was remarkable for her intelligence and good sense, urged Daulat Rao to give up low and frivolous amusements like hunting a kite-flying and to conduct himself in a manner worthy of his ancestry. In the initial four years of his region, the influence of the widows had some effect on him, but later on he came under the influence of his court advisors, like Sarji Rao and his bad habits revived.

Daulat Rao Sindhia had no experience of war and adversity, such as his predecessor Mahadji had to face in 1763, when he had to wander alone in the streets of Poona. He succeeded to the throne when he was completely ignorant of the rough and tumble of life and age had not given him any chance to develop sterner qualities.

"Cradled in luxury, called upon to assume the burdens of ruler at a tender age, he had no opportunity for developing the rough hardihood and spirit of enterprise which characterised his predecessor." But though void of military experience, he was not dull and unimaginative, he ably handled delicate negotiations even in his teens, and held his own against the astute diplomats of Poona."

50. Broughton Thomas D., *Letters written in a Maratha Camp*, p. 177.

51. Choksey, *A History of British Diplomacy at the Court of the Peshwas*, pp. 132-33.

Education and Environment

Daulat Rao Sindhia does not seem to have received much education. He was acquainted with reading and writing and fully understood Marathi and Hindustani, but during his childhood, he remained interested more in games and sports than in reading and writing. But he was not entirely devoid of literary taste, as Broughton has testified.

Daulat Rao was married to Durga Bai at the early age of about 11 years. Later on, he was married to Rukma Bai at the age of about 13 years. He married Baiza Bai after his enthronement.

Mahadji Sindhia died on 12th February, 1794 at 8 p.m., at the age of 67. After his death, the Sardars assembled and agreed to recognise Daulat Rao Sindhia as his successor.[52] He was at Tuljapur at that time, and was at once called to assume the reins of government.[53] On the 25th February, 1794, the Peshwa invited Daulat Rao and presented him with a Khilat.[54] Both Nana Phadnavis and the Peshwas Madho Rao Narain II condoled with him warmly and Daulat Rao made a suitable response.

Formal investiture by the Peshwa was done in a public Durbar on the 3rd March, 1794, though, according to Sardesai, this was done after some hitch on 10th May, 1794. It is interesting to note that none of the important Maratha Chiefs or the surviving members of the Sindhia family ventured to disregard the wishes of the dead king.

The ceremony of Daulat Rao's formal adoption took place in April (1794) and he was officially installed as successor on 10th May, 1794.[55] All the ministers of Mahadji swore fidelity to each other and to Daulat Rao.[56] Letters in his name were despatched to the officers of the provinces, forts, districts and to those commanding armies, to give them every assurance of the support and protection from Daulat Rao that they had enjoyed under their later master.

52. Foreign Political Index 1974, Sub Heading Resident with Sindhia, pp. 379-85.
53. *Ibid.*, p. 329.
54. *Poona Residency Correspondence*, Vol. II, p. 329, No. 215.
55. Sardesai, *New History of the Marathas*, Vol. III, p. 263.
56. *Poona Residency Correspondence*. II, No. 215, p. 321.

An 'Arzee' was also despatched to the King and letters to Shah Nizamuddin in Daulat Rao's name, soliciting a continuation in his person of the titles and honours enjoyed by his adoptive father.[57] Apparently, Daulat Rao Sindhia had inherited the throne peacefully, but it was an oily surface on troubled waters.

At the time of the death of Mahadji Sindhia, the Poona Darbar faced many problems. Holkhar, crushed by the armies of Sindhia, was endeavouring under Tukoji to collect tribute in North-Western Gujarat. In the North, there was constant dread of an invasion by Zaman Shah the ambitious successor of Abdali to the throne and fortunes of Kabul. Any such invasion would not only affect the countries on both banks of the Indus but even the dominions of Daulat Rao were exposed to it. The Nizam was trying to evade payment of Chauth by hook or by crook and the Poona Darbar sought the aid of Sindhia against him. Ali Bahadur was busy collecting tribute for himself in Bundelkhand. The Poona Court had to deal with a disputed succession to Kolaba on the death of the ruling Angria and the piratical depredations on the Malabar Coast of the Raja of Kolhapur. Furthermore, there was the irresponsible Ismail Khan smarting under a sense of defeat. The Rajputs were ready to seize any opportunity to efface their recent defeat. The most troublesome people in tackling whom (Mahadji) Sindhia had the greatest difficulty to experience were the Sikhs. "They had defied Mahadji by making marauding in-roads into the Mughal dominions, which Daulat Rao was bound to protect." There is hardly any necessity to mention the miserable shadow of the house of Timur consigned to blindness in a palace at Delhi. The Resident wrote : "It is fair to presume that new life will be given to the designs of Tooko Ji Holkar.... Nor can we suppose that Northern Rajas and Chieftains, nay the blind King himself, perhaps struggle to gratify the natural impulse of emancipation; in the pursuit of which recourse will be industrially to arms and intrigues and as Shah Alam has the credit of being a considerable adept in the latter."[58]

The death of Mahadji was sure to cause, as Malet wrote, "deep individual concern and regret at the loss of so great and

---

57. *Poona Residency Correspondence*, Vol. 1, No. 280, p. 398.

58. *Ibid.*, Vol. I, No. 288. C.W. Malet to G.G. Shore, p. 399.

so eminent servant of the State." Yet, Malet was of the opinion that it was a matter of doubt "whether on consideration of political convenience the Government of Poona would be much grieved by the removal of the member of the empire whose power, claims and pretensions were in some degree irksome and obnoxious. Circumstances had considerably changed and the Poona administration found itself as arbiters of the hopes and fortune of Mahadji's successor." The Patel's death at Poona placed his successor completely within the influence of the paramount power, and all the more so, when Daulat Rao's claims were far from indisputable. The death of Mahadji had also removed from the path of Nizam Ali of the Deccan "the author and executor of the most dangerous designs against the Independence of his state and power of his family".

Sir John Shore openly stated that if his delineation of Sindhia's character was just "the company had little reason to regret his death."[59] Thus, to every power Maratha, Rajput, British and Muslim, the death of Sindhia was a welcome relief and all these powers tried to take advantage of the immaturity of Daulat Rao Sindhia.

Thus, at his accession, Daulat Rao found dark clouds hovering over the political sky with no trace of a silver lining to relieve it.

---

59. *Life of Lord Teignmouth*, Vol. I, p. 318.

2

INTERNAL CONDITIONS OF SINDHIA DOMINIONS

With the approval and good wishes of the leading men in his own state and many of the contemporary rulers, Daalao had a smooth succession to the gaddi. This promised a successful reign but the sequel proved otherwise. It is proposed to probe in this chapter into the domestic conditions of Daulat Rao Sindhia's dominions at the time of his accession.

In the dominions that he inherited, he exercised only a vague territorial jurisdiction over Delhi, the Panipat Haryana region of the Punjab, the Upper Ganga-Yamuna Doab, Kol (Aligarh) and Agra as Deputy Vicegerent of the Mughal Emperor. He had a right only to tributes from the major Rajputana States. In Bundelkhand, he had ample opportunities to profit by the mutual quarrels of the almost fifty descendants of Chatrasal Bundela: only in Malwa, Gohad and Gwalior did he enjoy full *de jure* and *de facto* authority although there, too, the presence of numerous feudal chiefs and Pindari Sardars considerably disputed his authority.

The most troublesome people, in tackling whom even Mahadji Sindhia had to experience the greatest difficulty, were the Sikhs.[1] Cis-Sutlej Punjab was under a number of refractory chiefs, who lived largely by brigandage. The only noteworthy chief in the region, the Raja of Patiala, adhered to Ahmed Shah Abdali's interest.[2]

Delhi

Even in Delhi, held by the Sindhia's since 1785, Major James Brown was working desperately to bring the Mughal

1. Dr. H.R. Gupta, *History of the Sikhs*, p. 172.
2. *Ibid.*

Emperor once again under British protection.[3] Begam Samru ruled at Sardhana near Meerut as a feudatory of Sindhia, but intrigued continuously against him.

Agra

Agra too had been in the possession of Sindhia since 1785. These provinces of the North were potentially the most prosperous in North India, but Durrani attacks, wars among the Jats, the Rohilas and the Maratha for the control of Delhi had impoverished these lands and they lay waste and ravaged.

Gwalior and Gohad

Gwalior and Gohad were also seething with troubles. Mahadji Sindhia had neglected the government of these regions and conditions did not improve even under Daulat Rao Sindhia in the early years of his reign as he continued the arrangements made his predecessor there to begin with.

Bundelkhand

Bundelkhand, Narwar, and Chanderi were old feudal principalities and the Rajas of these places constantly troubled the Marathas. During the regime of Mahadji, these states remained unsubdued, until Daulat Rao Sindhia later on annexed them to his own dominions. The greatest difficulty that Daulat Rao had to encounter in this region came from the Raja of Datia, who supported the widows of Mahadji against him. Himmat Bahadur Gosain, and Ali Bahadur, the ruler of Banda and a grandson of Baji Rao I and Mastani, were at daggers drawn with the Sindhia family.

Malwa

The condition of Malwa was deplorable due to recurrent wars between the Sindhia and Holkar. This territory was at this time the happy hunting ground of a variety of adventurers and the Grassia Chiefs. The Bhils and the Pindaries proved the most troublesome to Daulat Rao Sindhia. The Khichchi Rajas of Raghogarh constantly gave trouble to Mahadji throughout his whole life and later on to Daulat Rao Sindhia also.

---

3. Dr. H.R. Gupta, *History of the Sikhs*, p. 172.

Ajmer

The Suba of Ajmer included the whole of Rajasthan, and it was a source of constant trouble to Mahadji and Daulat Rao Sindhia. The collection of tribute from the Rajput states by Mahadji created unending enmity between the Rajputs and the Marathas and the Suba became the cockpit of Maratha-Rajput wars. The fabulous wealth of the Raja of Jaipur, so assiduously amassed by Raja Jai Singh, and that of Raja Abhaya Singh of Jodhpur, melted away and the best lands of Jaipur, Jodhpur and Udaipur lay fallow. The Rajputs lost their former valour and love of human virtues. The proud descendants of the Sun and the Moon had degenerated to such a low state that in the words of J.N. Sarkar "the saddest aspect of the fall of the Delhi empire was, to my mind, the utter degradation of this chivalrous race and the hopeless misery of this land of the Rajas."[4] The task of collecting tributes from this war-torn territory was like squeezing oil from sand, but even in this ignoble pursuit, the Maratha Sardars quarrelled with one another. The constant warfare between the Marathas and Rajputs laid the whole of Rajasthan waste so that it presented a spectacle of utter misery and squalor. The Rajputs were naturally anxious to get an opportunity to throw over the Maratha yoke.

The Doab

The condition of the Doab was scarcely better. Thomas Twig, travelled through the Upper Doab in November and December 1794, gives a sad picture of the ruin of agriculture, reduction of population, and widespread brigandage throughout this region.[5]

In the whole of Sindhia's dominions, the condition of Broach, Ahmadnagar, Asirgarh and of the Deccan territories was slightly more satisfactory.

The Nobles of Gwalior State

The internal condition of Gwalior state was further weakened by refractory nobles of the state and its traitorous generals and

---

4. Sarkar, *Fall of the Mughal Empire*, Ch. IV, 29, Tod, A.A.R.
5. *Ibid.*, IV, p. 223 and for details Marathi Riyasat 55-57, Imp. Gzztt. of India, XIV 320, Ojha Rajasthan and Dr. Raghubir Singh: Purv. Adhunik Rajasthan.

officers. Indeed, Daulat Rao Sindhia's political difficulties were greatly increased by the intrigues and activities of the most important nobles at his court. These nobles may be divided into three categories : (1) Foreign Generals, (2) the Maratha Sardars and (3) other grandees.

Of the important foreign generals : (1) De Boigne, (2) Du Perron, (3) Jean Baptiste, (4) Michael Filose, (5) Louis Bourquein and (6) Jacob were the most noteworthy.

Conspicuous among the Maratha nobles were (1) Aba Chitnis, (2) Balloba Tattiya alias Pagnis, (3) Jeoba Dada Bakhshi, (4) Gopal Rao Bhow, (5) Sarji Rao Ghatge, (6) Ambaji Ingale, (7) Lakhwa Dada, (8) Bapu Sindhia, (9) Jagoo Bapu, (10) Jaswant Rao Bhao, (11) Devji Gaule, (12) Anna Shicknavis, (13) Babu Rao Angeria, (14) Gokul Parikh, (15) Hindu Rao Ghatge, (16) Munshi Kamalnain.

The third category consisted of Shah Nizamuddin and the leaders of the Pindarics.

Sindhia's Foreign Generals

1. De Boigne. A French soldier of fortune, born at Chambery in Savoy in 1751, first joined Mahadji Sindhia's army as an officer of his general Apa Khande Rao at the end of 1784. After the death of Mahadji Sindhia, he remained in the service of Daulat Rao only for a short while and handed over charge to De Perron in 1796. According to Roberts, his last advice to his master was to avoid all contest with the British Government."[6] According to Duff, "the force of De Boigne was gradually augmented to 18000 regular infantry, 6000 irregulars, Nujeebs and Ruhelas, 2000 regular horse and 600 Persian cavalry.[7] De Boigne has been praised highly by Sir J.N. Sarkar and Sardesai, but it should be remembered that he was a person who "made hay while the sun shone" and was partial to the British.*

---

6. P.E. Roberts, *India Under Wellesley,* pp. 222-223.
7. Duff, *History of the Marathas,* III, p. 74, Ed. 1912.

* He first served in the Bundelkhand Campaign of that chief. Along with Apa Khande Rao he came to Sindhia's camp before Lalsot at the head of two battalions of trained sepoys. After the departure of Lesteneau, he became the supreme officer of Sindhia's army. De Boigne achieved a remarkable victory in Rajasthan against the Rajputs at Patan on 20th June, 1790 and at Merta on 10th Sept., 1790. He also defeated Holkar's forces at Lakhari (1st June, 1793).

2. Du Perron. Francois Culliar alias Du Perron was also a Frenchman** and held a very responsible post under Daulat Rao. After the death of Colonel Freemond on 8th July, 1794, Du Perron became next to De Boigne. He distinguished himself at the Battle of Kharda and after De Boigne's resignation, he became his successor. On 12-2-1797, he was made a Mansabdar of 7000 and a military fief yielding Rs. 27 lacs was assigned to him. He rendered valuable military and political services to Daulat Rao between 1797 and 1804.+ His annual revenue was

---

He had his own gun factory and arsenal under European supervision. He made Aligarh and Meerut (Gurgaon) his head quarters. Firozabad, Hathras, Khurja, Aligarh, Palwal, Hodel and Gurgaon were allotted to him to meet the expenses of his army.

He was a good financier and he introduced the plantation of Indigo and export of saltpetre. He was a very good general and Sindhia's army became supreme in North India with the help of this fine military organiser. He helped Sindhia in gaining a decisive victory over Mirza Ismail Beg at Agra. He was not only a good general, but also a good administrator. De Boigne's contribution to the stability of the Sindhia family in general and Daulat Rao in particular was that by dint of experience and ability, he imparted remarkable efficiency to Sindhia's army. De Boigne was successful in realising tribute as he helped the tributory princes in putting down rebels. In a short career of seven years (1789-1795) he amassed 32 lacs of rupees.

** Driven by poverty, he first enlisted in the French Royal Service first as a soldier and later as a sailor in the East India Co. He ran away from Pondicherry and after reaching North India joined in 1781 Rene Medic' Corps which the latter sold to the Rana of Gohad. He worked in that corps as an artillery man in a Singster Canon factory. After the death of the Rana of Gohad, he joined Lesteneau's service as a quarter-master-sergeant on Rs. 60 per month in 1784. Lestaneau ran away with Gulam Qadir's Jewels and his corps was broken, but De Boigne employed De Peerron as a Captain. He was a servant after De Boigne's heart, being diligent, energetic and indefatigable taking a pride in bringing his battalion to the highest pitch of efficiency and discipline. In April 1793, at Kannud, Perron acted as De Boigne's deputy in receiving the surrender of Mirza Ismail Beg. In 1793, a second brigade was raised by De Boigne and he was appointed brigadier.

On 16-4-1799, he captured Agra, and on 27th April, Aligarh. He affected compromise between Ambaji and Lakhwa, after Lakhwa's re-appointment.

+ On 15th April 1800, he supported Lakhwa by sending an army under Poleman, in the battle of Manpura, in which the Raja of Jaipur was defeated. When Lakhwa took up arms against Sindhia, he crushed Lakhwa Dada in the Battle of Seondha, on 3rd May, 1801, he gained Ajmer from Lakhwa's partisans through Louis Bourquin and, on 8th May, held office as Subedar of Delhi. He defeated George Thomas

estimated at £16,32,000[8], and he held the most important territory, on the preservation of which hung the existence of the British Empire in India.[9] The part that he played in the Second Anglo-Maratha War has, however, laid him open to criticism from all sides.[10]

After his return from Ujjain in March, 1802, Du Perron started hoarding as much money as he could and made up his mind to retire to France.* History bears testimony that if he had not deceived Sindhia, it would not have been probably so easy for the British army to crush Sindhia. Lord Lake doubted of his victory at Lasswari and wrote, "All the sepoys of the enemy behaved exceedingly well, and if they had been commanded by French Officers, the event would have been extremely doubtful."[11] Grant Duff also subscribed to this view.[12] He proved a traitor to his master and his men, because at Aligarh, he ordered the army to defend the fort to the last and promised to help them, but failed to do so and the garrison met with a tragic end. He was a traitor to his nation because he delivered all his territory, worth Rs. 80 lacs to the East India Company, the most formidable foe of France and gave a death blow to the dream of Napoleon to conquer England in India. His treachery was only exceeded by his cowardice[13] and his

with the help of his forces and presented Rs. 15 lacs to Daulat Rao Sindhia. Foot Note: **Sarkar, *Fall of the Mughal Empire*, IV, p. 157.

8. P. Roberts, *India under Wellesley*, p. 223.
9. Review of Affairs of India from the year 1798 to 1806, London, 1807, p. 11.
10. *Poona Residency Correspondence.* Vol. IX letter Nos. 119 and 121, Hutton Wellesley p. 9, Mill — *History of British India,* Vol. VI. p. 353. Martin, *Wellesleys Despatches*, Vol. II, pp. 221 and 229.

* British Officers knew that Perron "anxiously desired to retire to Europe with his wealth." The British accused him of making a French State in the heart of India. The French denounced him as a traitor to France. According to Sarkar, he was not a traitor to France, but to Sindhia. In fact he was a traitor to France as well as to Sinohia. He lowered the prestige of France by his duplicity. To say that he knew that the victory of the English army was certain does not stand scrutiny. Footnote : 31. Sarkar, *Fall of the Mughal Empire*, IV, pp. 251-257. India Under Wellesley, p. 227.

11. *Martin's Wellesley Despatches*, Vol. III, p. 554. Roberts, *India Under Wellesley*, p. 227.
12. Duff, *History of the Marathas*, III, p. 264, Ed. 1912.
13. Sarkar, *Fall of the Mughal Empire*, IV, p. 267.

conduct assured to the English supremacy in Hindustan and did more harm to the name of France than 50 years of misconduct and misfortune could have accomplished.[14]

Grant Duff states that Perron who had for sometime been conscious (of the coming conflict) made overtures to General Lake even before the commencement of the war.[15] Skinner noticed with grief how Sindhia's cause was ruined by Perron and other French Officers.[16] According to Pioneer, it is asserted that he had savings to a considerable amount invested in the funds of the East India Company.[17] As Sarkar says, "the white rat hastened to leave Sindhia's sinking ship and came over to the British to surrender and share in the Governor General's promised bounty to deserters."[18] With his sickly wife, Madcline, whom he married at Agra on 16th December, 1782 and daughter, he eventually fled to France in 1804 with his hoarded wealth. To a great extent he was responsible for the downfall of Daulat Rao Sindhia. The example of Du Perron was followed by other foreign officers. Thus Mahadji's policy of appointing foreign generals proved suicidal to the Maratha nation.

3. Jean Baptiste

After the Second Maratha War, Jean Baptiste became the Chief Commander of Sindhia's European army. He was a half-caste Prussian "born in India." He was a son of Colonel Jean Baptiste Filoze and half brother of Colonel Filoze who betrayed Nana.[19] Jean Baptiste remained for a considerable period in Daulat Rao Sindhia's service. After the departure of De Perron, he became the most powerful commander of Sindhia's army. It is said that Jean Baptiste ruined the cause of the Marathas at Bharatpur, when Daulat Rao in alliance with Jaswant Rao Holkar tried to attack the British forces.[20] He also prevented

14. Crompton, Military Adventurers of Hindustan, pp. 334-35.
15. Duff, *History of the Marathas,* III, p. 249, ed. 1912.
16. Sarkar, *Fall of the Mughal Empire,* IV, p. 49.
17. Sunder Lal, *Bharat Men Angrezi Rajya,* I, p. 463, ed. 1960 Govt. of India Publication.
18. Sarkar, *Fall of the Mughal Empire,* p. 283, Vol. IV.
19. Malcolm, *Political History of India,* I, p. 410 Footnote.
20. General Lake's Private letter to Wellesly dated Agra 22nd Sept., 1804 and also see Sunderlal I, p. 508, ed. July 60.

Sindhia's cavalry reaching Bharatpur[21] Similarly, when he was sent to attack Bhopal, he quarrelled with Jaswant Rao Bhau, the Maratha commander, and missed the chance of capturing the place.

Jean Baptiste also tried to cross over to the British during the Second Maratha War. According to Malcolm, "Jean Baptiste...is desirous of coming to me (Malcolm) but requires a lac and half of rupees to pay his troops."[22] Although he scored a few victories for his master like the capture of Isagarh, etc., yet the record of his betrayals outnumbers that of his loyalty.

Jean Baptiste was neither a great general nor a good organiser. He was not even faithful to his master. But under the terms of the treaty of Sarji Arjan-Gaon, Daulat Rao was unable to employ other European generals, so he had to rely on Jean Baptiste, who remained in service even after the death of Daulat Rao Sindhia.

4. Louis Bourquien

Bourquien's greatest feat was that he succeeded in crushing George Thomas, the Irish adventurer, who had carved out an independent principality in the Punjab. He held charge of Delhi on behalf of Perron, but during the Second Maratha War, as soon as he heard about the war between Daulat Rao Sindhia and the East India Company, he repudiated Perron's authority and tried to make as much money as possible. He proclaimed himself Commander-in-Chief with a salute of 21 guns, and tried to come to terms with the English General, Lord Lake, but he was forced to fight. Eventually, he surrendered to the British army without fighting and Sindhia's army so betrayed and "abandoned by its chief and officers was easily defeated."[23] This victory led to the falling of Shah Alam's person into the hands of Lord Lake. Skinner called him, "not only coward but a fool, wicked as he was weak."[24]

With him Major Gaslo, Major Guriner, Del Perron and Jean also surrendered[25] and were allowed to go unmolested. In

21. Quoted by Sunderlal, *Ibid.,* p. 509.
22. *Ibid.,* p. 509.
23. Martineau, p. 173.
24. Gwaliour State Gazetteer Appendix.
25. Thorn, 118, Asiatic Annual Register 1803, Appendix 13.

1804, at the time when Perron retired, he went away to France and was reported to have carried away an immense fortune. As Crompton says, "There is no more contemptible character among the military adventurers of Hindustan."[26] He was incompetent, timid and treacherous.[27]

5. Filose

Filose was a Neapolitan[28] and was known as Batis Sahib. He was the son of Michael Filose.[29] The Resident described him as "a shrewd man, decidedly avaricious."[30] He quarrelled with S.R. Ghatge and captured him.[31] Grant Duff speaks of him as "a low, illiterate man of worthless character but of considerable address and cunning."[32] Filose was an indisciplined, treacherous person and inflamed the enmity between Nana, Baji Rao and Daulat Rao. He was a partisan of the British and possessed considerable property at Calcutta and Bombay. The Resident wrote to the Governor General that he was "very favourably disposed towards us."[33] Hessing[34] and Jacob[35] were other important foreign generals.

These foreign generals as shown above, proved thoroughly unreliable. Even in January, 1797 the Resident wrote, "I am inclined to think that in the event of our being engaged in war with the Marathas, the majority of them would not, under present circumstances, act against us."[36] Similarly the British hope for setting aside Daulat Rao and bringing Balloba Tattya to power with the help of these renegades. Balloba Tatiya's authority, said Palmer, depended upon the officers of Sindhia's brigades. There was reason to feel that if these officers continued

26. Crompton, *European Military Adventurers of Hindustan*, p. 342.
27. *Ibid.*, p. 309.
28. 'Dutch', *Poona Residency Correspondence*, VI, No. 72, p. 43.
29. Grant Duff, *History of the Marathas*, III, pp. 84.
30. *Poona Residency Correspondence*, VI. No. 72, p. 113.
31. Sardesai, *New History of the Marathas*, III, p. 340.
32. Duff, *History of the Marathas*, III, p. 84-85.
33. *Poona Residency Correspondence*, Vol. VI, No. 72, p. 113.
34. P. Roberts, *India Under Wellesley*, p. 227.
35. *Poona Residency Correspondence*, II, No. 11, p. 192.
36. *Ibid.*, Vol. VI, No. 11, p. 72, p. 113.

to support Tatiya, there was a possibility of his gradually establishing his power.[37]

How far these foreign generals worked as fifth columnists can be gathered from the fact that even in January, 1798, Resident Uthoff was of the firm opinion that "they would not fight against us."[38] Similarly when there was an apprehension of another rupture after the treaty with Sindhia, it was hoped by British diplomats that they would be assisted by these persons in the very citadel of the enemy.

The Maratha Nobles

The other pillar of Daulat Rao's power was the Maratha nobles. Was the pillar reliable? What did he do to repair or strengthen it?

Mahadji Sindhia generally patronised Maharashtrian Brahmins, particularly the Shenvi and Deshastha Brahmins. The leaders of Deshastha Brahmins were the three sons of Raghunath Malhar Kulkarni of Nagodi, known as Aba Chitnis, Krishnoba Chitnis and Gopal Bhau. Aba was a civil administrator and financial manager of extraordinary capacity. Krishnoba was a good secretary and accountant and Gopal Bhau was Mahadji's deputy in Hindustan.

Rival to the Deshastha party was the party of Shenvi Brahmins, consisting of Jivaji Balhil Kerkar, popularly known as Jiva Dada Bakshi, and his first cousin, Jagannath Ram Krishna, popularly known as Jagoo Bappu, Lakshman Annant Lad, popularly known as Lakhwa Dada, Balaji Anant Pingale, popularly known as Balloba Pagnis, and Sadashiv Malhar Barve popularly known as Bhau Bakshi were other leading members of the group. The widows of Mahadji favoured the Shenvis. To reduce the Shenvi influence at court, the Deshastha Brahmins tried to gain the favour of Nana Phadnavis. But the widows feared that the Deshastha Brahmins and Nana might unite against them. This brought about the downfall of Aba Chitnis[39] and Gopal Bhau, whose places were taken by Balloba Pagnis and Lakhwa Dada as Minister and Viceroy of the north respectively.

37. Choksey, *A History of British Diplomacy at the Court of the Peshwas.* p. 269.

38. *Poona Residency Correspondence,* Vol. II, p. 113, No. 72.

39. *Ibid.,* II, pp. 234, 238 Khare IX, pp. 48, 14.

1. Aba Chitnis

Aba Chitnis was a Minister of Mahadji Sindhia and occupied for a short time that post in the regime of Daulat Rao Sindhia also. The widows brought about his dismissal. De Boigne warned Daulat Rao against such a move and "it was, as Shah Alam argued, a ruinous mistake to replace a tried Minister, Aba, by a man of proved incompetence like Balloba."[40] Aba was a competent person and could have saved the Maratha Empire which was heading towards ruin.

2. Gopal Bhau

Gopal Bhau was a capable Deputy and Viceroy of Mahadji Sindhia in the north. He defeated Holkar in June, 1793 at Lakheri. After the accession of Daulat Rao, he again came into power when the widows rose against Daulat Rao, and his place as Viceroy of the north was taken by Ambaji Ingale. He fought bravely against the British during the Second Maratha War and was wounded in the Battle of Aragaon. In 1804-05, when Daulat Rao Sindhia tried to form an anti-British alliance, Jenkins, the Resident with Sindhia, and Walker, the Resident at Baroda, tried to win over Gopal Bhau but did not achieve any success.[41] He was later granted a pension for life by the East India Company. He and Aba again become Ministers in 1807 for a short time and conducted negotiations with the East India Company on behalf of Daulat Rao. He died on 8th January, 1815. The British Resident wrote : "Sindhia considered Gopal Rao Bhau his wisest statesman and his best soldier. He was remarkable for his bravery and coolness in action."[42]

3. Jiva Dada Bakshi

Jiva Dada Bakshi was "confident, competent and chief adviser of Mahadji."[43] In the Battle of Kharda, he commanded immediately under Daulat Rao[44] and showed personal bravery.[45]

---

40. Dilli Yethil Marathayanchin Raj Karncned by D.B. Parasnis I and II Supplementary 1913-14, 12, 133, 119, 121, Hingane Dafter Vol. I.
41. Secret Proceedings Fort William, pp. 19920-30.
42. *Poona Residency Correspondence*, XIV, No. 210, p. 247.
43. Dr. Raghubir Singh, *Purva Adhunic Rajasthan*, p. 221.
44. Duff, *History of the Marathas*, III, p. 112.
45. *Ibid.*, p. 114.

His death[46] gave British diplomacy a chance to sow the seeds of discord in the Maratha Confederacy by winning over Balloba to oppose Nana's plan of adoption. Grant Duff states : "Taking advantage...as the death of Jaoba Bakshi had taken place,"[47] the British diplomacy succeeded in bringing Baji Rao II to power. His son Narain Rao Bakshi along with other Shenvi Brahmins opposed Daulat Rao and met with a tragic end.[48]

4. Balloba Pagnis

Balloba Pagnis played a leading role in Maratha history. Dismissed by Mahadji, he later ingratiated himself into the favour of the widows and as a result of their intercession, he was appointed Prime Minister of Daulat Rao Sindhia. British diplomacy used him as a tool to oppose Nana Phadnavis's plan of a boy to set aside the succession of Baji Rao II. Grant Duff states that Baji Rao II "taking advantage of the favourable disposition evinced towards him by Balloba Tattiya, opened correspondence with him and in a few months gained him over to his cause."[49] To avoid a clash, Nana agreed that Baji Rao II should be made Peshwa, but Balloba opposed even this plan of Nana and set free Mashirulmulk, the Prime Minister of Hyderabad, a partisan of the British, who worked for the ruin of the Maratha state by taking advantage of the confused situation.[50] On 31st December, 1797, Nana Phadnavis was arrested but Pagnis failed to take advantage of the situation, as Sarji Rao Ghatge, father of Sindhia's wife Baizabai, became supreme. So he encouraged the widows of Mahadji to rise against Daulat Rao. To reconcile the widows, Daulat Rao again appointed him Prime Minister on April 11, 1799, but he and Lakhwa Dada conspired to dethrone Daulat Rao and even tried to win over Nana and later on Amrit Rao to oust both Daulat

46. Sardesai has mentioned his date of death 6th Jan., 1796, III, p. 333, Hindi Translation but Dr. Raghubir Singh mentions 4th January, 1796 : *Purva Adhunik Rajasthan*, p. 221.

47. Duff, *History of the Marathas*, p. 522, Vol. 1.

48. Sardesai, *New History of the Marathas*, III, p. 356.

49. *Ibid.*, p. 356.

50. *Ibid.*, p. 356.

Rao and Baji Rao II.[51&52] Daulat Rao, however, proved more than a match for Balloba. He lured him to attend the victory celebration after Malpura in a grand durbar on 16th April, 1800, and got him arrested. Balloba was ailing at the time and died at Ahmednagar on 1st December, 1800.

According to Major Basu and Sunderlal, these Shenvi Brahmins and the widows, were stooges of the East India Company.[53] Sir J.N. Sarkar also considered Balloba as an incompetent person and the same was the opinion of Emperor Shah Alam.[54] It is perhaps correct that the Shenvi party was favourably inclined towards the East India Company, though they seem to have been won over more by British diplomacy than by British gold. It was Balloba's opposition to the plan of adoption at Poona which created a rift among the Marathas, brought about the downfall of Nana and the succession of Baji Rao II, which ultimately paved the way for British supremacy.

5. Jaggoo Bapu

Jaggoo Bapu was one of the leaders of the Shenvi faction and revolted against Daulat Rao in alliance with Lakhwa Dada, when Balloba was dismissed, but later on he worked as a general and subedar of Sindhia in Rajasthan. He defeated Karim Khan Pindari[55] and crushed many other petty chiefs. He attacked Bhopal in alliance with Nagpur forces. He would have succeeded there, but he died during the siege of Bhopal in 1814,[56] leaving his task unaccomplished. He was not a very prominent figure.

6. Ambaji Ingale

Ambaji Ingale was born in 1730. Mahadji appointed him *Faujdar* of the districts situated to the north of Delhi and he succeeded in prevailing upon the Sikhs to make peace with

---

51. Foreign Secret Papers *Poona Residency Correspondence,* Vol. VI letter Nos. 298, 307 Sardesai also states Balloba Tattiya, Nana Phandnavis, Narain Bakshi and some others desired to bring about such a change, but their efforts were wickedly crushed, Sardesai : *New History of the Marathas,* Vol. III, p. 356.
52. *Ibid.*
53. Basu, *Rise of the Christian Power in India,* pp. 386-87 and Sunder Lal, *Bharat Men Angrezi Rajya,* p. 400 Ed. 1960.
54. Sarkar, *Fall of the Mughal Empire,* IV, p. 145.
55. *Poona Residency Correspondence,* XIV, p. 107, III.
56. *Ibid.,* XIV, pp. 90 and 92.

Mahadji on 30th March, 1785.[57] He worked as Kiledar of Gwalior,[58] as a deputy of Mahadji at Udaipur and amassed a great fortune there.[59] After the removal of Lakhwa Dada, Daulat Rao Sindhia appointed him Viceroy of the North. He became so powerful that in October, 1796, the British resident wrote, "Ambaji is rather a subsidiary chief than a servant.[60] When asked to repay the revenues of 147 lakhs that he had extorted and withheld, he conspired with the British, sent a secret agent to Lord Wellesley when he visited Fatehgarh in 1801,[61] requested Colonel Collins to allow him an asylum in the Company's territory.[62]

He tried to seek shelter at Banaras in 1802. British officers hoped that Ambaji,* his brother and Jado Bhaskar, might be brought over to the British cause.[63] In 1803, he opened negotiations with Lord Wellesley, "revolted against his master and joined the English."[64] "In order to reward him, the territories (Gwalior and Gohad) were divided between the Rana (of Gohad and Ambaji)."[65] He entered into a treaty with the British before the Battle of Laswari and was promised Marwar, Shivpuri, Koonch, Sabalgarh, Bijaypur Kolaras and Pauri, etc., so he deceived the Maratha forces at Laswari and at Gwalior,[66] but later on this treaty was repudiated. Later, he again joined Daulat Rao and

---

57. Dilliyethil, I, 134, 157; Maheshwar II 90, Parashis (New) 373, C.P.C. VII, 212 Imperial Records Secret Proceedings, 26th April, 1785 James Anderson to G.G., dt. 11th April, and 3-5-1785.
58. Sardesai, *New History of the Marathas*, III.
59. Tod, *Annals and Antiquities of Rajasthan*, Vol. 1, *Memoir* Chapter XVII, Ojha II, pp. 683-86.
60. *Poona Residency Correspondence*, VIII Resident to G.G. October, 1796.
61. *Ibid.*, IX 31, *Ibid.*
62. *Ibid.*, VIII 163, IX 64, Footnote M.M. III, 192.

* Broughton paints his picture in following words in 1809 : "Ambaji is a tall, hale looking man for his age, which is said to be upwards of eighty, his complexion is dark, and there is much humour and intelligence in his countenance. His dress was remarkably plain, almost amounting to meanness; consisting of common chintz jacket, quilted with cotton, a coarse red shawl and a white turban."

...Letters from a Maratha Camp, p. 68.

63. Duff, *History of the Marathas*, III, p. 168.
64. P.E. Roberts, *India Under Wellesley*, p. 230.
65. Sarkar, *Fall of the Mughal Empire*, IV, pp. 277-308.
66. Thorn 246 and Pester 237.

in cooperation with S.R. Ghatge tried to reconcile Sindhia and Holkar against the East India Company, but Malcolm again lured him and he along with Munshi Kamalnain, playing as convenient tools of British diplomats, brought about a compromise with the British, and created antagonism between the Sindhia with the Holkar.[67] In case of a rupture with Sindhia, the East India Company relied on him to side with it. But the East India Company did not give him any lands, so he joined Sarji Rao Ghatge and this action gave a pretext to the British Government to forfeit his claim.[68]

In spite of these somersaults, Daulat Rao still kept him under the sunshine of his favour and appointed him to several posts of trust and responsibility. He was entrusted with the task of realising tribute in Rajasthan, in which he failed, but he tried for the division of Mewar between Holkar and Sindhia.[69] Ambaji was a fair weather friend. Even British diplomats realised his slippery nature.

He was faithless, treacherous, miserly but luxurious and even at the age of eighty tried to marry a girl of a wealthy family in her teens.[70] He died leaving about "three crores of rupees,"[71] Daulat Rao said of him : "It was to him he had chiefly trusted for the well-ordered administration of his affairs."[72] He always played a game of double dealing[73] and died "in a wretched tent...with very thin attendance." Sarkar describes him as the worst sinner."[74]

---

67. Duff states "Lord Lake...seized on opportunity, consequent to Ambaji's appointment."
 * "Advantage may be derived" wrote Edmonstone Secretary to Government to Colonel Martindell from connexion with Ambaji. F.N. Foreign Secret Papers National Archives. Malcolm's letter to Ambaji written on 7th Sept., 1806, *Poona Residency Correspondence*, XI, Nos. 118, 123, 126, 127, No. 35, pp. 161-52.
68. *Poona Residency Correspondence*, XI, No. 95, pp. 151-52.
69. R. Singh, p. 239, ed. 1951, Broughton : Letters.
70. Broughton Thomas D., *Letters written in a Maratha Camp*, pp. 116-17.
71. *Poona Residency Correspondence*, XI, No. 286, p. 431 states night of 4th May, 1809; Broughton states morning of 5th May, 1809, p. 147.
72. *Ibid.*, IV, No. 318.
72. *Ibid.*, No. 286, p. 431.
74. Sarkar, *Fall of the Mughal Empire*, IV, pp. 308 and 7.

7. Jaswant Rao Bhau

Jaswant Rao Bhau was the son of Jinva Dada, the first cousin of Jaggo Bapu,[75] and became successor to his uncle Jaggoo Bapu after the latter's death.[76] He worked as a Commander or Subedar of Daulat Rao Sindhia at various places. As Subedar at Udaipur, he came into conflict with Bapu Sindhia and Amir Khan's Deputy, Jamshed Khan.[77] After the death of Jaggoo Bapu, the task of conquering Bhopal was entrusted to him, but he failed to do so owing to the non-cooperation of Sadick Ali Khan, commander of the Nagpur forces, the Pindarics and Jean Baptiste with whom he had a quarrel. Jean Baptiste resorted to arms and defeated him,[78] but afterwards a reconciliation took place between them by the intervention of Daulat Rao Sindhia himself. But a golden opportunity to conquer Bhopal was lost on account of this quarrel, as soon afterwards Lord Hastings took Bhopal under British protection.[79]

Later on, he again worked in Rajasthan and gained Kumbhalmer, Rypoor and Ramnagar from the Rana of Udaipur and even succeeded in seducing John Wood from the British service.[80] Though he was entrusted with the task of crushing the Pindaries in alliance with the British, and Captain Coulified was appointed to keep watch over him,[81] yet he gave shelter to Chitu and other Pindari leaders at Jawed. On account of this, he was deprived of his charge by General Donkin,[82] he was forced to leave Rajasthan[83] and General Adams stormed his stronghold at Jawed.[84] As the East India Company became supreme all over India, he sank into insignificance.

---

75. Thorn 346, Pester 237.
76. Malcolm, *Political History of India,* C.I.I, p. 410.
77. Dr. R. Singh, p. 254.
78. Malcolm, *Political History of India,* I, p. 411.
79. *Ibid.,* I, pp. 411-42. *Poona Residency Correspondence,* XIV, pp. 200 to 300.
80. *Poona Residency Correspondence,* XIV, No. 232.
81. Duff, *History of the Marathas,* III, p. 403 ed. 1912.
82. *Ibid.,* III, pp. 670-71.
83. Dr. R. Singh, p. 259.
84. Duff, *History of the Marathas,* III, pp. 464-65 ed. 1912.

8. Devji Gaule

Devji Gaule first worked under Gopal Bhau and Lakhwa Dada to check the Sikh raids on the Punjab border.[85] After that, he worked on different posts. He was on good terms with the British. It is said he was one of the leaders who connived at the murder of Sarji Rao Ghatge. After the latter's fall, he became a Minister and Subedar of Gwalior. Daulat Rao used to consult him on every occasion. Baiza Bai, wife of Daulat Rao Sindhia, was dead against him as she regarded him as one of the connivers of the murder of her father. On account of his failure in realising tribute from Gwalior and the enmity of Baiza Bai, he was dismissed and imprisoned. He was also suspected of bringing about a curse on Daulat Rao Sindhia with the help of a Pirzada.[86] He remained confined to the fort of Narwar and died or was poisoned on 16th January, 1812.[87] He received a regular pension from the East India Company but after his death, the East India Company refused to give the pension of Rs. 10,000 to his successors, though the last installment was paid. Devji Gaule remained supreme at Sindhia's court from 1809 to 1811.

9. Bapu Rao Angria

Babu Rao Angria was the maternal uncle of Daulat Rao Sindhia. Daulat Rao helped him in gaining the fort of Kolaba.[88] He entered the employment of Daulat Rao Sindhia in 1808, after the Peshwa had crushed the Angria family with the help of the East India Company. One Resident speaks of him as "the most competent person, fit for the post of Prime Ministership of Sindhia," but he never rose to that position, though he worked as a Minister along with Sarji Rao Ghatge. Later on he was appointed Subedar of Ujjain. People complained against him and he was suspended, but after a short time he was reinstated and worked for a long time. He was a man of luxurious habits, but of accommodating nature.[89]

---

85. Dr. H.R. Gupta, Vol. III, pp. 244, 348-49.
86. *Poona Residency Correspondence,* Vol. XIV, No. 96.
87. *Ibid.,* p. 115, No. 96.
88. *Poona Residency Correspondence,* Vol. XI.
89. Broughton Thomas D., *Letters Written in a Maratha Camp* and *Poona Residency Correspondence,* Vol. XI & XIV.

10. Gokul Parikh

Gokul Parikh was a great financier. His financial ability helped him to rise to the office of Prime Minister of Daulat Rao Sindhia. In the words of Prinsep, "the control of affairs had been in the hands of a banker of the name of Gokul Parikh, recommended to office by his financial ability and held in check by the counteracting influence and rivalry of Sindhia's personal favourites."[90] Broughton also confirms that "the Mahraj has concluded a loan for 10 lakhs of rupees with a rich banker named Gokul Parikh."[91] He was treated as a member of the Sindhia family.[92]

He was neither a general nor a statesman, but owing to financial difficulties, Sindhia could not dispense with him. However, after 1818, when pecuniary distress subsided, he lost his influence and Baba Rao Patankar[93] and Hindoo Rao Ghatge, respectively uncle and brother of Baiza Bai, became supreme.

11. Lakhwa Dada

Lakshman Annat Lad alias Lakhwa Dada was a general of Sindhia. He belonged to the Shenvi party, as he owed his rise to the patronage of Balloba Tattiya Pagnis.

Lakhwa Dada, along with Jaggoo Bapu, took charge as Sindhia's Viceroy in Hindustan on 1st November, 1794. He appointed Nana Rao to realize revenue from the Sikhs in the Cis-Sutlej area in October, 1795.[94] But he failed against the Sikhs. According to H.R. Gupta, "Lakhwa Dada, the Maratha Commander of Saharanpur, confined himself to his headquarters for fear of the Sikhs.[95] Being a partisan of the British he entrusted George Thomas with Sonepat, Panipat and Karnal Districts.[96] Later on this unfaithful Irish mercenary (George Thomas) tried to plant the British flag in the Punjab and became a

90. *Poona Residency Correspondence,* Vol. XI, Edited by N.B. Roy, p. 67.
91. Princep S. Transactions 1.2328, *Poona Residency Correspondence,* XI, No. 345.
92. Foreign Political Index 1820 under heading Gwalior 12, July, 22.
93. *Poona Residency Correspondence,* XIV, No. 344, p. 407.
94. Dr. H.R. Gupta, p. 256, ed. 1944.
95. *Ibid.,* p. 261.
96. *Ibid.,* p. 262.

menace to Daulat Rao. Lakhwa Dada failed hopelessly in the administration of the Punjab and against the Sikhs.[97] But he proved successful in Malwa and improved finance. In August, 1795, he captured Sawalgarh and laid siege to Bijapur. In October, 1795, he attacked the famous city of Narwar and succeeded in capturing the fort in March, 1796. In June, 1796, he attacked Datia but the Bundela Raja proved more than a match for him.[98] On 26th October, 1796 Daulat Rao Sindhia, on the advice of Nana Phadnavis and Sarji Rao arrested Balloba Tattya and Bhau Bakshi and recalled Aba Chitnis. This news reached Lakhwa Dada and he sent his family to Bithore in Oudh territory and himself marched to Gopal Garh on 7th November to take asylum at Banares in British territory as he was on friendly terms with the East India Company.[99] But Daulat Rao Sindhia retained him as Viceroy of the North, even though he did not discharge his duties sincerely. In February, 1798, Daulat Rao ordered Lakhwa Dada and Ambaji to attend on him at Poona in person, but Lakhwa Dada did not comply with that order and went to Bhopal with Jaggoo Bapu. Near Sagar, they were arrested by Hariji Sindhia on 10th March, 1798. In March, 1798, the war of the widows flared up and the widows urged for the release of Lakhwa Dada. He was released on 8th August, 1798. The partisans of the widows captured Ujjain without a blow on 15th September, 1798,[100] but Bala Rao Ingale recovered it three months later.

Lakhwa Dada strained every nerve to undermine the authority of Daulat Rao Sindhia with the help of the widows and the enemies of Sindhia like Durjan Sal and Raja Jai Singh of Ragho Garh. He defeated Bala Rao Ingale near Araun.[101]

On 20th January, 1801 the widows and Lakhwa Dada were joined by the Raja of Datia with 3000 infantry, 2000 horse, 6 guns, etc. He tried to capture Agra, but Perron attacked him

97. *Memoirs of George Thomas*, 44 Hamilton 450-52 and Dr. H.R. Gupta, pp. 262, 268, ed. 1944.

98. *Poona Residency Correspondence*, Vol. III, 24.

99. *Ibid.*, 9, p. 8.

100. *Ibid.*, 8, No. 47.

101. *Ibid.*, IX, No. 26.

on 3rd May, 1801 at Seondha and defeated him.[102] In the battle, Lakhwa Dada and the Raja of Datia were wounded; his adherents deserted him and the widows fled away with the remaining Sardars. Lakhwa Dada was offered shelter by the Rana of Udaipur, but this unfaithful, blunt and brave soldier expired on 7th February, 1802.[103] James Skinner mentions him as "the best Maratha General of his time."[104] British Resident Colonel Palmer admired him for his moderation.[105] and lamented his downfall.

Sarkar wrote about him : "His political sagacity equaled his generalship. Like his master Mahadji, he had the wisdom to treat the English with courtesy and friendliness."[106] He was "jealous of French influence in Hindustan.[107] Thus it cannot be denied that he was a brave soldier, but his policy of allying himself with the enemies of his master and of trusting the East India Company proved disastrous to the Maratha State. It is a pity that he did not use his generalship, tact and ability for the reconstruction of the State. He used it for its demolition.

12. Bapuji Sindhia

Bapu Sindhia was only Maratha Sardar of Daulat Rao who proved too tough for British diplomacy. He came into prominence when he was sent to help Colonel Monson after the latter's defeat by Jaswant Rao Holkar. He informed the British about the defeat and captivity of Lieutenant Lucan.[108] Later, he left the British forces to their fate and joined Jaswant Rao's Holkar. It is said that he joined Holkar with Daulat Rao's consent. General Lake demanded his punishment,[109] but Sindhia replied that Bapuji had to take recourse to such a path, because he was left alone and did not receive pecuniary aid from the East India

---

102. Seondha battle *Poona Residency Correspondence,* IX, 249-54, Frasers's Skinner I. 185-87, Gulgule D. Letter of 2nd May, 1801 and for settlement with widows Collin's letter of 5th October, 1801 and 10th Feb., 1802 not printed in *Poona Residency Correspondence.*

103. Dr. R. Singh, p. 221.

104. Fraser, I, 124, 131.

105. *Poona Residency Correspondence,* VIII, p. 217, No. 42.

106. Sarkar, *Fall of the Mughal Empire,* IV, p. 146.

107. Duff, *History of the Marathas,* III, p. 279, ed. 1912.

108. *Ibid.,* p. 299.

109. *Ibid.*

Company.[110] There appears to be more than a grain of truth in Daulat Rao's contention, because Resident Webb recommended to Lord Lake the payment of Rs. 1.5 lakhs to Bapu,[111] which was never paid. When Daulat Rao Sindhia interfered in the dispute between Jaipur and Jodhpur, Bapuji supported Dhokal Singh, the imposter, against Raja Man Singh of Jodhpur, and remained at Nagore upto 1808, but Amir Khan persuaded him to give up his alliance with Dhokal Singh.[112]

Thereafter, Bapuji was appointed Administrator of Mewar in place of Ambaji in 1811; he came in conflict with Jaswant Rao Bhau and Amir Khan's Lieutenant Jamshed Khan. He ruled with an iron hand and so Rana Bhim Singh of Udaipur sent Ajit Singh to complain against him in 1815, but Daulat Rao Sindhia refused to interfere.[113]

Bapuji also attacked Jaipur when the Raja of Jaipur refused to pay tribute. In June, 1808, he defeated the Jaipur forces, took Junara, Beejdara, and several other forts. In November, 1808, the Raja of Jaipur sent ambassadors to Daulat Rao and Bapuji desisted from further attacks. In 1817, he was instructed by Daulat Rao Sindhia to pursue a milder policy towards the Rajput Rajas. He was, however, no match for Colonel Tod and Metcalfe in diplomacy, and so Colonel Tod succeeded in entering into treaties with the Rajput rulers, which forced Daulat Rao to renounce his claims on the Rajput Rajas in 1817.

He was later ordered to cooperate with Major Ludlow to crush the Pindaries, but instead of cooperating with the British forces, he allied himself with their adversaries. However, he failed even to help the Pindaries.

In 1819, he attacked the Rajas of Ratlam and Sailana to enforce Sindhia's claims to tribute upon them but Malcolm intervened on the Rajas' behalf and assured realisation by and through the East India Company. He died soon after, probably in 1820. On the whole, he appears to be the most loyal servant of Daulat Rao Sindhia.[114]

---

110. Duff, *History of the Marathas*, pp. 299-300.

111. *Poona Residency Correspondence*, II, No. 16, pp. 24-25.

112. Dr. Raghubir Singh, p. 245.

113. *Ibid.*, 255.

114. Malcolm, *Political History of India*, II, p. 248.

13. Vithul Punt

Vithul Punt was the Chief Minister of Daulat Rao Sindhia during the critical period of the Second Maratha War. He was a very competent person, but too old, selfish and hot-tempered. Malcolm wrote : "Vithal Punt (is) neither destitute of ability nor deficient in energy, but he adds to bodily infirmity a very irritable temper and he has lately shown that he is capable of sacrificing the interest of the state to his private resentment."[115] Later on his death paved the way for the supremacy of Sarji Rao Ghatge, Ambaji and Babu Rao Angria. Malcolm said of him that "he never saw a man with such a face for the game of brag."[116]

Minor Personalities

Jadav Rao Bhaskar : He was a brave man who helped Daulat Rao during the upheavals of Poona. He remained Diwan for a short time and fell fighting against heavy odds at Assaye.[117] His younger brother, Annah Bhaskar, served Daulat Rao for a long time through all the ups and downs of his life, though in 1804 he had to face the enmity of Vithal Punt.[118]

Hindu Rao Ghatge : He was the son of Sarji Rao Ghatge. After the death of his father, he became supreme in the councils of Daulat Rao Sindhia. During the Pindari War, Chitu wrote to him for help, stating that "if such a favourable opportunity as the present (is) allowed to slip out of hand, it will not again readily occur. "Hindu Rao Ghatge urged Daulat Rao Sindhia to help the Pindaries to save them from complete extinction and advised him to adopt a bold policy, but nothing came out of this proposal.[119] During the last days of Daulat Rao, he became supreme, but his power diminished later on with the decline in the power of Baiza Bai.

Munshi Kamal Nain : He seems to have been a native of Northern India, probably of Kasimir.[120] He enjoyed the complete

---

115. *Poona Residency Correspondence,* II, No. 1 dated 1-5-1804.
116. Kaye, *Life of Malcolm,* Vol. I, p. 241.
117. Khare, XIV 6749.
118. *Poona Residency Correspondence,* XI, No. 1.
119. *Ibid.*, Vol. XIV.
120. Basu, *Rise of the Christian Power in India,* p. 578, Mill VI, pp. 454-58.

confidence of Daulat Rao Sindhia. He began to reside at Delhi after retirement during the period of the Second Maratha War. Lord Lake and Malcolm called him and urged him to send one of his relations to Daulat Rao to counsel him for negotiations with the British. Ambaji made a favourable response and Kamal Nain became the means of communication between the British and Sindhia's court. In the words of Sardesai, "he became the sole adviser of Sindhia and meekly carried out all that Malcolm desired."[121] He was amply remunerated in the form of a Jagir in perpetuity which his family still enjoys.[122]

Shah Nizammuddin : He was a confidential servant of Mahadji and on account of his religious influence, he was appointed Subedar of Delhi. He failed in the job owing to his harshness, and ruined the cause of Daulat Rao Sindhia, as we shall see later. His son Mohammad Khan was the companion of Daulat Rao from an early age and encouraged luxurious habits in the latter.

Review

A review of the lives of these Maratha Nobles and officers reveals that they lacked a national spirit and worked more for personal ends than for any higher objective. Their mutual bickerings and personal jealousies did not let them look beyond their noses. They took more pleasure in letting down their immediate rivals than in serving the cause of their master and country. Even those who were loyal and honourable were often dragged into these factious rivalries. They were no match for British diplomats, who were inspired by the mission of implanting the Pax Britannica in Indian soil. British officers had a better sense of discipline in their ranks and were emotionally more integrated than their Indian counterparts. Most of the Maratha nobles were at one time or another secretly in league with the British for the sake of securing their Jagirs and ill-gotten wealth under British protection.

Household Affairs of Daulat Rao Sindhia

Another serious difficulty that Daulat Rao had to face at the beginning of his reign was that of intrigues against him within

121. Sardesai, *New History of the Marathas*, III, p. 434.

122. Sardesai, *New History of the Marathas*, p. 435, Basu, *Rise of the Christian Power in India*, p. 579, Secret Papers 1805-06.

his own family. Historians pay little or no heed to the domestic affairs of a sovereign, but sometimes the power behind the curtain influences the course of history. The first marriage of Daulat Rao Sindhia took place on 1st June, 1792, when he was only 11 or 12 years old. According to Hindu traditions, this girl, Durgabai, being the eldest wife, was termed Maharani and was entitled to higher respect than Baiza Bai, but she failed to gain the love of Daulat Rao and died dejected, unwept and unknown on 4th May, 1812.*

Next to her was Sindhia's second wife named Rukma Bai. Daulat Rao's relations with Rukma Bai also were not cordial.[123] Daulat Rao Sindhia showed reluctance to adopt a child to the very end, as according to Maratha custom Rukma Bai the elder surviving queen, should have been the guardian of the minor Raja and in this way power should have passed to her which Daulat Rao Sindhia did not like for the sake of leaving all power to Baiza Bai after his death.[124]

The other important court ladies were the widows of Mahadji Sindhia, *viz,* Laxmi Bai, Yamuna Bai, Bhagirath Bai and Kesara Bai. Of these Luxmi Bai, was quarrelsome, and Yamuna Bai, a weather-cock, Bhagirath Bai, a partisan of Daulat Rao was gentle, mild, and sober, and Kesar Bai "highly praised for wisdom" was the chief adviser of Daulat Rao in 1794 and 1795.[125] All three widows possessed administrative and military experience.[126] In addition to these widows, Mahadji had left two daughters named Bala Bai and Chima Bai. Bala Bai was married to Ladoji Shitole, who worked as Resident for Sindhia at Delhi, but he died at a young age. Bala Bai's daughter was married to Yashwant Rao Dubberain in Feb., 1798.[127] Her son, Shitole Deshmukh,

* The British Resident wrote : "Her Highness died on the 4th instant after an illness of about ten days...this event from the terms which existed between the Maharaja and the late Bai is not one which occasions mourning, otherwise than in appearance." Footnote : 1. *Poona Residency Correspondence,* XIV, No. 115, p. 137.

123. *Poona Residency Correspondence,* Vol. XIV.

124. See Chapter X.

125. Sarkar, *Fall of the Mughal Empire,* IV, p. 141.

126. Sardesai, *New History of the Marathas,* III, p. 337 and Hindi Translation, pp. 360 to 366.

127. *Poona Residency Correspondence,* IV, No. 83.

was married to Yashwant Rao Dabade's daughter[128] and was supported as successor to Mahadji in the beginning. During her widowed life, Bala Bai passed her time in pilgrimages, in erecting temples and in planting trees.[129] Broughton states that "Bala Bai, the daughter of Mahadji Sindhia, a lady, who possesses great influence in camp has avowed herself as the supporter of those who oppose the present Minister (Sarji Rao). This shows that her influence over Sindhia was great. She belonged to the anti-Sarji Rao Group. She was given a Jagir at Pauri (now a tehsil in the district of Shivpuri) and passed her remaining days there.*

Jija Bai was the eldest daugher of Daulat Rao and was married to the son of Jaswant Rao Senapati in the Deccan. She died in 1820 and her claims were refused by the British Government.[130] Chumna or Chima Bai was his second daughter. She was granted a pension by the East India Company after the Second Maratha War, but she died while giving birth to a child at a young age and the East India Company stopped her pension. Maina Bai, the mother of Daulat Rao Sindhia, first used to live with her son, but later generally lived at Ujjain with her brother Babu Rao Angria. Shahjahanpur was granted to her for her maintenance[131] and after her it passed on to Baiza Bai.

Daulat Rao Sindhia, also kept concubines, slave girls and many female attendants, called Buktees.[132] Daulat Rao shared this vice with other rulers of the age, but it goes to his credit that they did not exercise any political influence. There was a great number of household servants and khasgi troops, who were called khidmatgars and used to work as confidential

128. *Poona Residency Correspondence*, VI, No. 2, 3-3-1797.

129. *Poona Residency Correspondence*, XIV and Broughton Thomas D., *Letters written in a Maratha Camp*.

* She sent for the Maharaj lately, and read him a long lecture upon the state of his affairs; adding abundance of good advice, and many exhortations to reform before it was too late, to all of which he listened very attentively and promised to give it his serious consideration.

130. Foreign Political Index No. 51, Oct. 14, 1820.

131. Malcolm, *Political History of India*, C.I.I. & Broughton.

132. Broughton has given a description of his meeting with Buktees in his book, p. 99.

servants of household affairs. Dhondava, Ysuwagh and Annah were great favourites.

Baiza Bai and Her Influence

Daulat Rao's relations with his third wife Baiza Bai need a little elaboration. It was only on Baiza Bai, daughter of Sarji Rao Ghatge of the famous Kagal family of Kolhapur, claiming Rajput descent, that he showered his favours liberally. She was married to him on 16th Feb., 1798 at the age 14, when Daulat Rao was 18. He was charmed by her beauty, elegance and tact. She did not interfere in the politics of her husband's court for a considerable time, despite the tumultuous fortunes of father. Only one or two instances of the interest in politics are recounted. Early in her married life, she opposed the annexation of Udaipur by Sindhia, on the ground, as supposed by Tod, that the most prominent Rajput state should not be annihilated.[133] She also opposed Sindhia's marriage with that famed beauty of Rajasthan, princess Krishna Kumari of Udaipur,[134] again on the ground that the proud Rajputs would never agree to such a misalliance without warfare.

The repercussions of the appointment of her father Sarji Rao Ghatge as Prime Minister were great. The Shenvi Brahmins and the widows of Mahadji Sindhia, who lost their former power with the advent of Sarji Rao, rose against Sindhia. The diplomats of the East India Company also hated and feared Sarji Rao, as it was not possible to get Court secrets and to weave the web of diplomacy during the regime of Sarji Rao. So the widows of Mahadji Sindhia and Balloba Pagnis, Lakhwa Dada and others rose against Daulat Rao and declared war against him. This was really a war for power. Sarji Rao Ghatge saw many political ups and downs later and was killed in 1809. His assassination distressed Baiza Bai most. Broughton writes : "The Baee (Baiza Bai) is in the deepest affliction at the sudden and shocking fate of her father. Sindhia sat up with her the whole of last night, endeavouring to console and comfort her;

133. Tod, *Annals and Antiquities of Rajasthan*, ed. by Crooke, Vol. I, pp. 533-34, ed. 1920.

134. Tod, *Annals and Antiquities of Rajasthan*, ed. by Crooke, F.N. Vol. I, p. 536, ed. 1920. *Poona Residency Correspondence*, XI Nos. 172 and 173, pp. 264-65 and Dr. R. Singh writes, *Purva Dhunik Rajasthan*, pp. 242-43.

and with his own hands wiping away the tears which she shed in abundance."[135]

Baiza Bai had to suffer further grief when her brother Hindu Rao Ghatge was ill-treated by the Raja of Kolhapur. In the treaty of 23rd November, 1805, the British Government granted her a Jagir of the value of two lacs per annum and of one lac to Chimna Bai, the daughter of Daulat Rao.[136]

Baiza Bai's marital life also was not happy, because Daulat Rao Sindhia suffered from the painful disease with which nature punishes promiscuous sensuality.[137] Baiza Bai suffered such indignities patiently and helped her husband faithfully through thick and thin. The most poignant tragedy of her life was that she bore many sons but all of them died in their infancy.

Daulat Rao Sindhia died without adopting a child and his rights devolved upon Baiza Bai. She selected for adoption one Mugat Rao, a distant relative, 11 years of age.* Baiza Bai tried to gain all power in her hands proclaiming herself "Regent" but owing to the intervention of the East India Company, she was expelled in 1833 and all power passed to Jankoji.[138] Later on she passed her days of long widowhood of 36 years *i.e.*, from 1827 to 1863 in secluded piety and kept herself aloof from all mundane affairs, though in 1857 she showed some actively.[139] She died on 16th September, 1863.[140]

Influence of Baiza Bai's Father Sarji Rao Ghatge

Sarji Rao Ghatge, father of Baiza Bai, was the most hated and determined enemy of the British. He was born in 1750. He

---

135. Broughton, *Letter from a Maratha Camp*, p. 226.
136. Malcolm, *Political History of India*, Vol. I. p. 34; 359.
137. Sarkar, *Fall of the Mughal Empire*, Vol. IV, pp. 149-50, *Poona Residency Correspondence*, XIV.

* The ceremony of adoption took place on June 17, 1827 and the boy was married the same day. The title of Alijah Jankoji Rao Sindhia was assumed by him when he sat on the throne.

138. See *Native States of India* by Maleson under Gwalior.
139. She deserves a place in Maratha History as a typical Maratha woman about whom Broughton wrote : "She has a bold look; which is to be observed in no other woman of Hindustan. Baiza Bai was conversant with horse riding."
140. *Journal of Indian History*, August, 1965, pp. 628-29, Vol. XL, III Article by Tilak Raj Sareen *Gwalior under Mutineers and Gwalior Residency* File No. 1361/1858.

first entered the employment of Daulat Rao Sindhia as a spy,[141] and soon earned a high place in Sindhia's estimation and became a trusted officer for the delicate duty of guarding eminent prisoners like Baji Rao, who was then in Sindhia's custody.[142] According to Grant Duff, Sarji Rao was persuaded to marry his daughter to Daulat Rao by Baji Rao.[143] Sardesai on the other hand, attributes the marriage to Sarji Rao's own ambitious design.[144] Daulat Rao was attracted by Baiza Bai's beauty and higher caste. After the marriage, Ghatge became Prime Minister of Sindhia. On account of the backing of Nana, the Peshwa, Baji Rao, and Daulat Rao himself, he became supreme in the latter's dominions. To realise the amount due to Daulat Rao, promised by Baji Rao II, he ruthlessly plundered Poona and committed cruel atrocities upon its innocent inhabitants.

His appointment caused resentment among the Shenvi party and annoyed the widows of Mahadji Sindhia also. They declared war against Daulat Rao. Daulat Rao connived at the capture of Ghatge by Michael Filose who tied him with strong ropes, paraded him through the bazar beating him with the butt ends of rifles. Later on, he was confined in Ahmednagar Fort:[145] but he still remained undaunted.

During the Second Maratha War, with the help of his relations; he tried to form an anti-British confederacy at Poona.[146] In October, 1801, he defeated Jaswant Rao Holkar, and plundered Indore.[147] After the treaty of Sarji Arjun Gaon, when Daulat Rao Sindhia tried to revive the war with the East India Company, he urged for a bold policy,[148] but he soon fell into the British trap laid by Kamalnain, the notorious agent of Malcolm. Ghatge worked hard to impart vigour to the Administration, but Daulat Rao Sindhia never acted on the vigorous policy of Ghatge. He even refused to pay the troops from his private funds and never cared for the Dharna of the discontented soldiers.

---

141. Sardesai, *New History of the Marathas*, III, p. 332. H.T. ed. Jan. 1964.
142. *Ibid.*, III, p. 321.
143. Duff, *History of the Marathas*, III, pp. 140, 141, ed. 1912.
144. Sardesai, *New History of the Marathas*, III, p. 322.
145. *Ibid.*, III, p. 340.
146. *Poona Residency Correspondence*, VIII, Poona Affairs.
147. Malcolm, *Political History of India*, C.I.I., pp. 217-19.
148. Duff, *History of the Marathas*, III, p. 302, ed. 1912.

He was a sworn enemy of the British. They planned his dismissal. British Residents contrived to hatch plots to oust Daulat Rao, but none of them could mature under the sleepless vigilance of Sarji Rao. Once he punished four persons mercilessly merely on suspicion of taking part in plots.[149]

Broughton has drawn a pen picture of Sarji Rao.[150] But he has painted him in the darkest dye.

Sarji Rao Ghatge met a tragic end.... "The circumstances which immediately led to the event of yesterday arose from Ghatge's determination, if possible, to procure Ambaji's succession to the Subashship of Gwalior. Maharaja showed reluctance...ordered *(Ghatge's) detention, but Ghatge ran away and his followers drew swords to defend him; troops followed him and he was speared by Anand Rao Sindhia."[151] Broughton writes that the minister had gone to the Darbar, and was earnestly pressing Sindhia to accede to some of his proposals to which "the Mahraj, as usual, returned evasive and unsatisfactory replies.... As he was about to depart, Sarji Rao repeated his remonstrances.... Sindhia escaped from the tent; giving an order, however to secure his person. He was followed and killed.[152]

After that Jawahar and other partisans were robbed of their wealth and punished.

Broughton, Grant Duff, Malcolm, Resident Jankins and Choksey have given a highly exaggerated picture of his atrocities and licentious character. Sardesai and J.N. Sarkar have also condemned Sarji Rao. According to Broughton, "he was bold and hasty in conception; but so little scrupulous in the means by which he endeavoured to attain his ends that instead of conciliating those whose concurrence was necessary to ensure success, he only inspired them with doubt and apprehension." Choksey says, "He (Daulat Rao) fell into the clutches of a wicked wretch, one Sarja Rao Ghatgey," "a character the like of

149. Malcolm, *Political History of India*, I, p. 328.

150. Sardesai, *New History of the Marathas*, III, p. 356 and Broughton, pp. 67-68.

* Broughton Thomas D., *Letters written in a Maratha Camp*, pp. 82, 83. Broughton says, that he presented Jawahar Nautch girl to his son-in-law and afterwards made her, his own favourite in his old age.

151. *Poona Residency Correspondence*,Vol. XI, No. 293, p. 446.

152. Broughton Thomas D., *Letters written in a Maratha Camp*, pp. 223-24.

whom is hardly to be found in the annals of India and who contributed to the material ruin of the Maratha States."[153] But, in fairness to him, we have to assert that he was more sinned against than sinning. Sarji Rao Ghatge was the only person whom the East India Company dreaded most and, had he remained in power, British expansion could not possibly have been so easy. He can be compared with Trimbuckji Dingalia, since both began their careers as spies, believed in the maxim that the end justifies the means, tried to infuse a fresh spirit of boldness in their masters, Daulat Rao and Baji Rao II respectively, spared no pains to whittle down British Imperialism and suffered for their country's sake, but destiny willed otherwise and they failed to avert the eventual disaster.

The influence of Baiza Bai and her father was so overwhelming that after a short period Babaji Patankar, her uncle, became minister of Daulat Rao and her brother Hindu Rao Ghatge continued the management of affairs upto 1832. After that all power passed to the adopted son Jankoji Sindhia.

The Widows' War

Another factor responsible for internal disturbances in the reign of Daulat Rao Sindhia was the hostile attitude of the widows of Mahadji Sindhia in the early years of his reign, resulting in a Civil War that lasted from 1796 to 1802 and had momentous repercussions.

Mahadji had married nine wives, five of whom had died before him, and three survived him, *viz.*, Bhagirath Bai, Yamuna Bai and Laxmi Bai and a morganatic wife Kesara Bai.[154] Sarkar mentions of one Kesra Bai, a morgantic wife of Mahadji as remarkable for intelligence and good sense. Laxmi Bai had opposed the adoption of Daulat Rao even during the lifetime of her husband.[155] Malcolm writes : "The succession of Daulat Rao was disputed by the widows of Mahadji who proclaimed another prince, and having assembled an army, did not give up the contest till they had been defeated in several actions."[156]

153. Choksey, *A History of British Diplomacy at the Court of the Peshwas*, p. 129, Ed. 1951.
154. Sarkar, *Fall of the Mughal Empire*, IV, p. 150.
155. Duff, *History of the Marathas*, I, p. 505.
156. Malcolm, *Political History of India*, I, p. 131.

A variety of causes are given by historians for the outbreak of hostilities between Daulat Rao Sindhia and the widows. Sardesai states that Daulat Rao did not fulfil his promise of sufficient provisions for them, and so they rose up against him.[157] Grant Duff and Palmer state that the widows demanded the "committing to their custody of a young wife of his late adoptive father whom he had forced to his bed."[158] The other view is that the widows were designedly set against Daulat Rao.[159] Basu, Sunder Lal, Kincaid and Parasnis and even Grant Duff do not seem to attribute the war to the scandal. Secret papers in the National Archives clearly establish the fact that it was the set design of the widows to oust Daulat Rao, as Sindhia's ambition appeared to Sir John (Shore) to be unbounded,[160] whose power had arrived at a most alarming eminence,[161] and the Britishers encouraged the widows to take up arms against their own adopted son. The real cause of the hostile attitude of the Widows appears to be that they desired to capture power in the state for themselves. "The Shenvi Brahmins, who held the principal offices under him, chafed at the expulsion of their accredited chief, Balloba Tatiya by Sakha Ram Ghatge, fanned the ill-will of the widows of Mahadji and leagued with the latter, excited disturbances in Sindhia's dominions. The Peshwa Baji Rao II fomented troubles by carrying on clandestine intrigues for the overthrow of Daulat Rao.[162]

Unfortunately they got the support of the Shenvi Party, the "Sarswat Faction"[163] led by Balloba Pagnis, who was the Prime Minister and of Lakhwa Dada, who was the Viceroy in the North and a leading general of Sindhia. Grant Duff states that the "Shenvi Brahmins...much disgusted by the elevation of Sarji Rao Ghatge espoused the cause of the two Byes"[164] and

157. Sardesai, *New History of the Marathas*, III, p. 237.

158. Palmer's Embassay, p. 166 and Duff III, p. 162.

159. Basu, *Rise of the Christian Power in India*, pp. 386-87, Sunder Lal, *Bharat Men Angrezi Rajya*, p. 400 ed. 1960.

160. Choksey, *A History of British Diplomacy at the Court of the Peshwas*, p. 196.

161. Malcolm, *Political History of India*, Vol. I, p. 188.

162. N.B. Roy, Introduction, *Poona Residency Correspondence*, XI, p. 11.

163. Sardesai, *New History of the Marathas*, III, p. 337.

164. Duff, *History of the Marathas*, p. 538, Vol. I.

they further got support of the East India Company, help of Amrit Rao, the assistance of the Raja of the Kolhapur and probably of the Peshwa Baji Rao II. The British Resident, Colonel Palmer writes, "It is reported that the enterprise of Muzaffar Khan was suggested by the Peshwa himself."[165] Even Sardesai asserts that "the forces of Nizam Ali and of the Bhonsleys of Nagpur also marched from their bases at the call of the ladies."[166] Thus the widows created complications unparalled in Maratha history, with the object of overthrowing Daulat Rao Sindhia.

Palmer also states : "The person to be intended to be raised to the Masnad in the room of Daulat Rao is to be selected by the principal Begam of Mahadji Sindhia, who it is supposed will make choice of a youth, possibly Maunaji Phaukaria who held the Raj several years under Raghunath Rao."[167]

Daulat Rao's absence from Poona provided a golden opportunity to the widows to form a formidable league against him. Being encouraged by British diplomats, Shenvi Brahmins, Jaswant Rao Holkar and probably also by Baji Rao II, they put forth a proposal to the Governor General for adopting a boy and this proposal was also forwarded to Jaswant Rao Holkar, Lakhwa Dada, Jaggoo Bapu etc. and circular letters were sent to the several Kiladars and Amils and to Perron....[168]

The Governor General, Lord Wellesley, desired that Daulat Rao Sindhia should anyhow leave Poona, as Grant Duff states that "the principal danger to the English in a war with Tipu, supported by their European rival, was the fear of his being joined by the other native powers." He further says, "it became a primary object to induce Sindhia to return to Hindustan to accomplish the annihilation of Mysore." Mill and Sunderlal also are of the same opinion. To avoid a possible collusion of Sindhia with Tipu, false reports of the invasion of King Zamanshah of Afghanistan were put forward, but this failed to achieve the purpose. Then, the officers of the East India Company, took advantage of the vanity of the widows and

165. *Poona Residency Correspondence,* VI, No. 102, 107 & p. 161, 170.

166. Sardesai, *New History of the Marathas,* III, pp. 337, 339.

167. *Poona Residency Correspondence,* 6 No. 107, p. 170.

168. *Ibid.,* VIII, No. 73.

worked up their feelings against Daulat Rao. The Resident, Collins, was sent to sow the seeds of discord and he reached Ujjain in the absence of Daulat Rao Sindhia, who was then at Poona.[169] He added fuel to fire and took full advantage of the ambitious, foolish, and ignorant ladies as well as of the disaffection of the Shenvi Brahmins to encourage the plot against Daulat Rao.

On 26th October, 1796, Balloba Pagnis and Bhau Bakshi Diwan were arrested and the widows, along with Lakhwa, took up arms against Daulat Rao Sindhia.[170] A regular civil war broke out over an extensive area from the south to the north, from Poona to Kolhapur, and from Ujjain to Bundelkhand. It was possible to capture the ladies but Daulat Rao did not consider this as prudent. Unknown to him, however :

> Muzaffar Khan, Pathan Officer in the interest of the Shenvi Brahmins, who commanded a choice body of Hindustan horse in Sindhia's service, suddenly assailed the escort, rescued the ladies, and brought them back to the neighbourhood of Sindhia's camp. This daring act would have been punished immediately but Sindhia had reason to believe that many chief persons in his army were involved, and he also hesitated to attack a party of desperate men, lest either of the females standing in such relationship to himself, should be killed in the tumult, an accident which would have entailed upon him the greatest disgrace and odium throughout the Maratha country.[171]

On 18th June, 1798, however, Daulat Rao made an attack on the widows, but the ladies took to flight and Daulat Rao being quite unable to suppress them, restored Nana Phadnavis to liberty on 18th July and threw Sarji Rao into prison in order to satisfy the widows. Nana Phadnavis did not interfere in the dispute, but Daulat Rao refused to accept Palmer's mediation, saying that it was a family dispute."[172] Though later on he

---

169. Basu, *Rise of the Christian Power in India,* pp. 368-379.
170. *Fall of the Mughal Empire,* V, IV, p. 161.
171. Duff, *History of the Marathas,* I, p. 539.
172. Palmer's Embassay, p. 161 letter No. 103 of 25th May, 1798.

accepted the offer.[173] But as Grant Duff states, "The widows became so extravagant in their demands that it was impossible to accede to them."[174] In order to satisfy them, Daulat Rao Sindhia appointed Lakhwa Viceroy of the North in 1799,[175] and tried his best to conciliate them.

With a large following, these ladies retired from Ujjain to Poona. Daulat Rao himself met them there and tried to compose their ruffled spirits by arranging for their residence at Burhanpur. But they refused to move.[176] On 8th June, their adherents attacked Daulat Rao at midnight.

According to Sardesai, the widows' cause was just and this view has received support at the hands of impartial observers.[177] According to Sarkar, these ladies were loved and honoured by high and low alike, and they could form a centre round which the growing discontent against Daulat Rao's tyranny could rally and thus raise a formidable opposition to his power.[178] It cannot be denied that the widows were highly respected by the people, but to say that their cause was just or they had popular support seems unwarranted by facts. According to Malcolm,[179] the foreign secret papers and Poona Residency correspondence,[180] as already stated, the widows desired to usurp all power and to set up another boy in place of Daulat Rao. It is difficult to consider this cause as just. The widows did not have any popular support either. It is true that they got the support of Balloba Pagnis and Lakhwa Dada, because they desired to grind their own axes by supporting the widows' cause. According to Dr. Raghubir Singh, "in the name of the widowed queens Lakhwa declared himself Chief Officer of the North."[181] Similarly they got the support of the British, who only pretended to be well-wishers of the State. "Colonel Palmer, the British Resident

173. Palmer's Embassay, p. 183.
174. Duff, *History of the Marathas,* I, p. 539.
175. Dr. Raghubir Singh, p. 227, states May, 1799.
176. Sardesai, *New History of the Marathas,* III, p. 338 and Palmer's Embassay, p. 159.
177. Sardesai, *New History of the Marathas,* III, p. 338.
178. Sarkar, *Fall of the Mughal Empire,* IV, p. 11.
179. *Central India Memoirs* I, p. 131.
180. *Poona Residency Correspondence,* Vol. VI No. and add. No. 107.
181. Dr. Raghubir Singh, p. 226 Ed. 1951.

at Baji Rao's Court offered his mediation to Sindhia, by whom it was declined[182] on the ground "that it was a family dispute and would be adjusted without the intervention of friends."[183] Amrit Rao was also a partisan of the British and Jaswant Rao supported the widows for his own selfish reasons. With the help of Jaswant Rao, the widow occupied Ujjain. But when they failed to pay money to him, he abandoned their cause. In Ujjain, too, nobody moved a finger in their support or contributed a single shell to help them. Similarly the support of the Raja of Datia and Chatrapatis of Kolhapur and Satara was not inspired by any high principles but by sheer self-interest. They married one daughter of Mahadji to an illegitimate son of the Chhatrapati of Kolhapur.

Bhagirathi Bai, the supposed cause of all this turmoil, died on 15th August, 1799, but even after her death, the widows continued their intrigues. Jaswant Rao Holkar, Durjan Sal and other Grassia Chiefs who had first joined the widows, now abandoned them. Only Lakhwa Dada and the Raja of Datia still continued to support them. At last, Du Perron defeated Lakhwa Dada and the partisans of the widows in the battle of Scondha on 3rd May, 1801,[184] Lakhwa Dada was wounded and he died on 7th February, 1802,[185] "at the temple of Salumber."[186] With his death the widows lost all support and had to come to terms. Ambaji Ingle on behalf of Daulat Rao Sindhia consented to give possession of Antri yielding a revenue of Rs. 2 lacs to the Byes.[187] Laxmi Bai survived till 1806 and Yamuna Bai till February, 1815.

According to J.N. Sarkar, "the Widows' War now ended, being engulfed in a colossal contest between Daulat Rao Sindhia and Jaswant Rao Holkar, whose final result was the loss of Maratha independence."[188] While it lasted, several thousands

182. Duff, *History of the Marathas*, III, p. 164, Ed. 1912.

183. Palmer's Embassy No. 103, pp. 161-62.

184. Gul Gule office, letter of 2nd May, 1801, Eraser Skinner, pp. 185-87, *Poona Residency Correspondence*, IX, pp. 249 and 254.

185. Rajya Adhyaksh's Jiwa Dada, p. 264 and letter No. 329.

186. Dr. R. Singh, p. 231.

187. *Poona Residency Correspondence*, Vol. IX, pp. 255-60 for detail letter of 14-2-1802, 5-10-1801, not printed in *Poona Residency Correspondence.*

188. Sarkar, *Fall of the Mughal Empire*, IV, pp. 177-78.

of persons died and much money was wasted. On account of this war, the English succeeded in annihilating the power of Tipu, winning over Jaswant Rao,[189] reducing the power of Sindhia, creating factions, and controlling the Nizam. In short, the war of the widows gave a severe blow to the tottering Maratha Empire.

Review

Thus we find that the European officers, the older nobility, the Pindari chiefs and the widows of Mahadji posed to Daulat Rao Sindhia a menace, which could have damped the bravest spirit into Pussilanimity. His dominions and government were clouded over with a climate of intrigue, internecine quarrels and self-seeking. From the day of his accession, Daulat Rao was faced with these formidable problems, which threatened the stability of his own power and indeed of the entire Maratha Empire. If he wanted to perpetuate his dynasty, Daulat Rao was bound to act on the prudent maxim : "discretion is the better part of valour," and, as we shall see during the course of present dissertation, he was probably not wrong in his final decisions.

189. Basu, *Rise of the Christian Power in India*, p. 228.

3

Relations of Daulat Rao Sindhia with Holkar

Introduction

Of Daulat Rao Sindhia's external problems, his relations with the Holkar family was the most troublesome. The rivalry between the Houses of Holkar and Sindhia dates from the time, when these two families began to come into prominence during the days of Baji Rao I. Malhar Rao Holkar forged ahead earlier to a higher rank in the Peshwa's army than Ranoji Sindhia, but the latter was luckier in his descendants. Malhar Rao outlived Ranoji Sindhia by 21 years and he was the sole elder Maratha statesman, who survived the Panipat disaster. He did not leave any direct male successor but the Sindhia family did better. Malhar Rao's daughter-in-law, Ahalya Bai, succeeded him, but during her regime the military power of Mahadji Sindhia was in the ascendant. The family chronicles of the Holkars claim that it was Malhar Rao's patronage that laid the foundation of the future greatness of the humble Mahadji Sindhia.[1] On the other hand the Sindhias assert that when Raghunath Rao tried to attack Ahalya Bai, Mahadji Sindhia and Jankoji Bhonsle refused to unite with him[2], and owing to this, the rule of Ahalya Bai was stabilised.

To begin with, the Sindhias and the Bhonsles maintained cordial terms[3] with her, but later on they fell out. Ahalya Bai

---

1. Malcolm, *Political History of India*, I, pp.181-82, Ed. 1832.

   Malcolm also asserts that a bond of 30 lacs of rupees of Ahalya Bai and 6 lacs of Horecarbai alias Mushia Bai was given as a loan to Mahadji.
2. Malcolm, *Political History of India*, I, p. 162.
3. *Ibid.*, p. 181.

was "a female without vanity, a bigot without intolerance"[4] and was very careful in financial matters, "but she could not command in the field, nor control distant province; hence her virtues counted for nothing in the manly games of war."[5] The evil of drink moreover, was the curse of the male members of the Holkar family.

Origins of the Rivalry

In 1787, on account of his defeat at Lalsot against the Rajputs, Mahadji had to ask for reinforcements and Nana sent Tukoji Holkar along with Ali Bahadur to help him. However, by his own efforts Mahadji regained his lost position in 1789. The help of Tukoji and Ali Bahadur was only nominal, but Tukoji demanded an equal share of the spoils of victory and encouraged Ali Bahadur also in opposing Sindhia. According to Kale Akhbarat, Mahadji gave 15 Mahals in North India to Tukoji Holkar, including Garh Mukteshwar, Khurja, Hapur, Dholpur, Achhnera, etc. Ali Bahadur was promised the Aligarh-Koil district. However, his refusal to divide equally the territory which he had won mainly through his own efforts became an apple of discord between the Holkar and Sindhia families. On the occasion of the conferment of the title of Deputy Vakil Mutlak on him, Tukoji sent only a servant to congratulate Mahadji, which was an insulting gesture. Further, he tried to exact tribute from the Rajputs and hindered Mahadji from doing so. Moreover, a historic feud between the two families still rankled. Malhar Rao Holkar I had not helped Dattaji Sindhia in the war against Ahmed Shah Abdali and had encouraged the Rajputs against Jayappa, and Najibuddula against Mahadji.

Nana Phadnavis was also apprehensive of Mahadji's supremacy. So he made no attempts to settle the quarrel between the two chiefs in the hope that he could check the ambition of Mahadji, by placing Tukoji and Ali Bahadur as counterpoises to him. But this was a fatal mistake, as Col. Palmer wrote on 23rd March, 1789 : "It is probably the expectation of Poona Durbar to preserve the influence of the state by the check which each chief will exercise upon the other. But, in my opinion, more will be lost by their dissensions than can be gained by

4. Malcolm, *Political History of India*, I, p. 195.
5. J.N. Sarkar, *Fall of the Mughal Empire*, IV, p. 76.

their mutual jealousies, and Maratha interests are exposed to be totally annihilated by such a delegation to them."[6] Ahalya Bai added fuel to the fire by constantly egging Tukoji on to claim equality with Mahadji. But ancestral glory or family tradition are of little avail in this matter of fact world. "The concerns of state depend for their success on character and capacity."[7]

The Course of the Struggle

Kama, a place 23 miles north of Bharatpur in Rajasthan, became a bone of contention between Tukoji and Mahadji. Differences further deepened by the overbearing attitude of Sindhia's Generals, Jeoba Dada and Gopal Bhau. At last, war clouds burst forth at Lakheri on 1st June, 1793, and a battle took place between the armies of Sindhia and Holkar in which Holkar's forces were routed.[8] After this battle, Mahadji became supreme in North India.

Thereafter the situation was reversed. In the previous generation, Malhar Rao Holkar I had died without a male successor, and now Mahadji died without a son, while Tukoji Holkar left four sons named Kashi Rao, Malhar Rao, Jaswant Rao and Vithoji Holkar. Jaswant Rao Holkar was the bravest of the whole lot. After the death of Tukoji Holkar in 1797, there ensued a fight among his sons for succession. Kashi Rao, the eldest was an imbecile, and all the other three brothers combined against him; but Daulat Rao "with Baji Rao's ready support"[9] availed himself of this opportunity and espoused the cause of Kashi Rao Holkar to exercise influence at Indore in his name.

On September 14, 1797, the armies of Daulat Rao made an unprovoked attack on Malhar Rao II and the latter died in the encounter.[10] His wife, who was pregnant, was captured with her son Khando Rao by Sindhia's army, but Jaswant Rao and Vithoji escaped. Jaswant Rao determined to avenge the wrong. He left Poona for Nagpur on 18th September, 1787, to gather opposition

6. *Poona Residency Correspondence,* I Nos. 246, 255.
7. Sardesai, *New History of the Marathas,* III, p. 213.
8. M.D. II 241, Gulgule Daftar, Holkar Kaif 64, Kala Akh.
9. *Ibid.*
10. *Poona Residency Correspondence,* VI No. 24 pp. 44 and 45.

to Sindhia. On 30th January, 1800, he was again arrested and imprisoned at the instigation of Sindhia. After a short imprisonment, however, he again escaped[11] and reached Dhar, where he was received kindly by Anand Rao Pawar, but dismissed again under the express instructions of Daulat Rao.

Jaswant Rao soon raised a large army of his own, as he was supported by all persons in his state for his opposition to the traditional enemy, Sindhia, and against his own brother, Kashi Rao who had became a tool in the hands of Sindhia.[12] The tribals, grassias, Pindaries, the Afghan soldiers under Amir Khan, Bhil chieftains, Jujhar Naik of Kherla, Goverdhan Naik of Mekhla and Bhan Singh of Arkani joined him and he soon had 2,000 horses, 5,000 foot under him. He routed two brigades of Sindhia's general, Duderenic, in December 1798. Fully equipped with men and money, unbeaten in battle, he turned to win his patrimony and reached Maheshwar, where he acquired Ahalya Bai's jewels and treasure. Then he joined the Widows and Lakhwa Dada in their insurrection against Daulat Rao Sindhia. William Gardener, a Scotch soldier of fortune tried to raise a brigade for Holkar, but he was captured by Sindhia's men.[13]

Daulat Rao and Holkar

Daulat Rao Sindhia left Poona on 5th December, 1800 to deal with Holkar, and reached Burhanpur on 15th February, 1801; but wasted his time in tiger shooting, Kite-flying and attending dances, and this delay ruined his cause.[14] All this while, Jaswant Rao Holkar was plundering Malwa and carried away all the wealth that he could find there. In the words of J.N. Sarkar, "For Malwa's misery, the responsibility lies primarily

11. For Jaswant Rao's early activities refer to Phalke's Kotah Papers Vol. II, 128-29-38-42, 43 his seal in 151.
12. Phalke's Kotah Papers. Vol. II, 128-29-38-42, 43 his seal in 151.
13. Basu mentions "Mr. Colerboke employed every means...to help Holkar against Sindhia." Rise of Christian power p. 336. Similarly Resident wrote to G.G. on 3rd August, 1978 vide, *Poona Residency Correspondence,* VIII No. 74 raising of brigade by Gardener vide, *Poona Residency Correspondence,* VIII No. 200, Mohan S. 76 A, Footnote Thakur II (Bhil) 13 Dipalpur 16 Mir Khan February 1799 and subsequent leading of troops at Headapsar by Britishers show some connivance of the Britishers in rise of Holkar's power.
14. *Poona Residency Correspondence,* VI 386-89, Gulgule Daftar.

on Jaswant Rao Holkar's unpatriotic ambition and in a lesser degree on Daulat Rao's insane desire to extinguish the power of the House of Holkar.[15]

Jaswant Rao in the north and Vithoji in the south practically destroyed all the vestiges of the power which the Peshwa and Sindhia had exercised hitherto in Malwa. The Peshwa sent Balaji Kunjar and Bappu Gokhale to suppress Holkar. Bappuji Gokhale succeeded in capturing Vithoji alive and brought him in chains before the Peshwa. The Peshwa immediately ordered Vithoji to be tied to the foot of an elephant and had him killed with horrid cruelty.[16] This was a blunder and the action sealed his doom. Jaswant Rao Holkar attacked Sindhia's general MacIntyre at Newari and defeated him. Next, he attacked Sindhia's army at Satwas, but failed to overcome it and called upon Amir Khan to unite with him near Ujjain for another attack.

The Battle of Ujjain

Jaswant Rao now attacked Sindhia's army, led by Hessing, and consisting of a corps of 8 battalions at Ujjain and after a hotly contested battle on July 18, 1801 defeated them; but did not plunder Ujjain immediately.[17] Entering Ujjain on September 1, 1801, he demanded fifteen lacs of rupees as war indemnity from the city, but he got only one-eighth of the demand, the rest having been pocketed by his officers.[18]

Sarji Rao Ghatge joined Daulat Rao's camp on 20th August and this supplied him with a counsellor of quick decision and driving power. In the meantime, Daulat Rao succeeded in seducing Dudere-nic and his son-in-law Plumet from Holkar's service. The combined army of the six battalions of Filose, six battalions of Brownrigg and 25,000 horses moved towards Ujjain. Holkar thereupon abandoned the city. Ujjain was recovered and Sarji Rao Ghatge proceeded towards Indore.

---

15. Sarkar, *Fall of the Mughal Empire*, IV, p. 167.
16. *Poona Residency Correspondence*, VI 405, Khare XII No. 6027, Thakur II 32, 34. Sardesai III, pp. 366-67. Duff-III, p. 199 Ed. 1912, Sarkar IV, p. 195.
17. *Central India Memories*, Vol. I, p. 215 and Mohan 593 A, *Poona Residency Correspondence*, IX, p. 28, Thakur II 38, Gulgule Basawan p. 159 of Sarkar.
18. Col. Collin's letter Holkar's letter to Barwal Dada, report of Saji Ballal of Daulat Rao's Camp, Baswan Sal's Amir Khan, Bhawani Shanker's narrative and Crompton's adventures, pp. 255-363.

The Battle of Indore

On 5th October, 1801, the rival hosts came face to face on the plain enclosed by the Sipra and the Kan rivers to the north of Indore and fighting lasted ten days. At last Ghatge and Browning advanced and came in conflict with Holkar's forces within two miles of Indore on the 14th. After a last desperate counterattack by Jaswant Rao himself, the struggle ended at sunset. Holkar was completely defeated, largely on account of the treachery of Amir Khan.[19] His 100 guns, camp and stores fell into the hands of Sindhia. Holkar fled to Kushalgarh and Jam Ghat and the remnants of the vanquished army followed him.

Sarji Rao exacted retribution from Indore and after some weeks the victors withdrew.[20] Grant Duff states : "Had Sindhia followed up the blow, the power of Jaswant Rao was by this victory annihilated."[21] Sardesai also states : "If Daulat Rao had the dash that Yashwant Rao was gifted with, he could easily have crushed the latter."[22] It is difficult to agree with these writers, because when a message for conciliation was sent to Jaswant Rao through Gen. Perron, "Jaswant Rao Holkar pointed to his horse and spear, and directed the men to tell their master that the former at all time afforded him a shade to sleep in, and the latter the means of subsistence."[23] Thus to hope for crushing the power of such a person in battle was an hopeless task.

Attempts at Reconciliation

The well-wishers of the Maratha nation desired reconciliation between the two chiefs, but their claims could not be reconciled by any ingenuity, as both of them lacked the spirit of compromise. Jaswant Rao demanded his recognition as regent at Indore and the restoration to him of every village and fort, in every part of India, that had ever belonged to the Holkars, and absolute parity between Sindhia and Holkar in respect of

---

19. Malcolm, *Political History of India*, I, p. 248, ed. 1832.
20. Mohan : S. 97 A, *Poona Residency Correspondence*, IX 33, Gulgule letter of 19th Oct. 1801.
21. Grant Duff, *History of the Marathas*, III, p. 201, ed. 1912.
22. Sardesai, *New History of the Marathas*, III, p. 365.
23. Gulgule, *Poona Residency Correspondence*, IX No. 50, Malcolm 1-220.

territory, income and power and resources through formal sanction by the Peshwa. He also demanded that Daulat Rao should cease to help Kashi Rao Holker in the latter's claim to the headship of the house of Holkar. On none of these points was Sindhia prepared to yield. The solution of hereditary rivalry between Sindhia and Holkar was a challenge to the statesmanship of the Peshwa. But such a feat of statesmanship was beyond the mental capacity and armed strength of Baji Rao II.

Jaswant Rao Moves South

The climax of the drama now began to approach fast. Finding Baji Rao II utterly impervious to his solicitations, Jaswant Rao moved south in April, 1802. He crossed the Tapti in May, 1802, reached Sangamner, about midway on the road from Nasik to Ahmednagar, in August. Holker's captains — Fateh Singh, Mane, Amir Khan and Shamat Khan — captured Nasik (June) Ahmadnagar (July) and Pandnarpur and Jamgaon, an ancestral village of Sindhia, 16 miles to the S.W. of Ahmadnagar.

The Battle of Baramati

Peshwa Baji Rao II appealed to Daulat Rao for help to oppose Holkar's forces under Nana Purandharao and Pandoji Kunjar. The Peshwa sent 25,000 men against Holkar hoping that his gold embroidered banner would overawe Holkar into retreat. Mane declared his intention of not doing anything against their common master till 50 shots had been fired. After the 50th discharge from Purandhare's guns, Mane opened his own fire and sent his horsemen forward on the gallop. At this, the Peshwas' army ran helter-skelter, leaving their guns and even the banner of the Peshwa. This complete victory of Holkar at Baramati on 8th October 1802, disabled the Peshwa from further action, but the Battle at Baramati was merely a rehearsal of the tragic drama soon to be staged at the battle of Hadapsar.

The Battle of Hadapsar

On 22nd October, Sada Shiva Bhaskar joined the routed forces of the Peshwa and took positions at Wonouri. Jaswant Rao Holkar now wrote to the Peshwa, begging him to send four front rank envoys for settling his feud with Sindhia on the basis of absolute equality between the two rival Houses. But without waiting for the Peshwa's reply, he crossed the Bor Ghat and reached Wanouri.

The Peshwa responded by sending a deputation of inferior rank and Holkar refused to meet them, declaring, "I cannot busy myself in this child's play." Baji Rao II's villainous favourites now again drove him to the suicidal course of further hostilities.[24] Holkar on his part declared that he would "die or conquer."[25]

At last, on Sunday the 25th October, 1802, the two sides clashed at Hadapsar with, it is said 1,44,000 men under Holkar and 80,000 in Sindhia's army. Holkar's battalions were commanded by British officers and Sindhia's army, now joined with the Peshwa's army, was also led by European officers. Holkar's however was superior in cavalry.

At about 8 o'clock in the morning, Sindhia's men opened a cannonade on Holkar's forces. Jaswant Rao restrained his own fire for a time. At 10 o'clock, the battle lines had come close together, and for a time Sindhia's forces pushed their opponents back. Seizing the advantage, Sindhia's massed squadrons fell upon the disordered Pathan ranks with fatal effect. The slaughter was great and it appeared as if Holkar's ranks were shattered. At this critical moment Col. Harding advanced with his brigade to the support of his chief's cavalry and by superior generalship, he shook the brigade which guarded the right flank of Sindhia's cavalry. At the same moment, Jaswant Rao himself rushed in to the thick of the battle, cutting down Sindhia's gunners and himself receiving four wounds in his arms. Capturing the enemy's guns, he turned them upon Sindhia's army with great effect. These men, already thrown into disorder by the steady fire of Harding's infantry, scattered like chaff before a sturdy gale. Baji Rao II retired from his position and proceeded towards Parvati and his forces followed his example. Sindhia's left, right and rear were all swept away with a rout by this time. His infantry put up stiffer resistance but had eventually to give way.[26] The personal bravery of Jaswant Rao had changed the whole course of the battle.

---

24. *New History of the Marathas,* III, p. 374.

25. Malcolm, *Political History of India,* I, p. 228.
    Asiatic Annual Register 1803, George Thomas's report in Mill, Memoirs of G. Thomas, 357, Resident Close to G.G. 26 Oct., 1802.

26. For details of battle see Asiatic Annual Register 1803 (Bombay Occur), p. 54, Bengal Occur, pp. 59-61, Mohan S.F. 109-110, Amioamah,

Results

Sindhia's army lost 5,000 men (killed and wounded) and all their guns and the whole of their camp equipment and luggage were destroyed. Holkar lost about 1,600 men, including Col. Harding. It was a decisive victory for Holkar and in one day Sindhia's power and prestige were destroyed beyond repair and the Peshwa had become a fugitive. In fact, it was a dooms day for the Maratha nation, fraught with far-reaching consequences. The backbone of Maratha power was broken. The demand of the hour was cohesion and consolidation of Maratha strength to resist British power, but the Sindhia Holkar struggle had rendered such opposition impossible. Henceforth, British expansion became irresistible.

The Peshwa wandered about for some time and at last took refuge in an English ship which landed him at their port of Bassein on 6th December, 1802, and here, on 31st December, 1802, he bartered away the independence of the Maratha Empire for his personal safety by the treaty of Bassein.[27] It is true that even before the battle Baji Rao II had secretly sent to Resident Close a secret agreement to cede lands worth 25 lakhs rupees a year in return for a British protective force of six battalions of sepoys[28], but this battle lifted the lid of secrecy and his surrender became complete.

There can be no two opinions that even in such straits, Baji Rao II committed a blunder by seeking British help. Had he gone to Sindhia or Bhonsle for protection, the fall of the Maratha Confederacy might not have been so precipitate. Holkar set up his puppet Amrit Rao as Peshwa in place of Baji Rao II, whose surrender to a foreign power was deemed equivalent to abdication. On 20th April, 1803, however, Arthur Wallesley entered Poona which had been vacated by Holkar and reinstalled Baji Rao II as Peshwa (as a British puppet) on 13th May, 1803,

---

Bhagwat's Holkar Patravyavhar First half pt. 1 Nos. 76-77, Khare XIV Nos. 6465-6471, Thakur-II 57, Holkar Kaif, p. 95 H. Crompton pp. 279-281, 352, Resident Close to G.G. 25 Oct. 1802.

27. Asiatic Annual Register for 1804, States Papers 68-70, Secret midnight interview with Resident Close on 17th April, 79 Wellesley's reply p. 80.

28. For Treaty of Bassein, full text in Wellesley's Despatches (i) 627-631, *As. An. Register for 1803*, State Papers, pp. 7-13.

History repeated itself and a drama like that of Mir Jafar's installation at Mursidabad was enacted at Poona.

Reactions of Sindhia

On learning of the victory of Holkar, Daulat Rao Sindhia issued letters, recalling his detachments in Hindustan to his side and intended to go to the Deccan in person. On 7th February, 1803, he reached the bank of the Narmada and arrived near Burhanpur on 24th February, 1803. On 27th February, 1803, Resident Collins demanded a categorical reply from Daulat Rao whether he accepted the Treaty of Bassein or objected to it; and he at the same time invited him to join in a general-subsidiary alliance with the English as the Peshwa had done.

Attempts for a Coalition

Daulat Rao Sindhia desired to make an anti-British coalition before the rupture with the English was complete. On 4th June, 1803, Raghuji Bhonsle joined Daulat Rao and both of them appealed to Jaswant Rao Holkar to join them. Holkar demanded the restoration of his territories and assured them of his readiness to join the Confederacy.[29] Daulat Rao Sindhia accepted nearly all the terms of Jaswant Rao Holkar and on 9th July surrended Jaswant Rao's nephew, Khanda Rao, to Holkar's men. But even then Holkar himself did not ally himself with Daulat Rao against the British. Daulat Rao Sindhia wrote to Holkar desiring a personal visit, to which the latter gave a curt reply : "The visit can take place as things come to be shaped."[30]

Several reasons have been advanced by various writers to explain why Holkar did not join Sindhia at this critical juncture. Major Basu and Sunderlal ascribe his reluctance to join Sindhia to Holkar's secret understanding with the British.[31&32] Grant Duff also points to British interest in these negotiations because "it was in the interest of the British Government to conciliate Holkar; and in order to prevent his joining the Confederacy, they wished to overlook any cause of complaint they had

29. Ait Patr, 373.

30. Sardesai, *New History of the Marathas*, III, p. 403.

31. Basu, *Rise of the Christian Power in India*, pp. 386-87. Sunderlal I, p. 400, ed. 1960.

32. *Ibid.*

against him."[33] J.N. Sarkar states that "Jaswant Rao Holkar though appealed to for joining a Maratha confederation against the English, knew the weakness of Sindhia's council and army and had no faith in Daulat Rao's promise of restoring Holkar's possessions. So like the realist in politics that he was, he withdrew to his own capital, after getting hold of his nephew, the child Khanda Rao, and Sindhia to his fate."[34]

None of these arguments stands close scrutiny, particularly Sarkar's argument that Jaswant did not join Daulat Rao because he was a realist. Jaswant Rao was an able general and competent soldier, but not a genuine realist in politics. Had he been so, he would have joined the anti-English coaltion at this critical juncture. Malcolm writes : "Jaswant Rao was willing to comply with Daulat Rao Sindhia's request for reconciliation, but while he was crossing the Narmada to join Sindhia, his conversation with Amir Khan turned the tables."[35] It remains inexplicable how Amir Khan persuaded Holkar not to join Sindhia at this juncture except by supposing that Holkar was gullible.

It is said that a letter said to be written by Daulat Rao to Baji Rao was intercepted by Amirit Rao and placed in General Wellesley's hands. Wellesley had it directed to Jaswant Rao. In this letter, Daulat Rao asked Baji Rao not to worry over Jaswant Rao. "Let us make a show of satisfying his demands. After the need is over, we shall both wreak our full vengeance upon him."[36] It is almost certain that no such letter was ever written by Sindhia. It is also most unlikely, if it was ever written, that it could have been despatched by an unreliable messenger from whom it could pass to a third party. It is possible that the whole affair was an intrigue of British diplomacy.

In the opinion of the present writer, three factors appear to be responsible for preventing the union of Jaswant Rao Holkar and Daulat Rao Sindhia :

(i) War psychosis,

(ii) Their deep ancestral jealousies, and

---

33. Duff : *History of the Marathas* III, p. 232, ed. 1912.

34. Sarkar, *Fall of the Mughal Empire*, IV, p. 255.

35. Malcolm, *Political History of India*, C.I., *A Memoir of Central India*, Vol. I, p. 232, Ed. 1832.

36. Owen *Despatches of Wellington*, p. 350.

(iii) British diplomacy

Protracted war had choked the stream of sympathies between the soldiers of the two groups. It was not easy to convert bitterness into sweetness overnight. Again, this reunion meant a step towards national integration, calling for great sacrifices for which nobody was prepared. Interested persons on both sides throve on this mutual jealousy, mistrust and parochialism. British diplomacy was determined to keep the Maratha chiefs divided and succeeded, where British armaments failed. It was in the interest of the British power to whittle down all attempts at the integration of Maratha interests. Their determination to establish British sovereignty over India could not succeed, if there was mutual love and confidence among the Maratha princes. They had no scruples where their major aim of the establishment of British supremacy was concerned. All these factors conspired to thwart all attempts at reunion and cooperation among the Marathas.

British Policy

British designs are clear from a letter of 16th July that General Wellesley wrote to Jaswant Rao Holker : "I am anxious to cultivate the good understanding which has subsisted between the Company's Government and you.... I have little doubt that you will conduct yourself in the manner which your own interest will dictate and that you will continue in peace with the Company. I send this letter with Kadir Nawaz Khan, a respectable officer, who enjoys my confidence and who will explain anything you desire to know, respecting my wishes," Kadir Nawaz Khan won Amir Khan to his side by arguments and by British gold and Amir Khan persuaded Holkar not to join Sindhia against the East India Company by clever tactics. The Second Anglo-Maratha War that now broke out between the East India Company and the Sindhia and Bhonsle will be discussed separately in the following chapter. However, it may be pointed out here that after the British had dealt with these Maratha chiefs, they turned upon Holkar. But the valiant Jaswant Rao was quite a tough customer. This does not directly concern us here, except in its later phases when, driven from the north, Holkar turned at bay against the Company in his dominance in Central India and by his unyielding defiance of the British once again revived the spirit of Maratha resistance.

Companions in the distress caused by a common enemy generally come close together and the same happened to Sindhia and Holkar. Sarji Rao Ghatge, whose influence with Sindhia was supreme, brought about a reconciliation and their armies joined together at Sabalgad.

So instable, however, were the political fortunes of Maratha politicians at this time that on 24th May, 1805, Jenkins, the British Resident with Sindhia, wrote to Lord Lake, "Sarji Rao Ghatge continues to exercise the functions of Prime Minister under the prevailing influence of Holkar, but my confidential communications with the principal officers of the government tend to impress a belief...that Ambaji Ingale will be his successor.... Ingale has been paid about 30 lacs of rupees.[37]

After the Second Anglo-Maratha War

From where Ambaji did get this gold to purchase his return to power? It is probable that it was British gold which brought about the downfall of Sarji Rao Ghatge and the first act of Ambaji on reinstatement was the restoration of the British Residency to its former footing.[38] The situation at that time was most critical in which context the return to power of Ambaji at Gwalior can be fully appreciated. Captain W. Sturrock, acting Resident, informed Malcolm about the possibility of an anti-British confederacy of Jaipur, Jodhpur and Udaipur.[39] Sindhia's army now purged of traitors like Perron and Lakhwa Dada was a formidable force of 20,000 cavalry, 10 battalions of Infantry and 64 guns, and was supported by Samad Khan, general of Amir Khan, with one battalion of foreign trained troops and 140 guns. There was growing discontent against the East India Company all over India and even attempts were made to organise anti-British rising in the Peshwa's dominions at Poona.[40] Holkar and Sindhia had united at Sabalgad and even the Chhatrapati of Satara was represented there. In the words of Sardesai, all the Maratha leaders flocked together at this critical juncture "in a grand concourse concerting measures towards undoing

37. *Poona Residency Correspondence,* XI No. 1114, p. 181.

38. *Ibid.,* XI No. 113, p. 182.

39. *Ibid.,* XI No. 115, pp. 183-85.

40. *Ibid.,* VI No. 170-180.

the recent British successes."[41] Acute financial distress and universal disaffection prevailed owing to Wellesley's policy of ceaseless conquest and annexation. "Our treasury" wrote Cornwallis "is completely exhausted."[42] The fall of Ghatge and the restoration of Ambaji to power, however, saved the situation for the British as the change of ministers was followed by a rupture between Sindhia and Holkar.[43] Jealousy between the two chiefs increased still further after and the breach was complete and Holkar had taken Ghatge into his service.[44]

On the other side, Malcolm and Lord Lake enticed Gopal Kishan, sent him to Ambaji and won over Munshi Kamalnain.[45] On 7th September, Ambaji wrote to Malcolm : "The firm establishment of amity with the honourable Company shall be accomplished, let your princely heart have confidence and consider me to be sincerely solicitous to prompt a cordial friendship."[46] Thus, with the help of Ambaji, Gopal Kishan and Kamal nain, Malcolm[47] and British diplomacy succeeded in winning over Daulat Rao Sindhia through a fresh treaty concluded on 21st November, 1805, known as Treaty of Mustafapur.[48]

Holkar proceeded north to secure the help of Patiala, the Afghans and Ranjit Singh against the Company. Ranjit Singh, however, refused to give him any help. "Being abandoned on all sides"[49] he was at least obliged to conclude the treaty of Rajghat with the East India Company on 24th December, 1805, by which he renounced all claims to the north and west of the river Chambal and the British Government restored to him his

41. Sardesai, *New History of the Marathas*, III, p. 430.
42. Ross, Correspondence of Lord Cornwallis 2nd Ed. Vol. III, p. 546.
43. *Poona Residency Correspondence*, XI No. 120, p. 196.
44. *Ibid.*, XI No. 124.
45. Secret Foreign Political Index 1805, p. 294. John Malcolm and Resident with Sindhia, *Poona Residency Correspondence*, XI Nos. 126, 135.
46. National Archives Translation of a letter from Ambaji to Malcolm 7-9-1805, see Chap. IV.
47. See *Poona Residency Correspondence*, XI Malcolm by B.G. Sharma, Secret Foreign Political Index 1805-1806, Kayee : Life of Malcolm I, II correspondences of Cronwallis despatches of Wellesley and Wellington.
48. See Chapter IV.
49. Malcolm : *Central India Memoirs* Vol. I, pp. 249-251.

hereditary possessions to the south and east of the Chambal and his possessions south of the Narmada.

Later Attempts at Reconciliation

Attempts were made for another Holkar-Sindhia alliance later, but nothing substantial emerged out of such efforts. Holkar devoted himself to increasing his martial strength, but in October, 1808, he became insane.* Holkar was now kept under strict confinement. Daulat Rao Sindhia sent doctors like the famous physician, Kundee Rao Joshi[50] to cure him. But the physician was not allowed to treat Holkar, owing to suspicions born of the ancestral feud. Holkar died near Bhanpura on the 11th of Hindu month Kartik Samwat, 1868 corresponding to 20th October, 1811 A.D.[51]

In the words of Sardesai, "He was the last typical soldier to make a name in history."[52] "His object", writes Malcolm was to restore the Maratha supremacy, but "instead of the falling empire of the Mughals, he had to contend against the rising fortune of the British."[53] Grant Duff praises his "hardy spirit of enterprise which though, like that of his countrymen, boundless in success, was also not to be discouraged by trying reverses."[54] "Holkar's statesmanship was short-sighted, his generalship was of a high order."[55]

The Government of the Holkar State fell into chaos after Jaswant Rao's illness and death. Several ephemeral favourites of Tulsi Bai exercised brief power. Amir Khan and his partisan, Ghafoor Khan, made matters worse in the state. Daulat Rao Sindhia and Zalim Singh of Kotah tried to improve conditions

* It is possible that Tulsi Bai who became his favourite mistress about this time had some hand in Holkar's illness, Balaram, a partisan of the British who rose to be Holkar's Diwan from the position of an ordinary shopkeeper on account of his successful negotiations with the East India Company is also suspected. (1) Malcolm Vol. I, p. 249, C.I.

50. Malcolm, *Political History of India,* Vol. I, p. 254.
51. *Ibid.,* p. 451.
52. Sardesai, *New History of the Marathas,* III, p. 436.
53. Malcolm, *Political History of India.* p. 457.
54. Duff, *History of the Marathas,* Vol. I, p. 607.
55. *History of the Marathas People* — III, p. 198, Kincaid and Parasnis.

but the party in power nullified all their efforts. Normally, Tulsi Bai continued to conduct the administration in the name of Malhar Rao II, the minor son of Jaswant Rao Holkar, born of his other wife named Lara Bai, but minor palace revolutions did not cease.

Two months after the death of Jaswant Rao Holkar, Emah Bai, the widow of Malhar Rao II, who was the legitimate son of Tukoji Holkar, and Larabai, the wife of Jaswant Rao, were put to death by Ghafoor Khan, falsely accusing them of alliance with Sindhia to oust the illegitimate son of Malhar Rao II, on whose behalf Tulsi Bai ruled. He then attacked the forces of Sindhia's General Jaggoo Bapu, but Daulat Rao Sindhia did not retaliate.

Ganpat Rao, an officer of Holkar, tried to establish understanding with Daulat Rao Sindhia once again, but Ghafoor Khan, who saw in such efforts the destruction of his own and his master's influence, called Tantia Jog and Amir Khan to his help to frustrate such plans.[56] Yet another scheme for an alliance with Sindhia, through Tantia Alikar, was foiled by the mutiny of the army and by Amir Khan and Tantia Jog. Latter on, Tantia Jog became the head of the Maratha faction and Ghafoor Khan of the Muslim faction at Indore, and both factions were at daggers drawn with each other. Tulsi Bai again sought the help of Daulat Rao in February, 1815[57] and the latter vainly requested Amir Khan to remove Ghafoor Khan from Indore.[58]

The fruit of this Civil War between Sindhia and Holkar was the loss of national liberty by the Marathas. The struggle between Holkar and Sindhia paved the way for the downfall of the Maratha Empire, but even after the loss of the Empire, the enmity between the two did not end.*

56. Malcolm, *Political History of India*, I, p. 287.

57. *Ibid.*, p. 315.

58. *Ibid.*, pp. 386-87.

* Party bickerings and factions at Indore and Gwalior continued to our own days and even Sardar Patel's plan to make Indore and Gwalior alternate capitals of the integrated Madhya Bharat for five and seven months respectively, could not satisfy the parties and finally the whole of the Madhya Bharat had to be merged into the Madhya Pradesh in November 1956 with Bhopal as its capital.

4

DAULAT RAO SINDHIA AND OTHER MARATHA STATES

Mahadji and the Peshwas

Ranjoi Sindhia and his descendents served the Peshwas devotedly. Mahadji did so with notable distinction and made the Maratha name great as never before.[1] Nana Phadnavis and he worked in close co-operation during the First Maratha War, faced the British challenge unitedly and succeeded in thwarting the British design to curb the Marathas. But Mahadji eventually entered into the treaty of Salbai without the concurrence of Nana Phadnavis.

By this treaty, Mahadji became virtually independent[2] and was recognised by the East India Company as the mediator between it and the Peshwas and guarantor of the honourable peace with the Marathas. He was virtually raised at once to the status of an arbiter between the Company and the Marathas.[3] The treaty of Salbai was, however, not beneficial to the Maratha Confederecy as a whole.

By Article 11 of the treaty, the East India Company and the Peshwa Madho Rao Pandit Pradhan, requested Maharaja Madhava Rao Sindhia to be the mutual guarantee for the proper observance of the condition of this treaty. If either of them violated the conditions thereof, he was to endeavour to punish the aggressor. This move of Mahadji Sindhia, though beneficial to him, not only saved the British Empire when the fortunes of the British in India had fallen to their lowest ebb,[4] but also

1. J.N. Sarkar, *Fall of the Mughal Empire*, Vol. IV, p. 127.
2. Duff, *History of the Marathas*, I, p. 455.
3. *Ibid.*, I, p. 503.
4. Hasting's: Letter to Wheeler, 22 April, 1784, Forest Imp. Records Vol. II, p. 1087.

proved to be an apple of discord between the Peshwa, as "Mahadji's friendship and intimacy with the English doubtless gave rise to the suspicion of his being disloyal to the Maratha national interests."[5]

In 1787, Mahadji met a reverse at Lalsot against the Rajput confederacy and he had to beg for the help of Nana Phadnavis. He wrote: "Not only Rajputs but the Rohillas, the Nawab Wazir and even the British are trying their hand against us; almost a repetition of the days of Panipat. It is essential that we should impress upon all that the Maratha power is still sound and solid."[6]

Nana Phadnavis sent Ali Bahabur and Takoji Holkar to help him, but a breach occurred between Ali Bahadur (who was helped by Tukoji Holkar) and Mahadji Sindhia, which culminated in the battle of Lakheri.

"Had it been possible to combine its (the Maratha Confederecy's) powers," writes Grant Duff, "The Marathas might have still extended their conquests."[7] Sindhia perceived the shadows creeping forward, "asserts Sardesai and" set his face towards resisting British supremacy.[8]* Macdonald after stating various reasons for Sindhia'a visit to Poona just before his death stated that "his views were directed to the establishment of his own authority at Poona."[9] A ballad composed by Ram Chandra states : "Sindhia has left Hindustan and Gujarat. Has now so journeyed to the Deccan at the behest of the Emperor."

---

5. Hasting's: Letter to Wheeler, 22 April, 1784, Forest Imp. Records Vol. II, p. 1087.
6. Sardesai, *New History of the Marathas*, III, p. 121.
7. Duff, *History of the Marathas*, I, p. 511.
8. Sardesai, *New History of the Marathas*, III, p. 81 and p. 226.

* For the death of Mahadji, Tarika-a-Muzaffari states that he was murdered by the assassins hired by Nana. Keene also states "Mahadji had been way laid the evening before by an armed gang" Keene's Mahadji Sindhia. Sunderlal accuses the British Govt. for this plot (vide Sunderalal : *Bharat Men Angrezi Raj*, p. 315 Ed. July 1960 Vol. I) Kincaid and Parasnis refute all these allegations. Ahalya Bai said before that the Patel would never return alive from Poona. She was a shrewd observer adept in Poona Politics and British diplomacy. Sardesai says Prophecy came true Vol. III, p. 213.

9. A. Macdonald : Nana Phadnavis, p. 81.

"Shah Alum played a dubious game as he gave support to Sindhia and intrigued with the British Agent at Delhi."[10]

"He was" writes Grant Duff "desirous of preserving a coalition, such as would unite the chieftains of the Empire against all foreign armies."[11] Keene, concurring with this point of view, states that "the great dream of Mahadji Sindhia's life was to unite all the powers of India in one great confederacy against the English, but death belied all his hopes."[12] According to Sardesai, Mahadji's successor Daulat Rao also for a time entertained a similar dream.[13]

With the death of Mahadji, the Poona administration found itself arbiters of the hopes and fortune of Mahadji's successor. No love was lost between Mahadji and Nana Phadnavis, but Daulat Rao Sindhia and Aba Chitnis reconciled themselves with the Government of Poona, in spite of the opposition of the widows of Mahadji,[14] who looked with abhorrence upon Nana.

Death of Madhava Rao II

Grant Duff has stated that in the battle of Kharda against the Nizam, "Daulat Rao Sindia's force was more numerous and more efficient than of any other chieftain."[15] It was at Kharda that the Maratha Chiefs assembled under the authority of the Peshwas for the last time. Soon calamity befell the Maratha nation as the young Peshwa died on 25th October 1795 by a fall from the roof of his palace at Poona. Whether the Peshwa committed suicide in a fit of despair owing to the over-weening tutelage of Nana Phadnavis, or he was thrown down by some hired assassin of the English or he fell down on account of some fault of his, is an unsolved puzzle of history.

Sindhia and the Attempted Revolution at Poona

The next heir to the throne was Baji Rao II, but Nana Phadnavis felt that Baji Rao II was not a fit person for the

10. *Poona Residency Correspondence,* I, p. 276 and pp. 128-32.
11. Duff, *History of the Marathas,* I, p. 503.
12. H.J. Keene : *Life of Madhav Rao Sindhia,* p. 174.
13. Sardesai, *New History of the Marathas,* III, p. 232.
14. *Poona Residency Correspondence,* Vol. II, p. 234, 238 Khare IX 4814 Sarkar, p. 144.
15. Duff, *History of the Marathas,* III, p. 112, ed. 1912.

exalted office of the Peshwa and brought forth a plan for the adoption of a child, which was accepted unanimously. On an enquiry by Malet, Nana Phadnavis told him that "the widow of the late Peshwa was to be considered the Head of the Empire and as fully authorised to adopt a son." In the absence of authentic information, it is difficult to say with any measure of certainty as to how Baji Rao II checkmated Nana's design. But Baji Rao freed himself from imprisonment, won over Balloba, and through him Daulat Rao also, by tempting them with the false promise of one crore of rupees in cash and lands worth Rs. 25 lakhs annually.

Sindhia's Part in the Recognition of Baji Rao as Peshwa

The Nana allied himself with Baji Rao II by agreeing that Baji Rao II should be the Peshwa and he should continue as Minister.[16] Balloba now decided to set aside Baji Rao II and instal Chimnaji Appa. On 2nd June, 1796[17], he detained Baji Rao II and attacked the Nana, who had to flee for his personal safety. Misfortune makes strange bed fellows. Undaunted by calamity, Nana now decided to win over Daulat Rao himself. Sakha Ram Ghatge was introduced to Sindhia by Nana and an offer of Rs. 2 crores and of marriage with Sakha Ram Ghatge's daughter, Baiza Bai, reconciled Daulat Rao. Promise of Prime Ministership of his Government and village of Kagal in inam to Sakha Ram Ghatge by Daulat Rao, confirmed the new alliance between Nana and Daulat Rao. Mushir ul-Mulk, Minister of the Nizam, and the Bhonsles were also won over by Nana and so Baji Rao II became Peshwa.

Daulat Rao was given the fort of Ahmednagar along with some other districts and the Bhonsle was also rewarded according to the promise, but Baji Rao refused to fulfil the terms of the treaty with the Nizam.[18] Under the influence of Daulat Rao, Baji Rao II also connived at the transfer of the fort of Kolabah to Babu Rao Angaria, the maternal uncle of Daulat Rao, by setting aside the claim of Manaji Angria, son of Raghuji Angria, who had died in 1793.

---

16. Duff, *History of the Marathas*, I, pp. 522-23.
17. Sardesai, *New History of the Marathas*, III, p. 317.
18. *Ibid.*, III, p. 147.

Baji Rao's Intrigues : Arrest of Nana by Sindhia

After his accession to power, Baji Rao II, according to Grant Duff, followed the maxim "trust none, and deceive all," "and like all who have ever done so, he never failed to lose."[19] He desired the destruction of Nana and to get rid of Daulat Rao, by removing him to North India as soon as possible. To kill two birds with one stone, Baji Rao II won over Daulat Rao to capture Nana, who was deceitfully invited by Col. Filoze[20] to dinner on behalf of Sindhia by a personal pledge for the Nana's personal safety. Nana visited Sindhia's camp and was arrested on December 21, 1797.

Sardesai surmises that the arrest of the Nana, with Sindhia's collusion, was caused by the suspicion that he was in league with the Widow, but he has stated no credible grounds for holding this opinion. Sarkar, on the other hand, holds that the Nana was in fact hostile to the Widows. It seems more probable that the capture of Nana was instigated by Filoze and Amrit Rao," the first traitor to the Maratha State,[21] who coveted the Nana's office for himself and even got a force under a British officer to be organised to prevent the Peshwa from ever favouring Nana again.

According to Grant Duff, Baji Rao II also tried to win over the Raja of Satara against Nana by promising to serve the Chattarpati loyally, but did not fulfil the promise after the arrest of Nana. So the Raja of Satara rose against him and Daulat Rao promised assistance to him,[22] Parashram Bhau quelled the Raja of Satara on behalf of the Peshwa, but his brother Chitoor Singh continued to intrigue with the Raja of Kolhapur to create disturbances.[23]

Baji Rao II and Daulat Rao, however, soon realised their mistake, and set Nana Phadnavis at liberty. His imprisonment had, however, been too severe a blow to his prestige for Nana to forget it, and he never thereafter genuinely reconciled himself to the Peshwa or Sindhia.[24] Baji Rao II not only freed the Nana,

19. G. Duff, *History of the Marathas*, Vol. III, p. 149.
20. *Poona Residency Correspondence*, Vol. VI, p. 64.
21. Sardesai, *New History of the Marathas*, Vol. III, p. 392.
22. Duff, *History of the Marathas*, Vol. III, p. 158.
23. *Ibid.*, Vol. III, p. 107.
24. Sardesai, *New History of the Marathas*, Vol. III, p. 341.

but in the night of 14th November, 1798, urged him "to protect and save this Brahman Raj."[25] It is said that at the same time he urged Sindhia to cancel his departure to the north to save him (Baji Rao) from the Nana.[26]

Baji Rao and Sindhia

Baji Rao II was however unable to pay the promised money to Daulat Rao and so allowed "Sarji Rao Ghatgay, on behalf of Sindhia, to realise money from the citizens of Poona. This thankless task of exacting money from the citizens was performed by Ghatgay with unusual severity and the populace of Poona looked upon him as "the God of Death incarnate."[27] Sindhia became very unpopular and taking advantage of his unpopularity, Amrit Rao, a partisan of the British and Baji Rao II, decided to arrest him. He was called to the Court and asked to declare whether he considered himself as master or as a servant of the Peshwa.[28] Daulat Rao's reply was couched in the humblest terms.[29] He acknowledged himself to be the Peshwas' servant but expressed his inability to leave Poona for lack of funds.[30] "Amrit Rao asked his brother that he should give the signal for Sindhia's arrest; but Baji Rao's courage failed him."[31] In the words of Grant Duff, he "thus gave his friends the first decided proof of that imbecility which swayed most of the actions of his life."[32] It is difficult to agree with Duff in this, as the arrest of Daulat Rao would have created civil strife and the East India Company would have immediately gained an upper hand in Poona affairs without a blow.

Grant Duff alleges "that Baji Rao II was the instigator of the (Widow's) revolt,"[33] against Sindhia, but Basu and Sunderlal[34] accuse the East India Company of it. The view of Sunder Lal

---

25. Sardesai, *New History of the Marathas*, Vol. III, p. 341.
26. *Ibid.*, p. 341.
27. *Ibid.*, p. 387.
28. *Poona Residency Correspondence,* 6 No. 100.
29. Duff, *History of the Marathas,* Vol. III, p. 156.
30. *Poona Residency Correspondence,* 6 No. 100.
31. Duff, *History of the Marathas,* Vol. III, Kincaid and Parasnis, p. 187.
32. Duff, *History of the Marathas,* III, p. 156.
33. *Ibid.*, III, p. 164.
34. Sunder Lal, *Bharat Men Angrezi Rajya,* Vol. I, p. 400, ed. 1907.

seems to be plausible, as Grant Duff himself says that "it became a primary object of the Peshwa to induce Sindhia to return to Hindustan", because his brigades occupied a dominant position in the Deccan and because he desired, "to obstruct the influence of the British with the Peshwa, over whom it was his policy to perpetuate his own ascendancy." He adds "The reported designs of Zaman Shah, King of Kabul, a grandson of Ahmed Shah Abdali, a name terrible to the Marathas, were strongly set forth by the British agents in order to induce Sindhia to return for the protection of his dominions in Hindustan; whilst to the Peshwa was offered a body of Company's troops."[35] To counteract this, Daulat Rao released Nana on 15th July,[36] but it did not bring the desired result as "Amrit Rao," wrote Palmer, "is attached to us by sentiment, Nana by policy."[37] Palmer further assured Wellesley that he would request Sindhia to leave immediately for Hindustan.[38]

The restoration of Nana to power antagonised Wellesley who wrote "that the restoration of Nana to power was never considered by me to be essential to the attainment of any object which I had in view.[39] Baji Rao and Daulat Rao both entertained Vakils of Tipoo and "in concert with Sindhia, a scheme was laid to attack Nizam Ally (of the Deccan) to declare the Marathas the ally of Tipoo Sultan."[40] Sindhia was perfectly well disposed to unite with Tipu.[41] It was known to Palmer that Tipu had sent a secret envoy to Sindhia[42] and East India Company "used the most strenuous endeavours to oblige Sindhia to leave Poona."[43] Sindhia's removal from Poona appeared to Palmer to be indispensable. Daulat Rao was regarded as the

35. Sarkar, *Fall of the Mughal Empire*, IV, p. 154, P.R.C., pp. 159-63.
36. Sunder Lal, *Bharat Men Angrezi Rajya*, Vol. I, p. 392, Choksey, p. 212.
37. Choksey, *A History of British Diplomacy at the Court of the Peshwas*, p. 212.
38. *A History of the British Diplomacy of the court of the Peshwas*, p. 212, ed. 1951. Wallesley's letter of 8th July, 1978 and Palmer's reply.
39. *Despatches of Wellesley*, Vol. I, p. 253.
40. Duff, *History of the Marathas*, Vol. III, p. 175.
41. Whilks; *History of Mysore*, p. 324.
42. Palmer wrote to Wellesley "Sindhia has not been very ingenuous in his denial of vakeel to him" Palmer's *Embassy*, p. 308, letter dated 12-1-1799.
43. Wilkes : *History of Mysore* Vol. II, pp. 323-24.

main obstacle[44] to the signing of a subsidiary alliance with the Peshwa. On 8th April, Palmer learnt about the proposal to invade the Nizam's dominions.[45] But while Daulat Rao and Baji Rao were conferring together at Poona about the course to be adopted for helping Tipu, the Widows along with Lakhwa Dada and Jaswant Rao Holkar started creating trouble in the territories of the Peshwa and Daulat Rao.

Death of Nana Phadnavis

Henceforth the Peshwa and Sindhia seemed to act like birds fascinated by the blazing eyes of a python and walking unresisting into its open jaws.[46] Sunderlal also seems to hold the view that it was a mistake of the Marathas not to help Tipu.[47] While this turmoil and vacillating policy was going on, Nana Phadnavis died on 13th March, 1800 and Palmer wrote "With him has departed all the wisdom and moderation of this Government." Balloba too died on 1st November, 1800 and his brothers were condemned to death. Baji Rao wreaked vengeance on other partisans of the Nana as well. Palmer had already been trying to ensure Baji Rao in a subsidiary alliance, but "the only obstacle...was Sindhia."[48] The Peshwa feared Sindhia and so he did not readily agree to a subsidiary alliance,[49] though he was in favour of it.[50] Lastly, Palmer remarked that certainty of destruction alone will reduce Baji Rao to make concessions.[51]

Sindhia Leaves for the North

All this while, Daulat Rao's position was worsening in the North and he had to leave for that region in November.[52] In the words of Sarkar, "His dream of controlling the Poona Government

---

44. Choksey, *A History of British Diplomacy at the Court of the Peshwas*, p. 247.
45. *Ibid.*, p. 250.
46. Sunder Lal, *Bharat Men Angrezi Rajya*, Vol. I, p. 392.
47. Duff, *History of the Marathas*, Vol. III, p. 190.
48. Choksey, *A History of British Diplomacy at the Court of the Peshwas*, p. 260.
49. *Ibid.*, p. 279.
50. *Ibid.*, p. 287. *Palmers Embassy and Sunderlal*, p. 397.
51. Choksey, *A History of British Diplomacy at the Court of the Peshwas*, p. 283.
52. Duff, *History of the Marathas*, III, p. 196, Raghubir Singh, p. 232, Sarkar also agrees, p. 179, Vol. IV.

as Regent of Poona had now vanished."[53] Sunderlal also says that Daulat Rao wanted to retain a hold on the Peshwa and committed the same mistake as his father had committed. Duff states that "in the end of November, he quitted the Peshwas' territory, leaving five battalions of regular infantry and one thousand horse under Sarji Rao Ghatge[54] at Poona.

Sindhia and Holkar

The specious alliance between the Peshwa and Sindhia naturally alarmed Holkar. Strong in men and money and undefeated in battle, Jaswant Rao now attacked Daulat Rao's forces at Poona. The ensuing events have already been discussed in Chapter III. After Holkar's victory at Baramati, and the failure of Sindhia's at a coalition with Holkar, the Peshwa immediatcly took the suicidal step of negotiating with the British Resident Col. Close.[55] He reached Bassein on 16th December, 1802, and signed the Treaty of Bassein on 31st December, 1802. With British help, he regained his Masnad at Poona on 13th May, 1803, exactly like Mir Jafar.[56]

The Treaty of Bassein and its Aftermath

Owen writes that "the Treaty of Bassein was the prelude to a new tragedy.[57] The treaty by its direct and indirect effects gave the Company the Empire of India."[58] But it was a treaty with a cipher. "Holkar declared that the Peshwa had sold the Maratha power to the English," Sindhia and the Raja of Berar realised that they were now face to face with the British power. But a general combination was frustrated by the neutrality of the Gaikwar and the withdrawal of the Holkar to Malwa.[59] This treaty was a flagrant violation of the treaty of Salbai, in which the East India Company had recognised Sindhia as mediator between it and the Peshwa. Sunder Lal goes a step further.

---

53. Sarkar, *Fall of the Mughal Empire*, Vol. IV, p. 179.
54. Sunder Lal, *Bharat Men Angrezi Rajya*, Vol. I, p. 396, ed. 1960.
55. Duff : *History of the Marathas*, Vol. III, p. 208.
56. Sarkar, *Fall of the Mughal Empire*, Vol. IV., *Poona Residency Correspondence*, 7, p. 67, p. 216.
57. Quoted oy Choksey, p. 294.
58. *Cambridge* : Vol. V, p. 216, p. 373.
59. *Cambridge* : Vol. V, p. 373.

According to him, the signature of Daulat Rao Sindhia and Bhonsle were necessary for the confirmation of the treaty.[60]

Sindhia's Reaction

Sindhia desired that "confidential persons on my part and the Raja (Bhonsle) be despatched to the Peshwa."[61] According to Grant Duff, "Baji Rao himself sent Balaji Kunjar to Sindhia to invite him and Raghoji Bhonsle to march to Poona with all speed...to deceive all parties."[62] But to quote Duff again, "(Sindhia's) own independence might be soon effected by the support which the Peshwa derived from a foreign nation."[63] "Baji Rao continued in constant correspondence with Sindhia and Bhonsle, secretly encouraging their views."[64] They, on their part were however still quite undecided on their plan of operations."[65] In the words of Sarkar, "Daulat Rao's imbecile political manoeuvers and the cowardly selfishness of his advisers, made him loose seven months in hesitation and secret intrigue, and then to go to war at the wrong time, like a moth that long buzzes round the candle and at last blindly rushes into the flame only to destroy itself."[66]

East India Company's Policy

Wellesley sought the destruction of the Maratha power and he wrote to the Court of Directors, on 24th December, 1802, "The recent distractions in the Maratha power have occasioned a combination of circumstances of the utmost importance to the stability of the British power in India." "Now that Sindhia was back south, Wellesley feared that Baji Rao may wish to be relieved from his alliance with the British."[67] Mill justified Daulat Rao's resentment at the treaty of Bassein.[68]

---

60. Sunder Lal, *Bharat Men Angrezi Rajya*, Vol. I, p. 411, ed. 1960.
61. Letter of Daulat Rao to Wellesley received on 21-7-1803.
62. Duff, *History of the Marathas*, III, p. 207, ed. 1912.
63. *Ibid.*, III, p. 228.
64. *Ibid.*, III, p. 229.
65. *Ibid.*, III, p. 238.
66. Sarkar, *Fall of the Mughal Empire*, Vol. IV, p. 262.
67. Choksey, *A History of British Diplomacy at the Court of the Peshwas*, p. 307.
68. Mill, *History of the British India*, Vol. VI, p. 451.

Meanwhile, "the Peshwa was quiet and happy with his routine of baths and prayers, eating, drinking and merry-making having no worry of any outside concern.[69] According to Khare, (No. 6655 and 6656)" Close Sahib came to visit Peshwa and said, "All the turbulent chiefs have coalesced. Do you then mean we should adopt whatever measures we deem proper?" The Shrimant replied "You should remain entirely at ease; I shall never desert you." The Peshwa was praised for supplying the stipulated quota of troops. The British kept him involved in the internal feuds at his court and with his Southern Jagirdars. This winning over of the Peshwa against his own chiefs was really one of the greatest feats of British diplomacy.

Sindhia and the Peshwa After 1804

The Second Anglo-Maratha War followed immediately. It will be discussed in the following chapter. But we may properly describe here the relations between the Peshwa and Daulat Rao Sindhia in the period after this war, that resulted in the deposition of the Peshwa by the East India Company in 1818.

Pinpricks continued from either side. The Peshwa had given no help to Daulat Rao in the late war. A village belonging to Lakshmi Bai, one of Mahadji's widows, was confiscated by the Raja of Kohlapur with the connivance of the Peshwa. It is said that two emissaries from Daulat Rao saw the Peshwa and correspondence passed between them for an alliance between the two.[70] Daulat Rao Sindhia offered Baji Rao the territory of Gurh Kota. But Elphinstone stoutly opposed the Peshwa's acceptance of any such terms.[71] It has been even alleged that a plan of confederacy was made but it did not materialise. Trumbuji is supposed to have entered into communications with Sindhia and Raghoji Bhonsle as far back as 1811, no doubt with his master's approbation.[72] By Trumbukji's advice, again, the Peshwa is said to have sent agents to Sindhia and Raghoji Bhonsle in 1814.[73]

69. Sardesai, *New History of the Marathas*, Vol. III, p. 393.
70. Choksey, *A History of British Diplomacy at the Court of the Peshwas*, p. 385.
71. Letter of 8th August 1811, Peshwa's Daftar and 24th Nov. 1811. Peshwa's Daftar.
72. Duff, *History of the Marathas*, III, p. 364, Footnote ed. 1912.
73. *Ibid.*, III, p. 364.

Baji Rao II had long since chafed under British control and finally rebelled against it. The Gangadhar Shastri incident at this time provided the occasion for the opening of the coflict. Taking advantage of the incident, Elphinstone forced the Peshwa to accept another treaty on 13th June, 1817. Baji Rao II grudgingly accepted the terms imposed on him, but the strain was too heavy to be tolerated and so a clash took place on 5th November, 1817. The Peshwa's forces attacked the British Residency but failed. He fought two more battles at Koregaon on the 1st January, 1818, and at Ashti on the 20th February, 1818, but was defeated in both and had to surrender to Malcolm on 20th February, 1818.

Before the surrender, Peshwa Baji Rao II turned to the North in the hope that Daulat Roa Sindhia and Appa Sahib would give him shelter. He wrote a piteous letter[74] to Daulat Rao, alluding to the kindness and generosity shown to his (Sindhia's) house by the Peshwa's ancestors, and supplicating for help in his present crisis, but Malcolm intercepted this letter. When charged by the British with disloyalty, Sindhia acknowledged his letter to the Peshwa promising him shelter and said that the promise was made out of consideration for the relations covering generations between the two houses, which could not be wiped out easily. As is well known, the Peshwa was disposed by the British in 1818.

Dhar and Dewas

The Pawars of Dhar and Dewas had long served the Maratha empire with distinction. They were of a Rajput clan, numbers of which had settled in Malwa in very early times. Their ancestors had been in the service of Shivaji, and Sahu Raja. On 5th January, 1741 one Yashwant Rao was entrusted with Dhar and

---

74. Baji Rao II wrote to Daulat Rao : "Your father, Mahadji Sindhia, agreeably to the order of the Sarkar, went to Delhi, was made a Wazir, and acquired a high reputation. He served us with his heart and soul when you became his successor you entered into alliance with the English : thus you govern in Hindustan and thus you show your gratitude. Thus serving us, it is befitting you to put bangles on your arms, and sit down like a woman. After my power is destroyed is it possible that yours should stand." But Daulat Rao grew too wise to risk the state.

Malcolm : C.I. Memorirs Vol. II, pp. 140-41, Kincaid Vol. III, p. 223.

vested with authority to collect a part of the Maratha share of the revenue of Malwa and Gujarat. He established himself at Dhar, but his power declined owing, to the rise of Sindhia and Holkar.[75] The weakness of Dhar attracted both Sindhia and Holkar and even the Pindaris, each of whom seized considerable territory of the chief of Dhar.

In the First Maratha War, Dhar helped Raghunath Rao. During the Second Maratha War, it was torn by internal strife and therefore, took no part in it. In 1817, Daulat Rao Sindhia returned Budhnawar, which he had formerly wrested from Dhar, and also promised to use his influence in effecting the recovery of Berasiah.

Dewas

The Rajas of Dewas belonged to the same family. Baji Rao had given Dewas, Sarangpur, Alloti in Malwa, Hammirpur in Bundelkhand and Kundelah in Hindustan to the younger branch of the Dhar family. Holkar, Sindha and even the Pindaris frequently attacked Dewas State and desolated its territories. The Pawars of Dhar claimed high rank as officers of the Raja of Satara and not of the Peshwa which "both Daulat Rao Sindhia and Jaswant Rao Holkar acknowledged."[76] But it was sheer vanity. The territories of Dewas were restored by Daulat Rao Sindhia along with Sarangpur through the intercession of the British. The States of Dhar and Dewas, though ancient, remained of little importance throughout. Their relations with Daulat Rao Sindhia were sometimes cordial and sometimes unsatisfactory, but nothing eventful happened.

---

75. Malcolm, *Political History of India*, Central India Memoirs Vol. I, p. 111. Anand Rao I was succeeded by Jaswant Rao who was killed at Panipat in 1761, and was succeeded by Khande Rao, who married the daughter of Govind Rao Gaikwar and was succeeded by Anand Rao II, but he died without a male issue. After the death of Anand Rao II, his widow Meena Bai gave birth to a posthumous son, Ram Chandra Rao Pawar, at Mandoo. Morar Rao, an illegitimate child of Jaswant Rao Pawar created trouble, but help from Gujarat under Sakha Ram who was later on succeeded by Bapu Raghunath saved this state from ruin. Misfortune never comes alone, so after a short time the son died. Meena Bai was not a lady to lose heart. She adopted another boy of her sister under same name of Ram Chandra Pawar.

76. Malcolm, *Political History of India*, Central India Memoirs Vol. 1, Part 100.

Sagar

Sagar came into the possession of Baji Rao I with other parts of Bundelkhand as a regard for helping Chatrsal Bundela or as the dowry of Mastani along with Kalpi, Hata, Jhansi, Sironj, Kanch, Garhkuta and Hirdaynagar.

Govind Pant Bundele, a Subedar of Peshwa Baji Rao I, selected Sagar for his headquarters to collect *chouth* from other rulers of Bundelkhand. He met a tragic death before the 3rd Battle of Panipat, when he was engaged in taking supplies to Sadashiv Rao Bhau.[77] After him, his successors continued to keep Sagar as their headquarters. In 1799, Amir Khan plundered it.[78] During the first Maratha War, the Subedar rose against the East India Company, but he was defeated and fell into the clutches of the British Government. After that, Daulat Rao Sindhia himself went to Sagar in 1804 and Sarji Rao Ghatge pillaged the town in January 1805. But after that a treaty was signed between him and the East India Company, and the state remained safe upto 1818. Sagar was situated at a strategic point; so Daulat Rao coveted its possession. The Pindaris under Sindhia also often used to ravage the territory. With the arrival of Lord Hastings, the possession of Sagar became absolutely vital for the British to crush the Pindaris. So it was taken under British protection, though nominally the Peshwa remained its suzerain. "Sagar was coveted because it linked the chain of military posts between the British possessions in Bundelkhand and the territory of their ally, the Nizam."[79] Govind Rao Nana, its ruler, signed a treaty with the East India Company on 1st November, 1818, under which his tribute and military service were transferred from the Peshwa to the Company. Daulat Rao Sindhia was unable to attack Sagar because of British protection.

Banda and Jhansi : (BANDA)

Banda was ruled by Ali Bahadur, grandson of Baji Rao I and son of Shamser Bahadur by his Muslim mistress, Mastani. If reliance is to be placed on Sardesai, Maratha leaders at one

---

77. XI. For details Rajwade Collections 6, p. 404, Sardesai, *New History of the Marathas*, II, pp. 562-63 Hindi Jr. ed. January 1964.

78. Sardesai, *New History of Marathas*, II, p. 135 Hindi Translation ed. January, 1964.

79. Duff, *History of the Marathas*, Vol. III, p. 391.

time, even thought of installing him as Peshwa in opposition to Raghunath Rao, if no son was born to Narain Rao's widow.[80] Ali Bahadur was despatched by Nana Phadnavis to help Mahadji after the battle of Lalsot along with Tukoji Holkar. In 1790-91, Tukoji enabled him to go to Bundelkhand, and with the help of Himmat Bahadur Gosain, Ali Bahadur found infinite difficulty in reducing the country and was perpetually involved in warfare and insurrections.[81]

During the Second Maratha War, it was alleged that Daulat Rao Sindhia tried to incite Goswami Himmat Bahadur and Ali Bahadur against the Company, but the former proved to be treacherous. He offered his services to the British and cooperated with them in the conquest of Bundelkhand. Ali Bahadur's son, Shamsher Bahadur II, fought the English in the Anglo-Maratha war of 1803 unsuccessfully.[82] After his defeat, Shamsher Bahadur II also became a British vassal, residing at Banda on a pension of 4 lakhs a year. After the death of Goswami Himmat Bahadur, his son was obstructed in gaming his father's possessions, and Daulat Rao Sindhia showed his displeasure when Thakur Das, Vakil of his son, Narain Giri, went to him to expostulate, but Resident Close wrote to Daulat Rao Sindhia about him : "It is undoubtedly well-known to your Highness that engagements of a family nature subsist between the British Government and Narendra Giri, son of Himmat Bahadur, by which my government considers him under its protection. Your displeasure towards him will accordingly no logger continue. In 1823, Shamsher Bahadur II requested for a Jagir, as the tribute payable by him was transferred to the British Government when the Peshwa signed the treaty and the British Government instructed the Collector to treat him as above civil and criminal jurisdiction. He died on 5th September, 1823,[83] and was succeeded by his brother Zulficar Ali.[84] In 1857, the Nawab of Banda revolted and suffered.

80. Sardesai, *New History of the Marathas*, Vol. III, p. 39.

81. Duff, *History of the Marathas*, Vol. III, p. 77, Sardesai III, p. 135 Hindi Translation, ed. 1964, Sarkar IV, pp. 7 to 14, P.R.C.I., 251-252, Satara 300, 308, Thorns Memoirs of the War, 240, 245, Atikson's N.W.P.G., 31-41, 130-132.

82. Duff, *History of the Marathas*, III, p. 239.

83. Foreign Political Papers 1823 No. 30.

84. Foreign Political Papers 1823 Bundelkhand No. 30.

Datia

Datia is situated near Jhansi in Bundelkhand. During the time of Daulat Rao Sindhia, Satra Jit Bundela was the ruler of Datia. The Raja of Datia sided with Lakhwa Dada against Daulat Rao Sindhia, and in 1799, the main army of Ambaji Ingale remained engaged at Datia.[85] In the last battle, which took place between Lakhwa Dada and De Perron,[86] Satra Jit Bundela and Lakhwa Dada both were wounded.[87] Daulat Rao Sindhia coveted the possession of Datia, but owing to wars with the widows and Jaswant Rao Holkar, he was unable to seize it. After that came the Second Maratha War which did not let him divert his attention towards Datia. Later on Datia came under British protection, and though Daulat Rao Sindhia's generals made several incursions into the territory of Datia, the British Government baffled them in their endeavours.[88]

Baroda

With the defeat of Senapati Dabhade by Baji Rao I in 1731, the Gaikwar family originally his dependents, became rulers of Baroda in their own right and in 1736, the title of Sena Khas Khel was conferred on Damaji Gaikwar.

During the First Maratha War, Mahadji advised the Gaikwars not to oppose their own kith and kin in alliance with the English, and during the Second Maratha War the possessions of Daulat Rao Sindhia in Gujrat were taken over by the British with the help of the subsidiary forces of the Gaikwar. Gopal Bhau, leading general of Daulat Rao, took shelter there and was reconciled through the Baroda Court.[89] By the treaty of Sarji Arjungaon, Daulat Rao Sindhia ceded Broach and all his other possessions in Gujarat to the Gaikwars, and through

85. Sarkar, *Fall of the Mughal Empire,* Vol. V, p. 154.
86. *Poona Residency Correspondence,* VIII, 198.
87. *Poona Residency Correspondence,* Vol. IX, pp. 249, 254, Fraser Skinner 1-185-187 Gulgule Dafter letter of 22nd May, 1801.
88. Grant Duff, *History of the Marathas,* Vol. I, p. 449, Camb. V, p. 269, Sardesai, Vol. III, pp. 100, 97 to 101.
89. Foreign Political Secret Papers, Government of India Secret Proceedings, Fort William, pp. 19920-30.

them to the East India Company.[90] In this way Gaikwar remained as faithful an ally of the British as Nizam.[91]

Relations of Daulat Rao Sindhia with the Bhonsles of Nagpur

The only two states which stoutly resisted Wellesley's aggression, as soon as they became aware of British designs to crush Maratha Power, were the Sindhia and the Bhonsles of Nagpur.

During the First Maratha War, the Bhonsles did not cooperate whole-heartedly with the other Maratha Chiefs, as they were bribed by Warren Hastings.[92] Not only this Chimnaji, the brother of the Raja, who was sent by Raghuji II, to invade Bengal "sank to the degradation of placing two thousand Maratha cavalry at the service of the British." Thus ended the last attempt of the Marathas to invade Bihar or Bengal.[93]

After the death of the Peshwa, Sawai Mado Rao Narain in 1495, the Bhonsles took no part in the dispute about the succession to the Peshwaship, Jaswant Rao took shelter with the Raja of Nagpur, when he ran away from Poona, after the attack of Sindhia on his brother, Malhar Rao. The Raja at the suggestion of Daulat Rao put Jaswant Rao Holkar under arrest on 30th January, 1800, communicated his step to Poona, but later on Jaswant Rao Holkar escaped from Nagpur.[94] Thus Daulat Rao Sindhia and Raghoji Bhonsle were in close political contact with one another.

Relations during the Second Maratha War

After the treaty of Bassein, Raghuji Bhonsle and Daulat Rao Sindhia rightly suspected that the reduction of the Peshwa, on whom they looked upon as the head of the Maratha confederacy, to a position of subordination to the British Government, would be a death-blow to the independence of the whole Maratha Raj, including themselves. Daulat Rao hastend to the western border of Berar.

90. The Gaikwars of Baroda by Gense and Banaji and Historical Selections from Baroda State Records V 1813-1820.
91. Choksey, *A History of British Diplomacy at the Court of the Peshwas*, p. 293.
92. Grant Duff, *History of the Marathas*, Vol. I, p. 449, Camb. V, p. 269, Sardesai, *New History of Marathas*, Vol. III, pp. 100, 97 to 101.
93. R.D. Banerji, *History of Orissa*, Vol. II, p. 203 and Gleig's Memoirs of Warren Hastings.
94. Phalke, *Kota Papers*, Vol. II, pp. 128, 129, 138, 142, 143.

Raghuji took upon himself the difficult task of reconciling Holkar with Sindhia and used every endeavour to effect a compromise but failed. "So long as British dominions last in India, it will not be possible to determine to what extent Jaswant Rao's action" writes R.D. Banerji, "was influenced by British gold."[95] The two Sardars, Sindhia and Bhonsle, were near Patan on 1st September. This created a sensation.[96] But they continued the endless discussion with Resident Collins to while away the time in the vain expectation of being joined by Jaswant Rao Holkar, and their plan of surprise attacks on the British forces by Gopal Bhau did not yield fruit.[97] They forgot that diplomacy only yields fruit, when it is backed by the power of the swords, and the struggle for power is aways decided by the force of arms, as a last resort. It is doubtful whether the forces of the Bhonsles co-operated with the Sindhia's forces at Assaye during the Second Anglo-Maratha War. The Maratha world certainly blamed Raghuji Bhonsle for his non-cooperation at Assaye,[98] and this suspicion caused a breach between the two Rajas and they separated their forces. Bhonsle's forces were routed at Aragaon, on 29th November, 1803. In this action Sindhia's army played a very indifferent role. Raghuji Bhonsle was the first to come to terms with the East India Company on December 19, by the treaty of Deogaon, and Sindhia followed suit.

When Daulat Rao Sindhia wanted to resume fighting in 1804 and sought the Raja of Berar's help,[99] he failed to get it. Being aware of this fact, Resident Jenkins sent a memorandum to Daulat Rao Sindhia : "Your Highness has likewise carried on negotiation with the Raja of Berar without the knowledge or participation of the Honourable Company's Government." "This proceeding" he remonstrated is as "contrary to the 8th Article of the treaty" and of "extreme unfriendliness."[100]

---

95. R.D. Banerji, *History of Orissa*, Vol. II, p. 264.
96. Khare, Vol. XIV, 1795 and 6708.
97. Khare, Vol. XIV, 6992, 6693, 6778 and Gurwood Vol. II, pp. 286-288.
98. Baswan Lal quoted in the Introduction of *Poona Residency Correspondence*, and Sardesai, *New History of Marathas*, Vol. III, p. 419.
99. *Poona Residency Correspondence*, Nagpur Affairs, May 23, 1805 and *Poona Residency Correspondence*, No. 72.
100. *Poona Residency Correspondence*, Vol. XI, No. 65, p. 108.

In purely Maratha affairs, however, same degree of co-operation continued to exist between them. Sindhia and Bhonsle desired to conquer Gurh Kota, which was in the possession of Arjun Singh. Sindhia sent his troops under Jean Baptists and Bhonsle under Sadic Ali Khan. Jean Baptiste occupied Gurh Kota and routed Sadic All's forces, which had to beat a retreat[101] but despite the rupture between the Commanders, relations between Daulat Rao Sindhia and Raghuji remained tolerable as they later on cooperated in the siege of Bhopal.

Raghuji Bhonsle and Daulat Rao Sindhia jointly attacked Bhopal, but Bhonsle's commander came away from Bhopal, when it was about to fall under the pretext of a bad dream, and later on even Sindhia's attempts to conquer Bhopal were foiled, as it was taken under British protection.

British diplomats in order to tempt Raghuji Bhonsle to a subsidiary alliance, created the menace of Amir Khan's attack on Bhopal as Resident Jenkins wrote on 10-12-1809 : "Bhonsle would not accept a subsidiary force for any temptation without a sense of immediate insecurity."[102] Sindhia prepared himself to help Bhonsle, and Resident Jenkins had to report that the discussion for a subsidiary alliance had taken an unfavourable turn, owing to the Raja having received assurance of support from Sindhia and Holkar." "From Sindhia's camp" he said "the Raja had received assurances that Baptiste, who had been nominated to command against the Pindaris, would cooperate with His Highness's forces against Amir Khan, should he dare to attempt anything against Nagpur."[103]

Now British statesman, knowing that Amir Khan would be crushed if he dared to attack Nagpur, and instead of gaining a subsidiary alliance with Nagpur, they would loose their most trusted fifth-columnist, they became supporters of Raghuji Bhonsle and in order to gain his favour warned Amir Khan and sent forces to help Bhonsle, without any request from him for assistance. In return, they only desired a subsidiary alliance, but the Raja refused to be lured by British diplomacy and he

---

101. *Poona Residency Correspondence,* No. 219 dated 19.12.1809, p. 4B.

102. *Ibid.,*

103. *Poona Residency Correspondence,* p. 421, No. 222 dated 13.5.1814.

refused "even to listen to anything that can be said in favour of it," "Not only this" writes Resident Jenkins to the Governor General, "His Highness asks" Will it (subsidiary alliance) give me Berar or Cuttack?[104] Thus, Raghuji thwarted the designs of the British to bring him under their tutelage upto the last breath of his life, and his relations with Daulat Rao Sindhia in spite of many differences remained cordial.

Daulat Rao Sindhia agreed to entrust Chanderi to Nana Sahib, the brother of Raghuji Bhonsle, on a nominal payment of Rs. 5 lakhs, but this proposal did not materialise.[105] Daulat Rao Sindhia and Raghuji Bhonsale in order to cement their friendship also desired to enter into a matrimonial alliance. Resident Jenkins wrote to Minto: "The Raja is prepared to give his sanction to the marriage of Appa Sahib (who later became Ruler of Nagpur)" the son of Nana Sahib, with Sindhia's daughter[106] but barriers of caste, vanity and social traditions foiled the attempt.

Later on, Appa Sahib, who was hasty, obstinate and revengeful,[107] fell into the trap of British diplomacy by accepting a subsidiary alliance, but he had to reap the harvest of his foolishness soon, as his pretended friends later on sent him in chains as a prisoner. He escaped from his guards and when pursued, tried to seek shelter at Asirgarh from the Kiledar of Sindhia. Cheetoo, the most formidable Pindari on Sindhia's side, and Jaswant Rao Lad, Sindhia's Kiledar of Asirgarh, desired to help Appa Sahib, but their efforts failed on account of the unfailing vigil of British spies. On 18th April, 1819, Asirgarh itself was captured. Even in 1823 Dahiji Gopal and Ghumnaji Deshmukh, Daulat Rao Sindhia's vassals tried to help Appa, but in spite of his sympathies, he was unable to do anything for him.[108] Appa Sahib died heart-broken and crestfallen on 15th July, 1840 at Jodhpur,[109] in abject conditions and in a situation in which Sindhia's help was of no avail.

104. *Poona Residency Correspondence,* No. 223, p. 429.

105. *Poona Residency Correspondence,* XI, No. 242 dated 13.1.1808.

106. *Poona Residency Correspondence,* No. 127, p. 231.

107. *Poona Residency Correspondence,* No. 220.

108. Foreign Secret Political Index 1823 No. 90 dated 15.1.1823.

109. Sardesai, *New History of the Marathas,* III, p. 504 Hindi Translation.

Review

The above review of Daulat Rao Sindhia's relations with different Maratha States shows how the Maratha Nation was riven from within. Their interests clashed and their prospects differed widely. It was difficult for them to cooperate with each other or co-ordinate their efforts. (An awareness of a common enemy was the only ground for their unity, but the common enemy was a past master in the art of diplomacy). This formidable enemy was the East India Company, whose agents pledged themselves to build up the British Empire in India. Wellesley was convinced when he came to India and saw the condition of these Maratha States, that the British must become the one paramount power in the country. Towards this end, he worked from 1799 to 1805. His Subsidiary Alliance system was the 'Trojan Horse' of British Imperialism." He was lucky to have gifted colleagues like John Malcolm, Charles Metcalfe, Elphinstone, Arthur Wellesley, and the like. After an interval of 8 years, his policy was pushed upto its logical conclusion. The decisive campaigns in which Lord Hastings crushed the Pindaris and finally broke the Maratha power carried the spread of the British dominion over Northern and Central India. The need of the hour was the emergence of a genius, who could weld the scattered Maratha powers close together to meet the British power, both in diplomacy and arms. Through diplomacy the British did not let the Maratha Chiefs integrate themselves emotionally, and when they raised their heads they were crushed by superior arms. Daulat Rao was too young and deficient in capacity to unite the Marathas on the one hand and to break through the barrage of British Diplomacy and military might on the other. The extremely difficult situation that he had to face from the very beginning also partially explains his failure to unite the Marathas to face and counteract British Imperialism.

5

Anglo-Maratha Relations from 1794 to 1827

Introduction

Daulat Rao Sindhia inherited "a greater, if not a more consolidated power than any Indian Prince had attained since the days of Aurangzeb."[1] During that period, "Maratha powers seemed to outward view, at any rate, to have better prospects of permanency and stability and to be governed by abler rulers" than those of other Indian States "which had proved unable to resist (our) advance."[2] It seems strange that a power, which gave a death blow to the Mughal Empire when it was at the height of its glory, should have collapsed like a house of cards before British Imperialism.

The Treaty of Salbai recognised Mahadji as an independent Prince and the guarantor of the peace with the Marathas. "An independent Sindhia would weaken the whole Maratha Confederacy."[3] This was proved by subsequent events and so it gave rise to factions in the Maratha Confederacy, as Mahadji's ambition to control the Peshwa now came into full play. He tried to outwit the designs of Nana Phadnavis, who sought to maintain the Peshwa's hegemony over the whole Maratha confederacy, he now utilised his position to extend and consolidate his authority in northern India. It is also otherwise very important in diplomatic history that the British Government appointed Residents at the Courts of the Sindhia and later on at Poona. These Residents with their diplomatic finesse wove a web of plots into which Maratha statesmen fell irretrievably

1. Malcolm, *Central India Memoirs* I, p. 127, ed. 1832.
2. P.E. Roberts, p. 187.
3. Hastings' Judgment quoted by Perceval Spear in *Twilight of the Mughals*, p. 25.

like flies. Mahadji came under the spell of European methods of warfare, organised his army on modern lines, which ultimately proved fatal to the Maratha Raj.

The British hatched plots and counterplots against Mahadji Sindhia in the North, to bring the Emperor Shah Alam under their tutelage, but they dared not to come into open conflict while Mahadji Sindhia was alive. Their plots failed for two reasons. One reason was that Emperor Shah Alam was annoyed with the British owing to the stoppage of the pension of 26 lacks, which Lord Clive had promised him. The other reason was that Warren Hastings and Lord Cornwalis were opposed to coming into open conflict with Mahadji Sindhia and of interfering in the affairs of the Indian States. Mahadji was also wise enough not to start hostilities with the British in spite of the fact that he knew that their jealousy and their power were prejudicial to his interests.

Warren Hastings desired to give a free hand to Mahadji Sindhia in the affairs of the North, so that he might not get breathing time to turn his attention to Bengal. Moreover, he thought that British interests were safer in the hands of Mahadji than in those of Gulam Kadir or any other Muslim noble, who was bound to divert his attention towards the Subas of Bihar and Bengal, which were under the East India Company.

The Marathas formed a triple alliance with the English and the Nizam against Tipu, obliging Tipu to accept the treaty of Mangalore in March 1792. Mahadji was not a party to this triple alliance and his offer of assistance was refused. Thus, we see that relations between Mahadji and the East India Company were of mutual watchful jealousy. Perhaps Sindhia's ultimate aim was the establishment of Maratha supremacy in the south also, his next immediate move was to revive and establish under his direct control a powerful Maratha Confederacy as a counterpart to the British.[4]

British Views on Daulat Rao's Accession

British duplicity is clearly reflected in the note of Sir John Shore which he wrote on the death of Mahadji : "The death of Sindhia and youth of Daulat Rao cannot fail to augment in

4. Choksey, *A History of British Diplomacy at the Court of the Peshwas*, p. 107 and also Sardesai, *New History of Marathas*, III, p. 272.

some degree the power and influence of the Poona Government". He further added, "I shall not enter into speculations upon the mode by which this object which is in itself conjectured may be pursued. To disunite the principal officers and adherents of late Mahadji Sindhia by disseminating suspicion amongst them or to secure their attachment by promises and expectations with a view to render Daulat Rao dependent upon the Peshwa, are acts not unlikely to be tried if necessary. But a speculation, which regards the augmentation of the Maratha power and more particularly the absorption of authority held by Sindhia in that of Poona administration, cannot be uninteresting to this Government...."[5]

He further added that "the influence of the Resident may be occasionally employed to impede or dissolve a combination unfavourable to the British interests and that it will generally tend to the disunion of the Maratha interests by diverting the political connection of Daulat Rao...by diminishing the necessity of his dependence on the court of Poona."[6]

Malcolm also said that Sindhia desired to obstruct the influence of the British[7], and that "Mahadji Sindhia had been the enemy of the British."[8] Grand Duff[9] asserts that the designs of Sindhia were to unite the chieftains of the Empire against all foreign enemies. Thus, Daulat Rao received in legacy the overt animus of the East India Company along with the pre-eminence that Mahadji had achieved.

Daulat Rao and the East India Company

The installation of Baji Rao II on the Pehwa's gaddi was a striking diplomatic feat of the British power, and Daulat Rao Sindhia, despite all his efforts, was never able to win over the Peshwa, Baji Rao II, fully. It is to his credit however, that upto the time he remained at Poona, he was able to checkmate all the attempts of the British for a subsidiary alliance with the Peshwa. But the rebellion of the Widows and the rise of Holkar

5. Sir John Shore to Malet No. 289, *Poona Residency Correspondence,* Vol. I, p. 402.
6. *Poona Residency Correspondence,* Vol. I, No. 228-229.
7. Capt. A Malcolm, *Life of Nana Phadnavis.*
8. Malcolm, *Central India Memoirs,* Vol. I, p. 121.
9. Grant Duff, *History of the Marathas,* Vol. I, p. 502.

and the concentration of British forces on his frontiers forced him to leave Poona, and the thing which was feared most came to pass. Jaswant Rao Holkar defeated the combined forces of the Peshwa and Daulat Rao in the battle of Hadapsar and the Peshwa entered into the treaty of Bassein instead of going to Daulat Rao Sindhia.

British relations with Sindhia rested on the treaty of Salbai, of which the 16th article is most important. It is as follows :

Article XVI

"The honourable East India Company and the Peshwa Madhav Rao Pandit Pradhan, having the fullest confidence in Maharaja Subadar Madhav Rao Sindhia Bahadur, have both requested the said Maharaja to be the mutual guarantee for the perpctual inevitable adherence of both parties to the conditions of this treaty; and the said Madho Rao Sindhia, from a regard to the welfare of both States, had accordingly taken upon himself the mutual guarantee. If either party shall deviate from the conditions of the treaty, the said Maharaja will join the other party and will, to the utmost of his power endeavour to bring the aggressor to a proper understanding."

Thus according to the treaty of Salbai, Sindhia was the guarantor of the observance of the treaty by both parties. Daulat Rao Sindhia knew the weakness of Peshwa Baji Rao II, so he remained at Poona to undo British designs to win him over. Lord Welleseley knew that it would not be possible for him to crush Tipu and win over the Peshwa, if Sindhia remained at Poona, so he strained every nerve to remove Daulat Rao Sindhia from Poona, or to create such a situation in the Maratha confederacy that Daulat Rao Sindhia might be unable to move against the British.

Attempts to Move Sindhia to the North

To divert Sindhia'a attention, a rumour that vast preparations were being made by the Afghans for the invasion of India was spread around.[10] As Grant Duff says, "It became a primary object to induce Sindhia to return to Hindustan...from his known desire to obstruct the influence of the British with the Peshwa."[11]

10. Mill, *History of the British India,* Vol. VI, p. 590.
11. Grant Duff, *History of the Marathas,* III, p. 169, ed. 1912.

Colonel Collins, the Resident, went to Ujjain and fomented disaffection and discontent among the troops and subjects of Sindhia.[12] In 1799, Lord Wellesley instructed the Resident, Kirkpatrick, to form an alliance with the Raja of Berar, Duff, *History of the Marathas* "of which Sindhia as well as Tipu should be the object."[13] In March, 1799, a large force was assembled on the frontiers of Oudh, that is, in territories adjoining to those of Sindhia, to induce him to Hindustan.[14] Wellesley personally wrote to Daulat Rao Sindhia about the attack of Zamanshah to induce him to return to the North. Wellesley even framed a charge against Daulat Rao Sindhia of a conspiracy with Wazir Ali of Oudh.[15&16] In addition to this, British diplomacy instigated Lakhwa Dada and the Widows against Daulat Rao Sindhia with considerable success.

Lord Wellesley wrote to the Commander-in-Chief, Sir Alaurd Clarke (8-3-1799) "to use every endeavour to incite the Rajputs and other tributaries of Sindhia against him, and to take proper steps for supporting and encouraging the Bais (Widows) and Lakhwa Dada together with all persons in the family or service of Sindhia, who may be disaffected to his Govenment."

On 24th December, 1802, Lord Wellesley wrote : "The increased distraction in the Maratha State, the rebellion of Jashwant Rao Holkar...against the combined forces of Peshwa and Sindhia, appeared to constitute a crisis of affairs favourable to the success of our negotiations with Poona."[17]

By the close of the year 1798, Wellesley had resolved to embark for Madras to supervise the war against Mysore. Under these circumstances, Wellesley naturally desired the departure of Sindhia to the North, as Palmer wrote that Tipu had sent a secret envoy to Sindhia and Daulat Rao had entertained this

12. Basu, *Rise of Christian Power in India*, p. 368.
13. *Ibid.*, p. 370.
14. Letter of Wellesley to Alaurde Clarks.
15. Sunder Lal, *Bharat Men Angrezi Rajya*, Vol. I, p. 400 dated 8.3.1799.
16. Article of N.L. Chatterji in *Journal of Indian History*, Vol. XI. III, Part I, April 1965, p. 287.
17. Letter to Secret Committee dated the 24th Dec. 1802, Bengal and Bombay papers.

envoy secretly in his camp. He wrote : "Sindhia had not been ingenious in his denial of a Vakeel to him from Tipu."[18]

The Nana collected 4000 troops to help the East India Company, but Palmer observed that "unless Sindhia withdraws and the Peshwa allows full scope to the abilities and experience of Nana Phadnavis, no reasonable expectation can be indulged of this state being in a condition to fulfil its defensive engagements to its allies."[19] Fortunately for the British, Govind Rao Kale who was so far responsible for inducing the Peshwa to turn down the Resident's approaches for a subsidiary alliance, was imprisoned on the Peshwa's orders for an intrigue against the Nana.[20] In an interview with Sindhia, on 23rd January, 1799, Resident Palmer pointed out to Daulat Rao "the repeated injury to which his presence here subjects the cause of the Allies." The British further feared that "Sindhia was perfectly well disposed to unite with Tipu."[21] The Resident protested to Sindhia, but the protest fell on deaf ears. The British Government used the most strenuous endeavours to oblige Sindhia to leave Poona and eventually, being forced by the rebellion of the widows, the depredations of Holkar and concentration of the British forces in Oudh, Daulat Rao was obliged to leave Poona. His departure gave an opportunity to the English to annihilate the power of Tipu, who faced the British forces single-handed and met a martyr's death.

Baji Rao II and the East India Company

Daulat Rao had failed to gain the goodwill of Baji Rao II, who preferred the British as allies. The Peshwa once declared to a British Resident : "I know you both (Marathas and English), I have tried you both and I speak from what I have felt. These men with turbans, who are my servants, sought my ruin. You who wear hats saved me from destruction and gave me back my home. While they were here, I was insulted and opposed. Now that you are here, I am at repose and do as I please. They

18. Palmer's Embassy Choksey, p. 308, Palmer to Wellesley, 12th January 1799.
19. Palmer's Embassy, p. 308 dated 12.1.1799.
20. Choksey, *A History of British Diplomacy at the Court of the Peshwas*. p. 289.
21. Wilks, *History of Mysore*, Vol. II, pp. 323-24.

took from their master crores of rupees and still ask for more. You have spent crores of rupees for a friend and demand no return."[22] The Company wanted to utilise the Peshwa in their design of expanding their power. He was the de jure head of the Maratha confederacy and it was easier to deal with him. If he could be won over, the other Maratha chieftains would be subordinated by other means. If the Peshwa was left to throw his weight on the side of any or all of the chieftains (Holkar, Sindhia or Bhonsale) he would become a greater menace to the British power. So the British representative, with his policy of divide and rule, openly sided with the Peshwa and gave him all assistance in pursuing his policy of fermenting unending quarrels among the Maratha chiefs.

The British Government reserved a considerable portion of the conquered territories of Tipu to be given to the Peshwa..., but acting for once on Sindhia's advice, the Peshwa rejected the offer.[23] However, the defeat of Sindhia's forces at Hadapsar gave a shattering blow to the influence which Sindhia exercised over the Peshwa and drove the Peshwa openly to cling to the British.[24] Malcolm asserts: "In the contest which took place in 1802, between Sindhia and Holkar.... Baji Rao had moved out of his capital before the action commenced, (but) immediately fled towards the sea coast, having previously sent his minister to the British Resident with a writing with his own seal containing his consent to receive a subsidiary force and to cede for its subsistence territory in Gujarat, or in the southern territory, yielding an annual revenue of 26 lakhs."[25]

The British Government hoped that their purpose would be achieved without a war, but their hope was frustrated by the advance of Sindhia and Bhonsle against the Nizam,[26] with the firm conviction that the Peshwa possessed no right to accept

22. National Archives, Delhi Duplicate No. 24, *Poona Residency Correspondence,* Vol. VII, No. 175, p. 233.

23. Malcolm, *Political History of India,* p. 246.

24. Early Proposal of the Peshwa in Asiatic Annual Register 1802, 1803 State Papers, pp. 68-70 and 7-13, Midnight Interview with Resident Close on 17th April 1802.

25. Malcolm, *Political History of India,* p. 250.

26. *Ibid.,* p. 251.

subordination to the British without the concurrence of the Maratha chiefs. But the British diplomats defended their aggressive policy and argued that the Peshwa possessed the full right to avail himself of the aid of the British power for his restoration and to make his present engagements with that power independently of the consent of feudal chiefs of the Maratha Empire.[27] In his letter he said : "The Vakil has assured Mirza Bakar that Ambaji had sworn to act in concert with him, and to support all his views."[28] Bala Kunjar also seemed confident that he would be able to detach Jadu Rai and the Berar Raja from the disaffected party, and declared that his Highness Baji Rao would soon deprive Daulat Rao Sindhia of the assistance of all the Sardars in his service, should that chieftain attempt to obstruct the completion of the engagements concluded between the head of the empire and the British Government. Internecine feuds within the Maratha Empire thus lent an opportunity for the successful consummation of British diplomacy.

The Treaty of Bassein

Wellesley was "desirous of comprehending principal branches of the Maratha Empire in a general system of defensive alliances."[29] The treaty of Bassein was signed on December 31, 1803, and the Peshwa Baji Rao was restored on 20th April, 1803 exactly like Mir Jafar. The treaty was harshly criticised by Lord Castlereigh as a treaty against the Marathas who "have hitherto respected our territory,"[30] but Lord Wellesley ignored the criticism. The result was that "it produced one of the most widely extended wars which India had ever seen...."[31] How the British diplomats forced war on Sindhia and succeeded in defeating him remains to be seen.

Sindhia's Attitude

Wellesley's aim was the pacification of India under British hegemony,[31] and he wrote to the Directors that "the crisis affords

27. *Poona Residency Correspondence,* Vol. VIII, No. 123, Edmonstone, Secretary to Governments to Collins (Instruction confidential).
28. Martin Wellesley, Despatches Vol. III, p. 6.
29. *Ibid.,* Vol. V, p. 303.
30. Mill, *History of the British India,* Vol. VI, p. 324.
31. S.J. Owen, *Selections of Marquis Wellseley,* p. 22.

the most favourable opportunity for the complete establishment of our power in the Maratha Empire."[32] So he was in search of a pretext to begin a war with Sindhia as will be amply borne out by the following extracts : "Yesterday afternoon I visited on Daulat Rao Sindhia and was immediately conducted to a private tent. The persons present on the part of the Maharaja were Anna Bhaskar, Raja Ambaji Rao, Vitthul Pant, Babu Chitnis and Munshi Kamal Nain.... The Maharaja then declared that he had no intention whatever to obstruct the completion of arrangements lately concluded between the Peshwa and the British Government, but, on the contrary, it was his wish to improve the friendship at present subsisting between the Peshwa and the British Government and his own Sirkar.... Maharaja said, these are my words and you are authorised by me to write to His Excellency."[33] Every kind of assurance was given on behalf of Sindhia to avoid war as he was aware of the British preparations," Anna Bhaskar took upon himself to say in reply that his master had no intention whatever to invade either the territory of neighbours, the Peshwa and of the Nawab Nizam.[34] But Edmonstone, Secretary to Government, instructed Collins to ask "Sindhia either to return with troops northward of the Narmada or to afford some other unequivocal proof." ...It was further said that "the Governor General had received news of a projected confederacy between Sindhia, Nagpur and Jaswant Rao (which) rendered it necessary in His Excellency's judgement that Sindhia should be required to disavow such intended confederacy." He further dictated that "His Excellency is disposed either to admit Sindhia as a contracting party to the treaty of Bassein or to conclude a subsidiary alliance with Sindhia." The Resident went on a step further and said that "the objects of the treaty of Bassein are...to provide at the same time for the safety of the several branches of the Maratha Empire."[35] Daulat Rao pleaded for conciliation and said to the Resident on 22.6.1803 "you by the bounty of God are sensible, wise and a well-wisher of the both the State; (Sindhia and the

32. S.J. Owen, *Selections of Marquis Wellseley,* p. 212.
33. *Poona Residency Correspondence,* Vol. VIII, No. 97, p. 165.
34. *Poona Residency Correspondence,* Vol. VIII, No. 148.
35. *Poona Residency Correspondence,* Vol. VIII, No. 159, p. 255.

East India Company) let not therefore, the delay of a day or two appear to you of any material moment."[36]

Daulat Rao Sindhia forgot that the treaty of Bassein was a move of the British Government for supremacy in India. On one side, Daulat Rao Sindhia believed in the British Government, and on the other Lord Wellesley believed in the maxim of catching opportunity by the forelock, as a chance once lost is lost for ever. British diplomats were aware that the Bhonsle could not cooperate with Sindhia. "It is possible that the Raja of Berar's...object in his taking the field may be merely to preserve the appearance of co-operation with Daulat Rao Sindhia."[37] They also knew "that Holkar will not join the confederates."[38] Further, the Resident succeeded in getting the assurance of Himmat Bahadur for assisting the English in Bundelkhand and of other traitors like Ambaji, Begum Samroo and European Officers like Perron. Collins collected all the information that could possibly be of any use against Sindhia[39] and utilized his time in intrigue, in getting information and creating traitors to Sindhia.

Wellesley and Sindhia

Lord Wellesley thus initiated an aggressive policy against Sindhia who was, as Mahadji's successor, the guarantor of the treaty of Salbai.[40] He wrote that "the entire reduction of Sindhia's power would certainly afford considerable security to our interest."[41] On the same day, Resident Collins was informed that "the Maharaja (Sindhia) entertained no thought whatever but that of friendship."[42] On the other side, Arthur Wellesley wrote, "It is my intention to commence my operations for which I am fully prepared."[43]

Thus Daulat Rao Sindhia's protestations of friendship for the British yielded no result, as the main object of the Wellesley

36. *Poona Residency Correspondence*, Vol. VIII, No. 178, p. 225.
37. *Poona Residency Correspondence*, Vol. VIII, p. 222.
38. *Poona Residency Correspondence*, Vol. IX — Introduction by Dr. Raghubir Singh.
39. *Poona Residency Correspondence*, Vol. VIII, No. 182, dated 27-6-1803.
40. *Ibid.*, No. 184.
41. *Ibid.*, No. 372.
42. *Ibid.*, p. 382.
43. *Ibid.*, p. 382.

brothers was to destroy Maratha independence and establish British supremacy in its place. Residents were sent only to divert the attention of Sindhia. Daulat Rao Sindhia blundered in delaying action and relying on the old British friendship. He does not seem to have been fully aware of designs of the East India Company, which aimed at the total extirpation of his power.

Another difficulty before Daulat Rao Sindhia was that he disliked to face the British forces alone, and naturally had to wait for Raghuji Bhonsle, who made a great delay, and pressed Sindhia for reconciliation with Holkar. They both waited for Jaswant Rao Holkar and passed their time in vain talks. Both chiefs met on 8th June, and on 12th June. Collins gave a warning by leaving Sindhia's camp and thus created a crisis. The two confederates were then negotiating with Holkar who was not within easy reach. Collins again pressed for a categorical assurance and the confederates again demanded time. Sridhar, Vakil of Bhonsle, was of the opinion that the British had no business to contract a treaty with the Peshwa without reference to all the chiefs.

When Sindhia and Bhonsle assured the Resident of their peaceful intentions, Daulat Rao Sindhia was accused of instigating Gosain Himmat Bahadur, Jani Beg, Bambook Khan, and the Nawab Ghulam Mohammad Khan of Rampur against the British. This accusation was false and groundless. In the meantime, Amir Khan was seduced by the British from the side of the Sindhia through the Nizam. On 3rd May, 1803, General Wellesley wrote to Major Kirkpatrick that "Amir Khan should be kept in employment of the Nizam with all his soldiers." Arthur Wellesley himself states that "On 8th July, they (Sindhia and Bhonsle) declared they had no intention to attack the British Government or their allies or to impede the treaty of Bassein. They further assured the British that they would return to Burhanpur."[44] On the same day "I then commenced hostilities.[45] On the 23rd...I received a report that Sindhia and the Raja of Berar had moved off in the morning and that the infantry was

44. Gurwood, Selections from the Despatches of Willington, p. 80, ed. 1851.

45. *Ibid.*, p. 80.

about to follow (to avoid a clash)" writes Arthur Wellesley from his camp at Assaye, "but he marched on to attack."[46] There was thus wanton and naked aggression.

According to the treaty of Salbai, the Peshwa did not possess the power to enter into treaty with the British Government without the consent of the other chiefs as Mahadji was the Guarantor. Further according to Maratha usage, its ratification by the Chhatrapati was necessary. Baji Rao II urged the British Government to "let the child (Sindhia) be preserved"[47] and further says "he (Holkar) is a monster and must be destroyed,"[48] but what the British did was to let off Jaswat Rao Holkar, to destroy Sindhia and to reward Amrit Rao, the arch enemy of Baji Rao II with a pension of Rs. 8 lakhs per annum, and all this was done in the name of fulfilling the treaty of Bassein! Jaswant Rao Holkar, too, must have been rewarded, had he not shown an independent attitude after Daulat Rao Sindhia's defeat.

The East India Company did not possess any right to prevent the Peshwa from meeting Daulat Rao Sindhia and Raghoji Bhonsle. Wellesley's instruction about the aims of the war and seduction of the officers of Sindhia's army clearly show that war preparations had been made long before the war. The Maratha forces were not willing to go to war with the Company. Further, the predecessors of both Daulat Rao Sindhia and Raghoji Bhonsle had helped the British and they never apprehended any such naked aggression on them by the British.

War Aims of the British

Lord Wellesley wrote to Arthur Wellesley "In the event of hostilities, you will take proper measures for withdrawing the European officers from the service of Sindhia and Holkar and of every other chief opposed to you."[49] You are at liberty to incur any expense requisite for the service and to employ such embassies as may appear most serviceable.[50]

46. Arthur Wellesley to Governor General on 24th Sept. 1803, pp. 82-85.
47. *Poona Residency Correspondence,* VIII, No. 178 Baji Rao II's request to Resident communicated to Governor General on 27.5.1805.
48. *Ibid.,* No. 178.
49. *Poona Residency Correspondence,* IX, p. 293.
50. *Ibid.,* p. 292.

In his letter to Lake, Wellesley clearly stated the following aims of the war :

1. To seize all the possessions of Sindhia between the Ganges and the Doab.
2. To take the person of the Mughal Emperor under our protection.
3. To form alliances with the Rajputs and other inferior States.
4. To occupy Bundelkhand.

He further instructed that Sindhia's European officers should be induced to resign his service by the offer of the present subsistence and of further emoluments. British officers were asked to open negotiations with Perron, and other European officers, with his troops, with the Rana of Gohad and with Jat Chiefs of Bharatpur and Kumbulmer, and with Jaipur and Jodhpur.[51] A proclamation was issued that all British subjects, holding employment in the military service of Sindhia and Holkar, who joined the Company "shall receive a pension equal to the amount of their fixed pay and allowances." Collins was sent to lure Sindhia into inactivity till British preparations were complete.

In the face of these facts, it can never be doubted that Wellesley sought the destruction of the Maratha power. The accusation of Lord Wellesley that Daulat Rao's proceedings since accession had manifested a systematic design of establishing an ascendancy in the Maratha state upon the ruins of the Peshwa's authority, was merely an excuse for aggression, as he considered it a tempting opportunity for intervention, and "improving the British interests on solid and durable foundation."[52] Mill said, "Were Sindhia the greatest lover of peace and justice on earth, he would have still reason to resent the treaty of Bassein."[53] The Governor General himself wrote that "it gave power over all the other governments of the Maratha nation, to the British."[54]

---

51. *Poona Residency Correspondence,* IX No. 182.
52. Mill, *History of the British India,* Vol. VI, p. 451.
53. Choksey, *A History of British Diplomacy at the Court of the Peshwas,* p. 307.
54. *Despatches of Wellesley,* Vol. III, p. 2 to the Secret Committee dated 24.12.1802.

Now that Sindhia was back in the south, Wellesley feared that Baji Rao might wish to get rid of his alliance with the British. The Maratha chieftains, Wellesley knew, feared the restoration of the Peshwa to the Musnud by the British.[55] Wellesley therefore proposed that Holkar be offered a sum of money on condition of his immediately withdrawing his army from Poona.[56] Wellesley even deceived the Directors also. In a despatch to the Secret Committee of the Court of Directors, he himself wrote that if any confederacy was formed, "its object (is) probably restricted to the purpose of a defensive nature without involving any view of hostility towards British power."[57] On the other hand, he sent instructions to Collins at Sindhia's court and to the Resident in Berar and Colonel Close at Poona to foment intrigues.[58] Holkar and Amrit Rao were to be appeased and Baji Rao lulled into inactivity. Bhonsle and Gaikwar were to be kept from joining the opposition. Sindhia alone with his formidable army was to be broken and controlled. His power in Hindustan was to be ended. Thus, we see that war was inevitable. British Imperialism desired only an excuse to declare it and did so when they got an opportunity for it, relentlessly and without any scruples.

British Preparation

While on the one hand we find incredible folly, weakness and discord among Maratha leaders in the face of threatened subjugation, on the other hand, we see on the English side the most amazing sagacity and efficiency in preparing for the coming contest.

Wellesley's first step was to create a belt of British territory on the Western flank of Oudh, so as to intercept any Maratha invasion from Sindhia's part of Hindustan. By a treaty forced on Nawab Saadat Ali Khan of Oudh on 10th November, 1801, he secured, for occupation and administration by the British, the nine districts of Rohilkhand, Mainpuri, Etawah, Kanpur,

55. Despatches dated 20th June 1803, Bengal and Bombay Papers p. 98, also quoted by Choksey, p. 313.
56. Despatches dated 20th June 1803, Bengal and Bombay Papers, p. 98.
57. Letter of 5th May to Collins, letter to the Raja of Berar of 15th May through the Resident, letter of 13th May, to Col. Collins.
58. *Ibid.*

Allahabad, Azamgarh, Basti, Gorakhpur and Farrukhabad (this last was ceded by its Bangash Nawab a year later).[59]

The British could now maintain large additional forces on that frontier at the expense of the Nawab of Oudh. Fatehgarh was made the headquarters of the British Resident to Sindhia. In Northern India, General Lake organised another army with its headquarters at Kannauj, 50 miles north-west of Kanpur, where cavalry regiments of the British Indian army exercised together under the eyes of the Commander-in-Chief himself throughout the winter months of 1802-3, particular emphasis being laid on the use of galloper guns which had been introduced in India by De Boigne. Two of these six-Pounder guns were attached to each regiment of horse.[60] In the South, Arthur Wellesley was also actively preparing for war. He made arrangements for proper supply and perfected the plan of using coracles for ferrying his troop over the rivers of the south, which Marathas lacked. Generals Lake and Arthur Wellesley were instructed by the Governor General before hand and invested with plenary powers to conduct military operations and diplomatic negotiations and settlements necessary for the fulfilment of the main object.

Wellesley's preparations were unprecedented. "Never before in Hindustan and seldom in the most renowned nations of Europe, have so many separate armies been supplied and equipped for actual service from points so distant."

Weakness of The Maratha Confederacy

The Maratha leaders naturally regarded Baji Rao's acceptance of the treaty of Bassein with open alarm and anger, particularly the provisions regarding British arbitration in disputes between the Peshwa and other Indian rulers, and realised that at last they were face to face with the British power. Wellesley's system of subsidiary alliance would reduce them to impotence as surely as the Maratha claim to Chauth had ruined the Mughal Emperor. But a general combination was frustrated by the

59. Pearse 132, 416-15-154, Pester War and Sport, Shipp's Memoir Chapter 6-8. For detail see, Mill, *System of the Marathas and History of Farrukhabad,* Thorn 80.

60. Pearce 151, Thorn 80, *Pester War and Sport, Shipps's Memoir,* Chapter 6 and 8.

neutrality of the Gaikwar and the withdrawal of Holkar to Malwa.... War was declared in August, 1803, with the avowed object of conquering Sindhia's territory between the Ganga and the Yamuna, destroying the French forces which protected Sindhia's frontier, capturing Delhi and Agra and acquiring Bundelkhand, Orissa and Broach.

Further, to the misfortune of the Marathas, Dhar was torn by internal feuds and its Jagirdar were won over by British diplomacy. Many officers of Sindhia also were seduced.[61]

Lord Wellesley gave first priority to capturing the Emperor Shah Alam, and for this purpose, false promises were held out to him. He wrote a letter purporting to show the good wishes of the British Government towards him. The principal agent in this scheme was Syed Raza Khan, a courtier of Shah Alam. It was claimed that Lord Lake even gave a written contract to Shah Alam on 2nd December, 1803. But when Akbar Shah represented his case through Raja Ram Mohan Roy in England, the Company declared that "the document...called an 'Ikrarnama' was nowhere to be found in the records of the Court, or in those of the supreme Government of India."[62] Sullivan, however, affirmed : "in my judgment, a gross breach of faith has been committed in the case of the Mughal."[63] But the emperor Shah Alam was successfully lured by these false promises of the East India Company's officers to desert Sindhia in the ensuing war.

Seduction of the Sikh Chiefs

As to the Sikhs, Wellesley wrote that "the only support to be expected from Raja Ranjit Singh is the exertion of his influence with other Sikh chieftains to induce them to favour the cause of the British Government." Such of those chiefs as are subject to the control and exactions of the Maratha power may perhaps be detached from the interest of the nation by promises of protection from the British Government and of exemption from payment of tribute in future. Lord Lake acted accordingly and succeeded in winning over the Sikh chiefs.

61. *Asiatic Annual Register for 1803*, pp. 337-39.

62. Speech of the Chairman of the Bored of Directors at the East India House on 18th December, 1828.

63. Sullivan, at the East India Company House, 18th December, 1828.

Seduction of Begum Samroo

Begum Samroo of Sardhana was a Christian Lady of the most licentious character. She was an imperial fief-holder, her army was legally under the orders of Sindhia by virtue of his office as Bakhshi of the empire. But she was eager to assert her independence. Being a Christian, she always leaned to the side of the British and during her intrigue of love with Lauassoult (1795) she had tried to flee for refuge to British Indian Territory. More recently, she had agreed to receive British protection with a guarantee for her Jagir.

Four of her battalions (all under European officers) were now attached to Sindhia's army in the Deccan. The Governor General wrote to Arthur Wellesley "to continue means to win over those battalions to him (his side)," and they did deceive Sindhia at Assaye at a critical stage. Lord Wellesley also wrote to Lake : "She (Begum Samroo) would be required to recall her battalions, now serving in the army of Daulat Rao Sindhia." Eventually, she was won over wholly to side with the British.[64]

Seduction of Ambaji

Ambaji, Sindhia's Deputy in North India, seemed a "Subsidiary Chief rather than a servant of Sindhia."[65] Being jealous of Perron and fearing demand for the money misappropriated by him, which amounted to Rs. 147 lakhs, he sided with the British and desired asylum in British territory.[67] British diplomats hoped to win them (him and Jado Rao Bhaskar) even to their interests.[68] The Governor General empowered Lake to guarantee territory to Ambaji.[69] Thus, moved by personal interest, Ambaji delivered Gwalior to the British and deceived his chief at Laswari.

Other Defections

The Rajput Rajas were also approached. The chiefs of Bundelkhand were torn into factions. So it was very easy to

64. Sarkar, *Fall of the Mughal Empire*, Vol. IV, p. 274.
65. *Poona Residency Correspondence*, Vol. VIII, No. 123 dated 4.3.1799.
66. Mewar Collection Tod : 1st Mewar Chapter XVII, Ojha I, pp. 683, 636.
67. *Poona Residency Correspondence*, IX, No. 31.
68. *Poona Residency Correspondence*, VIII, 163, IX 64, M.M. III, 192.
69. M.M. III, 192, 409-11.

secure the service of one against the other. British forces defeated Shamsher Bahadur with the help of Goswami Himmat Bahadur.[70] The dispossessed Jat chief of Gohad was set up against his hereditary enemy, the House of Sindhia.

Thus, with the withdrawal of Ambaji, Shah Alam, Begum Samroo, Sikh chiefs, Bamboo Khan, the Rajput and Jat Rajas, Daulat Rao Sindhia was completely cut off from his moorings. By their policy of seduction, British diplomacy made Daulat Rao Sindhia a solitary figure, ploughing a lonely furrow against the foreign aggressor.

Treachery of European Officers

De Boigne left Daulat Rao Sindhia's service in 1796, and De Perron became Commander-in-Chief of Sindhia's European forces. How Perron deceived Daulat Rao has already been narrated. Louis Bourquin also deceived Sindhia later on. George Hassing, who held Agra and Col. Pedron were also seduced.[71] To narrate the treachery of all the European Officers would be a tedious task. In short, the edifice of Sindhia's power "of most alarming eminence,"[72] received a serious blow.

Treachery of Indian Officers

In this crisis even Indian officers also fell a prey to British charms. It was a clerk of Sindhia who supplied all information to Collins, owing to which Arthur Wellesley succeeded in routing Sindhia's army at Assaye,

The fort of Ahmadnagar was captured with the help of traitors.[73] Bheel chiefs were seduced by the promise of foregoing tributes. The fort of Bhroach also came under British occupation by unfair means. The fort of Pawangarh was gained more by bribery than by force.

Above all, Daulat Rao Sindhia was deceived by his confidential adviser, Munshi Kamal Nain, who proposed a compromise between Daulat Rao Sindhia and the British army, when the

70. Satara 1, 300, 308. Thorn's *Memoir of the War* 240-245, Atikson N.W.P.G., pp. 31-41, 130-32.

71. M.M. IV 190-93, M.M. III 190, 284, M.M. V, Maratha War Supplement Crompton 277, Martineau, P.R.C. IX.

72. Malcolm, *Political History of India,* I, p. 189.

73. Ahmadnagar Gazz. ed. by Hames, p. 695.

former had agreed with Holkar to make a common cause against the British. The Rajputs, too, formed a confederacy opposed to Sindhia. Thus, the diplomatic isolation of Sindhia was complete.[74]

Proclamation of War

On 29th August, Wellesley published two long prepared proclamations. By the first, all British subjects were called upon to give up the service of Sindhia, Bhonsle or any other chief and deliver themselves upon the British military officers nearest to them. In return, they were promised by the Company, provision for their actual pay and allowance which they were getting in the Maratha army. All subjects of France or any other foreigner, European or American, in the service of the hostile Maratha powers were promised continuation of their existing pay and allowances, if they surrendered to the English. By a supplementary proclamation issued on 16th September, all British subjects continuing in the enemy's armies after the Ist of November, were threatened with prosecution for treason.

By the second proclamation of 29th August, all natives of British India or Oudh employed in the military service of hostile Maratha chiefs were called upon to resign and deliver themselves to British officers on promise of employment in the East India Company's army or of being given a provision equal to their pay in the Maratha army.[75] Thus, Daulat Rao Sindhia not only lost his European officers but also the Purbias, men of Oudh and the upper provinces.

At the same time the army of the East India Company was greatly increased by the addition of large subsidiary forces (under British officers) free of cost to the Company, Oudh, Mysore, Hyderabad, Gujarat and the Peshwa's Government.

War With Sindhia

Then war was formally declared on 7-8-1803.

A British army numbering nearly 60 thousand men assembled in different quarters of India. The army in the Deccan and Gujarat numbered 35,596 men, of whom 3,595 were left for the protection of Hyderabad and Poona and 7,826 formed into

74. M.M. III, 192, 228, 229, 243, 409-412.

75. *Asiatic Annual Register 1804, State papers,* p. 276, M.M.V. 73.

a combatant army under General Stuart. The forces under the personal command of Arthur Wellesley numbered 8,930 men and those under Col. Stephenson numbered 7,920 men. Out of 7,352 men in Gujarat, 4,281 were under Col. Murrary. In Northern India, 10,500 men were under General Lake, 2,500 men were assembled at Allahabad to operate in Bundelkhand and 5,216 men for attack on Orissa.[76]

Arthur Wellesley attacked Ahmadnagar on 8th August, 1803. This important fort, which had defied Akbar The Great during the regime of Chand Bibi, surrendered on 12th August, 1803. This was achieved by bribery. Sindhia's European Killadar marched out with his private property and 1,500 men.[77]

Capture of Asirgarh

The fall of Ahmadnagar was a decisive blow to the Marathas. It not only marred their reputation but also gave possession of an important strategic point to the British. When after capturing the town, General Wellesley reconnoitered the fort at Ahmadnagar on 9th August, the complete protection which its western walls afforded made it difficult to fix on a spot for bombardment. Ragho Rao Baba, the Deshmukh of Bhingar in return for a bribe of four hundred pounds about Rs. 4,000/- advised an attack on the east face. Sindhia's nine European officers and British soldiers sided with the British and the Kiledar handed over the fort on cash payment of Rs. 7 lakhs and a promise to pay him the arrears of salary.

Fall of Baroach and Pawagarh

The Gaikwar's subsidiary forces and the English army under Col. Waddington marched out on 21st August from Baroda and on the 25th it surrounded the fort of Baroach. The fort was not in a very good defensive condition. The Arabs fought bravely and put up a stubborn resistance, but had to yield to British arms and it was occupied on 29th August. Thus the district of Baroach yielding an income of Rs. 121 lakhs fell into British hands.

---

76. *History of British Army,* Vol. XV, also Gurwood II, 302, 303, Khare XIV, 6693 supp. Despatch III 173.

77. Ahmednagar Gazetteer edited by Sir James Campbell, p. 695 and Raiwade, Sardesai III, pp. 440-41, Hindi Translation ed., 1964.

The same party proceeded thereafter to the east and captured the town of Champaner together with the adjoining fort of Pawagarh on 17th September. In this operation, the Bhils were seduced by promising them exemption from tribute. Thus, Sindhia's power in Gujarat came to an end and the gains of Mahadji in the First Maratha War were wiped out.

War in North India

General Lake left Kanpur on 17th August and learnt of the intention of Perron to flee. Maratha troops had the great strategic advantage of holding interior lines against the British forces, but this advantage was nullified by the treachery of European officers. Perron had already treacherously dispersed his troops to Delhi and only 2,000 irregular militia were left to garrison the important depot of Aligarh. The troops put up a gallant fight and refused to surrender the fort. Lake kept up his assaults from 29th August to 3rd September. An Irish officer of Daulat Rao Sindhia joined General Lake and told him all about its defences. Col. Monson opened the assault with thrice the number of troops within the fort. A fierce battle took place, but British valour prevailed.[78] The entrance was forced. Lucan, the Irish deserter, showed the way and the army advanced. Colonel Pedron, the Commandant surrendered himself. All the two thousand of its defenders were massacred and most of the military stores belonging to the French party including 281 guns fell into the victor's hand.[79]

Lake's Capture of Delhi

According to J.N. Sarkar, Perron planned to invite the Emperor to his camp and force him to cede the Doab in full sovereignty to France exactly on the model of the subsidiary treaties by which the English had created their empire in Bengal, Oudh and the Decca. But his plans failed, as Bourquien repudiated the authority of Perron and set himself up as an independent agent of Sindhia.[80] It is difficult to agree with Sarkar's supposition, as all the records show that Perron had planned to go to France long before and he had no such plans in his mind.

---

78. *Pester*, p. 155.
79. *Thorn* 101, *Pester* 157.
80. Sarkar, *Fall of the Mughal Empire*, Vol. IV, p. 289.

Louis Bourquin, who under Perron was incharge of Delhi on behalf of Sindhia, repudiated the authority of Perron, struck the Emperor's flag, unfurled Sindhia's and proclaimed himself Commander-in-Chief under a salute of 21 guns. After that he plundered the city Delhi and the public treasury. Major Geslin, who was sent by Perron, was captured and Harsukh Rai Vakil of Perron, was roughly treated. Bourquien attacked the Red Fort, as the Kiladar Drudgeon, a Savoyard, refused to surrender it to him. This made the Mughal Emperor Shah Alam nervous. In the meanwhile, two couriers of the English reached Delhi to seduce Sindhia's army, which put Bourquien (suspected of being shaky in his allegiance to Sindhia) into confinement.

Lake hurried his advance to face Sindhia's army of 12 battalions. The British army numbered about 4,500 men of which one-third were Europeans. Sindhia's forces fought bravely, but being abandoned by its chief (Bourquien) and officers, they were defeated.[81] Sindhia's entire field army was destroyed. The battle was witnessed from the ramparts of Delhi by Shah Alam, who sent a messenger to Lord Lake as soon as British victory was inevitable. On 14th September, the British army entered Delhi. Lake paid a visit to Shah Alam and took him under British protection. Thus, the second aim of the war was achieved. Louis Bourquien, Major Gaslin, Major Guerinner, Del Perron, and Jeen Pierre surrendered to the British army.[82]

Capture of Agra

After making arrangements for the defence of Delhi, Lake set out for Agra on 24th September. Agra was, in fact, the real capital of Sindhia's North Indian dominions. The defence of Agra was in the hands of a Dutch officer, Colonel George Hessing, and Colonel Sutherland, a Scotsman, who were related to Perron by marriage. In this historic fort were stored vast quantities of ammunitions, stores, equipments and artillery, besides 22-1/2 lakhs of public money.

Lake reached Agra on 4th October, 1803 after takirg Mathura on 2nd, October and tried to gain the fort by bribery, but Indian forces put their foreign officers into confinement and

81. *Martineau*, p. 173.

82. *Thorn 118 As. An. Register 1803*, Appendix 13.

decided leaderless to resist, but on 13th, 2,500 sepoys went over to the English.[83] The fort was occupied by Lake on 18th October, 1803.

In order to defend his north Indian possessions, Daulat Rao had despatched an army on 17th July, 1803. Due to the desertion of Dudrene, Smith and Larpent, the command was given to the treacherous Ambaji Ingale. This army was joined by the remnants of the defeated army of Delhi under Sarwar Khan and Gulab Rao Kadam with 1250 Deccani horses. They decided for a junction with Vaman Rao (nephew of Khande Rao), having 8,000 or 9,000 men near the Mewat hills.

Their junction would have created a formidable force under Ambaji Ingale, but instead of attempting to recover Delhi and making alliance with the Rajputs and local Maratha chiefs, Ingale employed himself in looting the villages of Bharatpur, and Macheri State. This annoyed the Raja of Bhartpur, who made a treaty with the English on 29-9-1803. Bakhtawar Singh, the Raja of Macheri, also entered into an alliance with Lake under the influence of his Vakil, Ahmad Baksh, who was made Nawab of Loharu in Haryana, as a reward for his services to the Company.[84] This alliance gave much help and supplies and information to the British force for the Battle of Laswari.

The Battle of Laswari

Laswari, correctly called Naswari, stands near the Barki Nala, 20 miles due east of Alwar city. The Maratha commander at Laswari was Ambaji Ingale, and there were 10,250 Deccani horses under Gulab Rao Kadam and 13 French trained battalions under Sarwer Khan. At Laswri, sepoys of the same race and religion with equality in armaments fought on either side.[85] Few, if any of these men were natives of Maharastra. They were chiefly from Oudh, Rohilkhand and the Doab.[86] R.D. Banerjee and G. Duff confirm this racial composition of Sindhia's disciplined infantry.

The Maratha cavalry and transport marched in the front, and nine battalions of infantry followed them. The first British

83. Thorn 182, Fraser 302; Pester 207.

84. *Rajputana Gazetteer*, 1880, Vol. III, 184.

85. *Historical Account of Bengal Native Infantry*, 1817, p. 292 Williams.

86. Grant Duff, *History of the Marathas*, III, p. 256.

brigade, under T.P. Vandeeur, broke through the Maratha line in spite of heavy fire. Lake attacked by advancing troops along the north bank of the Nala. Sarwar Khan tried to forestall the British advance and a fierce bombardment was carried on and the Maratha artillery proved superior to British fire.

The situation was critical, but Lake rose to the occasion. The superiority of the British cavalry proved a decisive factor, and he succeeded in defeating the Maratha forces. About 2,000 sepoys and 45 officers surrendered. The setting sun revealed an extensive plain covered with the bodies of the dead and many thousands of the wounded, who also died owing to explosions and a hurricane.[87] Had the army of Sindhia been led by a competent commander, it might have succeeded. But the army was led by the cowardly and treacherous Ambaji Ingle, who sent a proposal for surrendering his guns if favourable terms were granted to him. The soldiers in the rank fought with great stubbornness and bravery and suffered tremendous losses. "The resistance was more determined than at any other place."[88]

The Victory at Laswari was decisive. It annihilated the whole of Sindhia's regular force trained by French officers. On the British side, 822 men were killed and about 553 were missing. The conquerors were so tired that they lost all zeal for pursuit.[89] Lake reported to the Governor General : "All sepoys of the enemy behaved exceedingly well, and if they had been commanded by French officers, the event would have been extremely doubtful...." "These fellows fought like devils, or rather heroes."[90] Grant Duff also states that, "They fell with their arms in their hands."[91]

Causes of Defeat

The causes of Sindhia's defeat were many, but the following are most important. Both at Patharganj and Laswari the Maratha forces had to fight without capable and experienced leaders. Secondly, Ambaji Ingale was the worst sinner. He first tried to

87. Thorn, 227.
88. Martin Wellesly's *Despatches,* III, p. 554.
89. Khare XIV, p. 7938, Parse p. 241.
90. Martin Wellesley's *Despatches,* p. 445, Pearse p. 249, Sardesai III, p. 416.
91. Grant Duff, *History of the Marathas,* III, p. 256.

gain favourable terms for himself and then abandoned the field as soon as the battle turned against him. Maratha officers of high rank did not show full enthusiasm. In Sindhia's forces, there was no regular cavalry organised into brigades and trained to deliver shock charges. Their equipment and tactics fitted them for light raiding only. Moreover there was no co-ordination between the cavalry and the infantry. There were no galloper guns with Sindhia's forces[92] either, and they also lacked mobile batteries. Their musketry was weaker in comparison to that of the British forces.

The Defeat of Sindhia in the South

Arthur Wellesley was not only a great general, but also master of diplomatic tactics. He seduced Muslim Jagirdars like Subhan Khan of Partur, Salabat Khan of Ellichpoor and Amir Khan Pathan[93] to his side. The force under his command was estimated at 2,164 British and 8,989 Indian soldiers and 2,174 horses. The contingent under Stevenson consisted of 890 British, 8,569 Indian sepoys and 1,022 horses.[94] In addition to this, there was the army of the Nizam under Sukhu Rudra.[95]

At first, Daulat Rao Sindhia and Bhonsle were in an advantageous position, but this advantage was soon lost as they waited for the arrival of Jaswant Rao Holkar. They proposed to go to the Peshwa along with Holkar to induce him to dismiss his British protectors, but the Peshwa only desired to return "to his former place of asylum."[96] Jaswant Rao Holkar also did not join them, nor did the Peshwa show any willingness to encourage them as even their envoy to him was kept at arm's length at Poona.

During this period, Arthur Wellesley was busy ensuring his supplies and Stevenson organising the defence of the Nizam's frontiers. Gopal Bhau was sent by Sindhia to attack Aurangabad,

92. *Poona Residency Correspondence,* Vol. IX, p. 112.

93. Gurwood III, pp. 274, 264, 178 and 228.

94. Fortesque's *History of British Army,* Vol. V, p. 15.

95. *Gurwood II,* pp. 302-03, Edition 1837. Khare XIV 6693, Supplementary D IV 73.

96. Khare XIV 6692.

which was in the possession of the Nizam. He fought a bloody skirmish with Stevenson's forces.[97]

The Battle of Assaye : (September 23, 1803)

Arthur Wellesley got full information about Sindhia's army and his movements through a "Munshi" (clerk) in the pay of Collins.[98] Thus strengthened, Arthur Wellesley made a surprise attack on Sindhia's army, when Sindhia was away,[99] and when only five battalions were able to meet the surprise attack of the British forces at Assaye.[100]

Arthur Wellesley reconnoitered the position and convinced himself about the enemy being in an unready condition and off their guard. Gun bullocks had been sent away for grazing. Soldiers were busy preparing their meals. Only a small advanced guard was in a position to face the attack. Sindhia himself was away for consultations with Bhonsle.[101] Arthur Wellesley decided to attack at such an opportune moment. "On the 23rd" he stated, "I arrived Baulniah and there received a report that Sindhia and the Raja of Berar had moved off in the morning and that the infantry were about to follow but were still in Camp about 6 miles from the ground on which I intended to camp. It was obvious that the attack was no longer to be delayed, and having provided for the security of my baggage and stores at Baulniah I marched on to attack the enemy."[102]

The British army crossed the Khelna at a chosen ford. The fork of two rivulets, which united a mile below the ford, defended the rear of the British battle line against any Maratha attack. The Marathas at first sight hurriedly drew the forces facing the Khelna and parallel to the two rivers, but they changed, their plan to bar the attack on their left flank. Arthur Wellesley also changed his plan of attack accordingly.

97. Khare XIV 6678, 6692, 6693, *Gurwood* II, pp. 286, 288.

98. *Supplementary Despatches* IX, p. 175.

99. Khare XIV 6749, 6734, Gulgule Dafter Letter of 15.10.1803.

100. Gulgule Daftar, Khare XIV 6720, A.W. in *Gurwood*, 434, 456.

101. Khare XIV 6734, 6749, Gulgule Daftar, 15.10.1803.

102. Arthur Wellesley to Governor General p. 85, *Gurwood Despatches* from Camp at Assaye dated 24.9.1803.

The actual battle can best be described in the words of Arthur Wellesley. "The enemy had altered the position of their infantry previous to our attack; it was no longer as at first, along the Kaitna or Khelna, but extended from that river across the village of Assaye upon the Nullah, which was upon our right. We attacked them immediately and the troops advanced under a very hot fire from cannon. The piquets of the infantry and the 7th regiment, which were in the right of the first and second lines suffered particularly from the fire of the guns on the left of the enemy's position near Assaye. The enemy's cavalry also made an attempt to charge the 74th regiment at the moment when they were most exposed to this fire, but they were cut up by the British cavalry which moved on at that moment. At length, the enemy's line gave way in all directions."[103]

According to Elphinstone, "the enemy's cavalry broke the 74th regiment and this was the critical moment of the engagement. But, at that instant, our cavalry appeared on the right, charged them and drove them with great slaughter into a nullah (or river) in front...and turned them back."[104]

The battle of Assaye was a brief but hotly contested one and treachery was active in some brigades on Sindhia's side. "Pohlman, whose conduct throughout the day bears strong marks of treachery to his master, seized the opportunity to retreat."[105]

In this battle, two notables, named Jado Rao Bhaskar and Anand Rao Nimbalkar, lost their lives.[106] The infantry fought well, but the cavalry did not fare well.[107] Raghoji Bhonsle left the field without delivering any attack or sending his army to help Sindhia's army.

198 Europeans and 230 Telingas were killed on the British side. 1,200 sepoys of North India and about two hundred Marathas with their leaders Jado Rao Bhaskar and Anand Rao Nimbalkar were killed on the Maratha side. The wounded

103. *Gunwood Despatches*, Arthur Wellesley to Lord Wellesley.

104. Elphinstone to Adams, 25th September 1803, Selections of G. Forest, p. 17.

105. *Macveigh Historical Records of 78th Highlanders* (1887) p. 53.

106. Gulgule 15th October, Khare XIV, p. 749.

107. A.W. in *Gurwood* II, 337.

were 3 or 4 times of this number,[108] but this estimate does not seem to be correct, as Elphinstone wrote, "The army's loss in men is almost equal to our own in number but very different in value."[109] Owen says "Loss in officers and men, has been very great."[110]

J.N. Sarkar has estimated that 644 Europeans and 940 Indians were killed, wounded or missing, 401 Highlanders, and 402 in casualties, 200 men and 715 horses were lost in the cavalry. The Sindhian army left 1,200 dead.[111] The Maratha Infantry of which there were three companies fought well and stood by their guns to the last. Their execution, however, was principally by their cannon. Colonel Wallance, Col. Harness and Arthur Wellesley himself had their horses killed under them.[112] The infantry showed bravery but the cavalry disgraced itself. The artillery of Sindhia proved its excellence. Grant Duff gives a similar account,[113] and describes the battle as "a triumph more splendid than any recorded in Deccan History."[114] But Sardesai states that the victory was won by the British at such an enormous cost of men that pursuit was found impossible.[115]

The Result

The battle of Assaye was obviously a hotly contested battle, but not a decisive victory. In the words of Elphinstone, after the action there was no pursuit because our cavalry was not then in a state to pursue.[116] But its repercussions were great. Never did such a hotly contested battle like that of Assaye take place again between the Marathas and the East India Company.

The cowardly flight of Bhonsle sowed the seeds of discord among the Marathas, as they accused Raghuji Bhonsle of selfishness and of giving his ally the least help. So Sindhia did

108. Khare XIV, 6749.
109. *Gurwood Selections*, p. 17.
110. Owen, *A Selection from the Despatches...Marquis Wellesley, and Wellington*, No. 172, p. 299.
111. Sarkar, *Fall of the Mughal Empire*, IV, p. 331, ed. 1950.
112. *Gurwood Selection*, Arthur Wellesley to Gen. Stuart on 24.9.1803.
113. Duff, *History of the Marathas*, I, p. 564.
114. *Ibid.*, 574, III, p. 173.
115. Sardesai, *New History of the Marathas*, III, p. 410.
116. G. Forest's Selections from Elphinstone 13.

not properly help him either at Aragaun or on any other occasion against the East India Company.

This battle made such an impression on Sindhia that he always avoided coming into direct clash with the East India Company, nor did Bhonsle and Sindhia make combined efforts to face the British ever after. This battle paved the way for British supremacy in Central India by humbling Sindhia, who was considered to be the most powerful Maratha ruler.

The Orissa Campaign

The possession of Orissa had been for a long time by the British Government. They wanted to connect the possessions in Bengal with Madras. So British operations were directed to Orissa also.

A force commanded by Lt. Col. Harcourt invaded Orissa. Munnickpattam was taken of without resistance on the 14th September, Jagannath Puri on 18th September and Cuttack surrendered on 10th October. A detachment under Capt. Morgen occupied Balasore on 21st Sept., Sooring on the 3rd October, and the fort of Barabutte on 14th October. Thus the whole of Orissa came under British rule.[117]

Conquest of Bundelkhand

Lt. Col. Powell crossed the Yamuna on the 6th Sept. and Himmat Bahadur joined him on 16th September. After reducing various forts, they crossed the Ken on 10th Oct. 1803. On 13th October, Shamsher Bahadur S/o Ali Bahadur, great-grandson of Baji Rao and Mastani, came to oppose them but was defeated. Himmat Bahadur helped the British forces against Shamsher Bahadur and was rewarded. The Maratha chief of Jhansi was won over, and Shamsher Bahadur made peace, thus Bundelkhand came under the control of the British Government.

Armistice

The Rana of Gohad had been already won over. Daya Ram Jat of Hathras and the Jat Raja of Mursan were also defeated. Some Rohila Chiefs and some other Rajas of Bundelkhand helped the British forces. So only Daulat Rao Sindhia and Bhonsle had to bear the burnt of war. Under these circumstances,

117. R.D. Banerji, *History of Orissa*, Vol. II.

Sindhia now sought peace and Jaswant Rao Ghorpare was sent to solicit an armistice for both the parties. Daulat Rao's request was granted, but an attack was made on Venka Jee Munya Bappu, who was at Aragaon in spite of the request of Daulat Rao's Vakil.

The Battle of Aragaon

On November 29th, the Battle of Aragaon took place and in this the confederates were again defeated. In this battle, in spite of the truce, Daulat Rao Sindhia secretly supported Bhonsle's forces. A body of 500 persons was killed to a man. The British army lost about 346 men. The British army next attacked Gowilgarh and this fort fell into British hands on 25th December, 1803. This brought Bhonsle to his knees and he sued for peace.

Wellesley wrote, "I could not have hoped for a completion of plans at once so rapid and so secure."[118] The astonishing victory of the British forces was achieved partly by the treachery of Sindhia's foreign officers and partly due to their excellent spy system. The superior British diplomacy, their pertinacity in fighting and their better tactics and strategy further explain their success. On the other hand, the Marathas had been weakened by mutual dissensions. But, perhaps, another reason for the defeat of the Marathas can be discerned in their abandonment of their national tactics of guerilla warfare and adoption of the western organisation and methods of fighting, in which at best they were dependent on foreigners.

The Peace

General Wellesley dealt separately with Bhonsle and Sindhia, the only two chiefs who came forward to defend the Maratha Empire. This move of General Wellesley was not appreciated by the Governor General, whose instructions were that "Daulat Rao and Raghoji be captured and sent to Calcutta personally to beg peace at the feet of the Lord."[119]

General Wellesley in reply showed his inability to carry out the order and wrote "I believe that I have made a better peace than the Governor General expected." On 17th December

118. Martin, *Wellesley Desptches*, Vol. III, p. 420.

119. Sardesai, *New History of the Marathas*, Vol. III, p. 417.

1803, Bhonsle affixed his signature at Devgaon by which he ceded the province of Orissa and parts of Western Berar upto the river Wardha to the British, but the Nizam retained some districts. He bound himself to respect the treaties concluded with his feudatories by the East India Company and not to entertain any enemy of the English in his service.

Daulat Rao Sindhia was now isolated. He endeavoured by every means to avoid making the cessions which the British Government demanded, and it was not until he was certain that compliance with these demands was the only means of averting the entire conquest of his territories that he at length yielded.

The Treaty of Surji Arjungaon

Overwhelmed by a sense of failure and frustration, Daulat Rao Sindhia sued for peace through his Chief Minister Vithal Pant and Munshi Kamal Nain, and after some diplomatic shuffling signed the Treaty of Surji Arjungaon on 30th Dec., 1803, on the following principal terms :

1. He ceded to the East India Company and its allies, in perpetual sovereignty, all his forts, territories and rights in the Ganga-Yumuna Doab, and his rights and claims in countries north of Jaipur and Jodhpur States and the territory of the Rana of Gohud.
2. He also ceded to the East India Company the forts of Baroach and Ahmednagar with their dependent territories and also lands lying south of the Ajanta hill.
3. He renounced all claims in the ceded districts upon the Peshwa, the Nizam and the Gaikwar.
4. Asirgarh, Burhanpur, Pawagarh and their dependencies were restored to him.
5. He renounced all claims and rights of interference in the affairs of Shah Alam.
6. He confirmed all treaties made by the British Government with his feudatories.
7. He agreed to abide by the decisions of the East India Company in his disputes with the Peshwa regarding his rights in Malwa and elsewhere.

8. He agreed not to entertain in his service any French man or any other enemies of the British.

The most controversial article was Article 15 by which the British Government had agreed to furnish a substantial subsidiary force of infantry, artillery and ordinance for the protection of the State of Daulat Rao Sindhia (Article 15).

Arthur Wellesley hastened to enter into these engagements in opposition to the Governor General's views, because he was conscious that Jaswant Rao Holkar would not submit to the British yoke without a blow.[120] Baji Rao, too, was hostile to the British and was engaged in intrigue against them as a "correspondence" was found to be carried on between Holkar and Sindhia's camp, Poona and the southern Jagirdars.[121] This news made the British eager for peace. The terms with the Raja of Gohud and Ambaji were similar to those with the Rajputs, except that the Raja agreed to subsidise three battalions of sepoys, paying for them at the rate of Rs. 75,000 a month. The treaty with Ambaji became null and void later on. The treaty of Sarji Arjangaon of 30th December 1803 was a striking feat of British diplomacy and a blow to Maratha sovereignty. It practically liquidated the power of the Sindhia and increased proportionately the power of the British.[122]

The Treaty of Burhanpur

On February 27, 1804 this matter was further clarified by the defensive alliance with the East India Company under the Treaty of Burhanpur, the East India Company undertaking to maintain a subsidiary force of 6,000 infantry and artillery to be cantoned in British territory near his border and the expenses of the forces were to be borne by the East India Company. In the words of Dr. B.G. Sharma all inducements were held out to him to agree to it, as it gave him all the benefits without causing any loss of revenue for the maintenance of the British subsidiary forces. This bogus display of generosity was merely a crafty device to cajole Sindhia into taking the bait.[123]

---

120. *Poona Residency Correspondence,* Vol. VII, p. 193.
121. *Ibid.,* p. 189.
122. Dr. B.G. Sharma's unpublished thesis "Sir John Malcolm in Madhya Bharat," pp. 33-39.
123. *Ibid.,* p. 34.

The most important Articles of the Treaty were as follows :

Article I

If any person or a State whatever shall commit any act of unprovoked hostility or aggression against either...in compliance with the requisition of the Maharaja would come to his assistance.

Article III

The Maharaja (Daulat Rao Sindhia) agrees to receive, and Honourable Company agrees to furnish, a subsidiary force.... This force is to be stationed at such place near the frontier of Daulat Rao Sindhia as may hereafter be deemed most eligible by the British Government.

Article VI

The subsidiary force, will at all times, be ready, on the requisition of Maharaja, to execute services of importance such as the care of the person of the Maharja, his heirs and successors, the overawing and chastisement of rebels or exciters of disturbances in Maharaja's dominions; but it is not to be employed on trifling occasions.

Article VIII

The Maharaja engages neither to commence nor to pursue in future any negotiation with any principal states or powers, without giving previous notice and entering into mutual consultation with the Honourable Company's Government...and it is further agreed that no officer of the Honourable Company shall ever interfere in the internal affairs of the Maharaja's Government.

Article IX

The Company was given power to adjust differences between Sindhia and other powers. By the other Article each party dared itself from interfering with tributaries of the other.[124]

The Treaty and Its Consequences

Malcolm was appointed Resident with Sindhia, and Elphinstone with the Raja of Berar. It might be pointed out

124. *Aitchson-Treaties...and Sanads*, Vol. IV, pp. 50-56.

here that these Residents had the status of an Ambassador merely and did not exercise any power of control or interference in the internal affairs of the State to whom they were accredited. Daulat Rao Sindhia resented this treaty and his subsequent deprival of Gwalior and Gohad added fuel to fire. He mustered up courage to protest against this last injury. Consequently the British avoided to mention this treaty in subsequent alliances. Accrding to Mr. C.E. Luard writer of the Chapter XXXI of Cambridge History of India Vol. V "The Treaty of Burhanpur of 1804," which though never denounced, had been objected to by Lord Cornwallis and treated as a dead letter, when new compacts were made with Gwalior in 1805 and 1817.[125] Similarly P.E. Roberts also states "Wellesley's treaty with Sindhia of 1804 establishing a subsidiary force, which had remained a dead letter from the day it was signed and been ignored in subsequent diplomatic relations."[126]

But later on Lord Ellenborough took advantage of Article VI of this treaty, attacked Gwalior in 1843 and imposed British tutelage over Gwalior. He was recalled due to this rash act but Gwalior became fully a dependent state after 1843.

This treaty is one of the most controversial treaties of India in respect of its consequences. Did it reduce Daulat Rao Sindhia to the status of a dependent ally of the East India Company? He, on his part, considered himself free from British tutelage. British diplomats also avoided open clash with him, but perhaps it is permissible to say that this treaty proved disastrous to the Gwalior State and British diplomacy took full advantage of this treaty when the occasion came. It is true that Daulat Rao suffered serious losses of territory by the treaty of 1803 and agreed to place his foreign relations under the East India Company's tutelage by that of 1804. Further the promise by the East India Company of unilateral assistance to him in case of internal or external disturbances was indication of Sindhia's reduction to a dependent status. But, it might be equally pointed out that

125. *Cambridge History of India,* Vol. V Chapter XXXI by Ma. C.E. Luard, p. 580 ed. 1929. Mr. Luard also edited Gwalior Gazetteer. For Treaty see Aitchson IV 53, Parliamentary papers p. 146. G.G.P. 315 and A.C. Banerji Document I, pp. 321-23.

126. P. Roberts : *History of British India*, p. 331, ed. 1943 Oxford University Press.

(i) the subsidiary force for his assistance was not stationed within his territories as in the case of other dependent allies and (ii) that the British Resident at his Court was still mere the envoy of a friendly power rather than the representative of a superior controlling power. In these respects Sindhia's status did probably differ from that of other dependent allies of the East India Company.

Subsequent Developments

The Maratha powers had no peace even after Sindhia and Bhonsle's war had ended. In April 1804, that stormy petrel of Maratha War politics, Jaswant Rao Holkar singly commenced hostilities against the British, defeated Col. Monson at the Mukundara Pass in Rajasthan, then besieged Delhi though without any success, and clashed with the British forces at Dig (November 17, 1804) but was defeated. The Raja of Bharatpur was leagued with him and when the British Commander Lord Lake besieged the fort of Bharatpur, he suffered a resounding reverse. The Raja, however, considered discretion the better part of valour and made peace with the Company on 10th April, 1805. Holkar might have been crushed thereafter, but Wellesley was suddenly recalled from India by the Directors, and the pacific Lord Cornwallis was sent out as Governor General to reestablish peace in India. We are not directly concerned in this *book* with the war between the Company and Holkar, except in so far that during its course, Sindhia's hopes for recovering his losses in the late war were again mildly revived though, eventually, the course of events brought him no gains.

Rupture with Sindhia

On May 31, Webb demanded Sindhia's help against Holkar, but Vithal Pant, expressed his inability to do so, owing pecuniary difficulties and a fear of Holkar's attack on his own dominions, and demanded monetary assistance before any help could be provided. Instead of helping Sindhia, Lumsden, the Secretary, arrogantly wrote to Webb that "our friendship with that chief must rest on the basis of our power."[127]

On 25th June, 1804, Vithal Pant, Bapoo Chintanavis and

---

127. *Poona Residency Correspondence,* Vol. XI, No. 17, p. 27.

Munshi Kamal Nain met Webb and complained about Holkar's attack on Ahmadnagar. On July 2, 1804, Vithal Pant again demanded pecuniary assistance from Resident Webb[128] and assured him of taking the field himself. Instead of helping Sindhia, Col. Murray occupied Ujjain, though he abandoned it in August.

Increasing Tension

Resenting the treaty of 1804, and deprived of Gwalior and Gohad, Sindhia came naturally to entertain unfriendly sentiments against the British. He did send his commander, Bapu Sindhia, with 10 thousand horses to cooperate with Lord Lake,[129] but a rupture took place between Col. Monson and Bapuji. According to British sources, Bapuji Sindhia did not cooperate with Lake, did not execute his orders, but rather "Excited disturbances, burnt and destroyed the taluka of Rampura, intercepted Col. Monson's dak and detained Harkaras. He treated Mr. Gront with great indignity, a musket was put to his shoulder and he was threatened with death." But according to Maratha sources, it was Lake, who refused to keep them with him and directed them to march to Col. Monson and Mr. Lucon to oppose Holkar. Bapuji Sindhia demanded pecuniary assistance from Col. Monson and on his refusal, wrote to Lard Lake but Lake directed him to go to Ujjain and now Bapuji wrote to Daulat Rao Sindhia for orders.

Under pecuniary distress, Bapu sent Sada Shiv Rao for collecting funds and himself remained with Col. Monson with 3000 horses. Col. Monson instructed Bapuji Sindhia to march with Mr. Lucon to oppose Holkar. In the subsequent encounter, notwithstanding the immense superiority of the enemy in numbers, Bapuji fought with the utmost vigour, but the combined forces of the British and Sindhia were repulsed by Holkar. The loss sustained by Bapuji in killed and wounded amounted to 700 horses and much of his camp equipage was also lost. Col. Monson was reported to "have taken no share in the action," and retreated and Bapuji joined him on the road. With his remaining forces, Col. Monson crossed the Chambal in boats at Kotah.

128. *Poona Residency Correspondence,* No. 18, p. 29 dated 11.6.1804.

129. *Ibid.,* p. 27.

Bapuji Sindhia requested him to send the boats back for conveying his own troops across the river so that they might be able to join him, but Col. Monson never returned the boats. Bapuji Sindhia remained behind. Raja Zalim Singh of Kotah sent a message to Bapu informing him that if he did not visit Holkar, he would inevitably lose his life. Bapuji again asked for pecuniary assistance, but Webb took no steps to furnish such help to him. Under these circumstances, Bapuji Sindhia was forced to espouse the cause of Holkar.[130] The complaints of Bapuji Sindhia seem to be more justified than those of Col. Monson. Webb, the Resident to Sindhia, recommended to Lake to pay 1.5 lakhs to Bapuji Sindhia,[131] but the sum was never paid.

Thus, the main cause of the tension between Sindhia and the British was that Webb refused to give financial assistance to Sindhia to fight Holkar. Besides this, Daulat Rao Sindhia demanded the restoration of Chamargoonda, Jamgaon and some other places, but these were not restored to him.[132]

Lord Lake further incensed Sindhia by giving away the territories of Gohad and Gwalior, together with the fort of Gwalior to the people of Bhootpoongre which was nowhere provided in the Treaty of Sarji Arjangaon.[133] Names of all ceded Territories with names and annual values were entered in the Treaty, but Gwalior and Gohad with the Gwalior Fort were not mentioned at all — This was a breach of the treaty[134] and Daulat Rao Sindhia naturally complained of this action. The name of the Raja of Jodhpur, was inserted without the consent of the Raja of Jodhpur though on enquiry by Sindhia, the Raja refused to admit any connection with the British Government.

Sindhia also complained that the amount of 15 lakhs on account of territory in Hindustan was not paid to him, though he was willing to be paid in instalment.

Moreover, the parganas of Dholpur, Baree and Rajkhera were not delivered to him as promised in the treaty. The

130. Various letters of *Poona Residency Correspondence,* Vol. XI, No. 59, of 14-10-1804, p. 90.

131. *Poona Residency Correspondence,* IX No. 16, pp. 24-25.

132. *Ibid.*, p. 92.

133. *Ibid.*, p. 93.

134. Treaty of Surji Arjangaon.

collections from Chamargoonda, Dahood, Pawagarh etc. and other places were also not paid to him. To these parganas, tehsildars were allowed to be posted to collect taxes, but the Bhils and others robbed these parganas. Daulat Rao Sindhia was not allowed to assist these tehsildars, nor did the British help them in the discharge of their duties. Neither were the promised jagirs in Hindustan handed over to him on various pretexts, even after the expiry of ten months from the signing of the treaty.

Col. Murray remained at Ujjain, but did not save Bhilsa from plunder by Amir Khan, though according to the treaty, British forces were bound to do so. Holkar plundered other territories of Daulat Rao Sindhia and the British Government did not help him to stop this pillage.

The financial condition of Daulat Rao Sindhia became so bad that he was unable to move from Burhanpur.

He wrote to Lord Wellesley : "My determined resolution now is, after having collected a numerous army consisting both old troops and new levies, to proceed to chastize the enemy (Holkar)."[135] But when his complaints fell upon deaf ears, he was forced to adopt another course against the East India Company which apparently desired to treat him as a vassal rather than as an ally. Guessing wrongly that the East India Company was growing weaker, Sindhia inclined to take more decisive action against it.

Finally, the arrival of Sarji Rao Ghatge, the death of Vithal Pant on 9-11-1804,[136] the arrival of Holkar's Vakils in his camp, and the hostile attitude of Col. Jenkins, British Resident at his court, forced him to chalk out a new line of action for himself. The timidity and hesitation which had characterised the policy of the Gwalior Government under Vithal Pant was flung aside and he launched on a bolder and independent course of action.

At Ghatge's initiative Sindhia's army attacked the fortified village of Seoni in the Bhopal State in the last week of October, and in the first week of the next month, burst upon Hoshangabad. Jenkins sent a hectoring letter to Sindhia on 17th November,

135. *Poona Residency Correspondence,* Vol. IX, No. 59, p. 96.

136. *R.C.,* Vol. XI Introduction, p. V.

1804 demanding to know "what has been the nature of your intercourse with the Raja of Berar? What is the object of your advance through the territories of Bhonsle."[137] The British victories at Deeg and at Khudaiganj near Farrukhabad in the middle of November still further increased the arrogance of the Resident and he asked Daulat Rao to dismiss his minister, Sarji Rao Ghatge, and retrace his steps to Ujjain via Bhilsa. Daulat Rao Sindhia cloaked his resentment. Ram Chandra Bhaskar *alias* Anna Sikkanavis, Keeper of the Seal, affirmed to the Resident the utter dependence of his master on the favour of the British Government, reaffirmed his master's sincere desire to return to his capital, and humbly placed the various obstacles to Ghatge's dismissal.

Daulat Rao's ministers continued to flatter the Resident during the absence of Daulat Rao Sindhia at Sagar and the pillage of that town. Jenkins failed to penetrate the wiles of the Maratha and acquitted Sindhia of any complicity in the late outrage but fulminated against Sarji Rao Ghatge, whose insidious counsels, "he declared" directed to pervert in the weak and despicable understanding of Daulat Rao Sindhia, every exertion of a specific and friendly tendency. "Ghatge, he said, was wanting in no art of cunning, knavery or malice to inspire the Maharaja with high notions of his own power and with most disrespectful and ungrounded suspicion of the generous and liberal principles of His Majesty's policy towards this court."[138]

The Resident's wrath was aggravated by the junction of Sindhia's army with that of Jean Baptiste Filose. Jenkins announced his fixed determination to leave the court on 17th January, 1805. On 25th January, Jenkins and Lieut. Stewart went to Daulat Rao Sindhia's court to bid him farewell. In the meantime, the camp of the Resident was "overwhelmed and plundered by the whole body of the Pindaris, who attacked it within about a mile from Sindhia's camp." All apparel was either robbed or destroyed and Dr. Wise and Lieutenant Green were wounded. Jenkins wrote to Wellesley : "The particulars of this affair which exceeded the most infamous atrocity that was

---

137. *Poona Residency Correspondence,* Vol. X and XI Letters 63, 64 and 65.
138. *Ibid.,* Vol. XI, Letters 77 and 71.

ever recorded in the annals of the most barbarous nation."[139] He held S.R. Ghatge responsible for this mischief. The British Resident estimated a loss of property amounting to Rs. 1,40,298.

Lord Wellesley was softened due to British failures in the war against Jaswant Rao Holkar coupled with the refusal of Lord Castlereagh to send even a single soldier on account of the death-grapple with Napoleon. Acute financial distress, news of hostile intrigues at Poona and of a Rajput-Maratha coalition against the British forced Wellesley to come down from his high pedestal. The wheel of destiny had taken a strange turn and the Governor General had to be particularly regardful of the feelings of Sindhia.

Sindhia marched to Serai Kachner, forty miles north of Sagar on the Kali river, after exacting 2-1/2 lakhs from the Killadar of Sagar. Towards the end of February, the British Government entered into a treaty with the Raja of Jhansi and Kalpee[140] and this interference further annoyed Daulat Rao Sindhia.[141]

Two weeks later, the Maharaja announced his intention to proceed direct to Bharatpur with a view to "putting an end, by amicable inter-position and negotiations, to the war between the British Government and Jaswant Rao Holkar."[142]

The entrusting of Gwalior to the Company and of Gohad to the Rana antagonised Ambaji Ingale, who was the active abettor of Sarji Rao Ghatge. Daulat Rao Sindhia refused to punish Bapuji Sindhia and Sedasheo Bhow Bhaskar, as suggested by Lord Lake, and complained against the treatment meted out to Bapuji and lack of pecuniary assistance to him.

Tension Reduced

A division of the British army under Col. Maratendele in Bundelkhand had been directed to reinforce the army at Bharatpur and it reached Gwalior about this time. On hearing of the recent outrage at the Resident's camp, he fell back to

---

139. *Poona Residency Correspondence,* Letter 88.

140. *Ibid.,* No. 139, p. 223.

141. *Ibid.,* Vol. XI, No. 87, p. 139.

142. *Ibid.,* Vol. XI, No. 59, p. 96.

Jhansi, as the Company's provinces from Calcutta to Kalpi were completely exposed. Sindhia proceeded towards Bharatpur and the Governor General accepted his promise of compensation for the outrage, and agreed to provide pecuniary aid to him provided Sindhia would return and employ himself in taking possession of Holkar's unoccupied districts in Malwa.

Sindhia pretended to acquiesce and retired 8 miles towards Sabalgarh, but sent a part of his cavalry and the Pindaris towards Bharatpur. The arrival of this force at Bharatpur was delayed on account of the treachery of Jean Baptiste who fell into British snares.[143]

Sindhia's army was now swollen to a mighty force of 9,000 cavalry, 20,000 pindaris, 18 battalions of infantry and 140 guns (including those of Amir Khan).[144]

Renewed Attempt of An All-Maratha Coalition

The British, having separated the Jat Raja from Holkar, could now direct all their energies against Holkar. While Jaswant Rao Holkar was occupied in the north, all his possessions in the South such as Chandwad, etc. were seized by the British during September and October, 1804. A similar fate befell his territory in Bundelkhand, though for a time Ambaji and Amir Khan joined hands and resisted the British there with considerable success.

The Governor General first called Arthur Wellesley and later on Malcolm, for consultations but was unable to decide any thing. He removed Malcolm from Sindhia's Court.[145]

The Sablgarh Meet

At Sabalgarh, Sindhia was joined by Holkar with a huge force of about 60 thousand men. Here the best brains of the Marathas assembled in a grand concourse for adopting measures to counteract the recent British successes. Even the Chhatrapati

---

143. *Rise of the Christian Power in India*, p. 568. *Malcolm's Political History* Vol. I and II Kayee's Life of Malcolm Vol. I and II Thorn, Maratha War and Sports in India, Robert's India under Wellesley etc.

144. *Poona Residency Correspondence*, Vol. Introduction.

145. *Kayee's Life and Correspondence*, Despatches of two Wellesley brothers and Sindnia's letter of 18.10.1804, Vol. VI, p. 502.

of Satara was represented by his intrepid brother Chatar Singh.

Jaswant Rao Holkar joined Sindhia at Sabalgarh on 15th April, 1805. Daulat Rao Sindhia also admitted Bapuji Sindhia "who stood in the light of an open enemy to the British Government on the 14th April, to all the honours of a Sardar in his service."[146]

The rendezvous of Sindhia, Holkar and Amir Khan exposed the British territories and those of their allies to the danger of an attack.

Two months afterwards, the Commander-in Chief braced himself up to call upon Daulat Rao Sindhia to "remove his army to a distance of 50 Kos from the frontiers of the Company's allies" and to separate his troops from those of Jaswant Rao Holkar. In case of refusal to comply with his demand, the Commander-in-Chief requested him to sent back the British Resident with proper escort. Knit together in alliance with Holkar by the treaty of Sabalgarh, Sindhia refused to accept these demands and also kept Jenkins in a state of semi-captivity.[147]

Return of Cornwallis

Meanwhile, Lord Wellesley had been recalled and Lord Cornwallis had arrived on 30th July, 1805, as Governor General. On 30th August 1805, he wrote to Lake. The Raja of Barar and other chiefs, who have suffered great deprivation of territory can certainly entertain no friendly disposition towards us. Even the Raja of Jaipur had adopted a dubious attitude and his officers prevented supply of rations to the camp of General Jones at Tonk Rampura. There was even a talk of a Rajput confederacy of Jaipur, Jodhpur and Udaipur against the British, because it was rumoured that the British were bent upon exterminating the Indian States, whereas the Marathas only desired for plunder.[148] Under these circumstances, Lord Lake wrote that he could not "look forward with any sanguine hope for the establishment of a happy permanent peace unless a great change can be effected in the minds of the natives of

146. *Poona Residency Correspondence,* Vol. XI, Letters 85, 89, 91, 94.

147. *Ibid.,* Letters 108 and 120.

148. *Ibid.,* Vol. XI, p. 183 No. 115.

India." The financial position of the British Government was very distressing. "Regular troops" Cornwallis wrote "whose monthly pay amounted to Rs. 5 lakhs are short of five months pay and many of the police departments are still more in arrears."[149]

Sindhia's Breach with Holkar

The task of the new Governor General was facilitated by the recrudescence of the old jealousy and rivalry between Sindhia and Holkar. Sarji Rao Ghatge, who had drawn the two chiefs into an alliance, was driven out of power by Ambaji Ingale, who paid Rs. 30 lakhs to Daulat Rao Sindhia to be appointed to the office of Prime Minister in the middle of July, 1805.[150] Ambaji was tortured by Holkar and Ghatge to make him disgorge his hoarded wealth. The change of ministers was followed by a rupture between the two allies. Holkar employed Ghatge in his service and Sindhia reciprocated by admitting Shamat Khan and Wahid All Bangash, two deserters from Holkar's army to his camp.[151]

Ambaji Ingale was pro-British. He had earnestly solicited the protection of the British Government for himself and had signified his readiness to concur in any arrangement which might be proposed to him with regard to his future place of residence or to the settlement of his districts. Resident Jenkins wrote that "from every information which I can obtain the councils of the Durbar which, since the accession of Ambaji to power, have never assumed any settled aspect, have been continuously distracted between the dread of the immediate consequence of a rupture with Holkar and of the more remote but more certain ruin which attends the contrary line of conduct; and in this dilemma it is easy to conceive that no decided steps are likely to be adopted by Daulat Rao Sindhia."

Munshi Kamal Nain[152] had since become the sole adviser of Sindhia in foreign affairs and meekly carried out all that Malcolm desired. On his advice, Sindhia finally separated from

149. *Ross Correspondence of Cornwallis,* Vol. III, p. 546.

150. Chapters II and III of this book.

151. *Poona Residency Correspondence,* Vol. XI, p. 118 and p. 123.

152. *Ibid.,* Vol. XI.

Holkar by a fresh treaty concluded between him and the Company on 21st November, 1805, known as treaty of Mustafapur signed by Munshi Kamal Nain.[153] Overtures had been made by Malcolm[154] to Kamal Nain and by Lord Lake to Ambaji. Lord Cornwallis grasped at the opportunity, and smoothened the way for peace which was facilitated by Kamal Nain, who signed the treaty on behalf of Sindhia.

The Treaty of Mustafapur

The Treaty of Surji Arjungaon was to remain in full force with the following alternations :

1. The fortress of Gwalior and Gohad were given to Daulat Rao Sindhia.
2. Daulat Rao Sindhia relinquished the pension of Rs. 15 Lakhs granted to certain officers in his service and to forego his Inam (reward) districts of Dholpur, Bari and Rajkhera, which were reserved to him by the Treaty of Surji Arjungaon.
3. The river Chambal, from Kotah on the west to the extremity of Gohad territory was declared the boundary of the two States.
4. Daulat Rao Sindhia was assigned a Jagir of four lakhs, Baiza Bai of two lakhs and his second daughter, Chimna Bai of one lakh annually.
5. The two districts of Bhadelkand Soosepoorah to the Chambal were given to the Company.
6. Daulat Rao Sindhia renounced all claim to tribute from the Raja of Bundi or from any other State North of the Chambal and to the Eastward of Kota.
7. Sindhia pledged "never again to admit Ghatgay" but this was honoured more in the breach than in the observance.

The British Government pledged themselves not to enter into any treaty with the Rana of Udaipur, the Raja of Jodhpur, and other chiefs and tributaries of Daulat Rao Sindhia in Malwa,

153. *Poona Residency Correspondence,* Vol. XI, No. 143, p. 227.

154. For influence of Malcolm see B.G.C. Sharma's Thesis on Malcolm Kaye's *Life of Malcolm* and *Poona Residency Correspondence,* Vol. XI, No. 91, 126.

Marwar and Mewar, nor to interfere with the arrangements which Sindhia might wish to make with them. The British promised not to desire restoration of such districts of Holkar between the Tapti and the Chambal as Sindhia had taken or interfere in any manner with their arrangements, wars or disputes. According to Sardesai the words 'defence' and 'offence' were deliberately omitted, so that Sindhia might consider himself as independent as he was before.[155] The treaty did in fact restore to Sindhia a status of semi-independence and freedom to deal with foreign states not in alliance with the Company.

Restoration of Gwalior and Gohad to Sindhia

About the restoration of Gwalior and Gohad to Sindhia a great controversy had already ensued after the treaty of Surji Arjungaon between Malcolm and Lord Wellesley in which Malcolm favoured restoration and Lord Wellesley refused to do so.[156] With the exit of Wellesley, British policy took a different turn and Lord Cornwallis even favoured the idea of giving still more territories and even Delhi to Sindhia. Malcolm protested against this and succeeded in consoling Sindhia with Gwalior and Gohad only.[157] The Fort of Gwalior was delivered by the British, but Kirat Singh, the Rana of Gohad and his adherents refused to hand it over either to British forces or to Sindhia. So, the fort of Gohad had to be stormed on 21st and 22nd February, 1806 and Col. Bowil reconciled the insurgent Chief of Gohad to Sindhia's officers on 12th May, 1806. To compensate him for the loss of Gohad and to create a buffer state between the dominions of Sindhia and the East India Company, Dholpur, Bari and some more territories were assigned to the Rana. Thus, a new state of Dholpur was created and the Rana of Gohad became the Rana of Dholpur. Subsequently, Gwalior was selected by Daulat Rao as his place of residence and capital. Jagirs to Ambaji, Gopal Bhau, Bapoo Chitnis, Jagoo Dada, Jaswant Rao in Mynpore of one lakh, 60 thousand, 45,000 respectively to each and of Rs. 25,000 to Kamal Nain were given.

155. Malcolm, *Political History of India*, P.H. Vol. I, pp. 357-59, Kaye's, *Life of Malcolm*, Vol. I, p. 352.

156. Sardesai, *New History of the Marathas*, III, p. 467, Hindi Translation, ed. 1964.

157. Keye's, *Life of Malcolm*, pp. 270-71. Sharma's *thesis*.

Evaluation of the Treaty

Assignment of Jagirs was a great feat of diplomacy, as it made officers of Sindhia favourable to the British. On the whole Sindhia's position in Malwa despite its acquisition of Gwalior and Gohad, remarks Dr. B.G. Sharma, "remained as fluid as before."[158] The terms of the treaty cautiously guarded against any possible conferment of real power to Sindhia.... Both Daulat Rao Sindhia and Jaswant Rao Holkar have lost to him (Malcolm) and the treaties he concluded with them reflected the onward march of British Imperialism in Central India.[159] Similarly Dr. B.N. Mehta remarks "Fresh arrangements made by Sindhia did not depart from the Wellesley's treaty of Surji Arjungaon and that even the retrocession of Gwalior and Gohad which Barlow made to Sindhia was already in the contemplation of Wellesley."[160]

But the main difference which Dr. Sharma has failed to notice and Dr. Mehta noticed was that no defensive engagements were to be renewed with Sindhia.[161] Dr. Mehta says "Sindhia had lately accepted a subsidiary alliance, although of a modified type, from Wellesley, but Barlow could not in principle renew it." He adds "but the idea of contracting any subsidiary alliance with Sindhia or Holkar was ruled out by the policy laid down, the main spring of which was the abandonment of Wellesleyan system of subsidiary alliance."[162]

We are here concerned only with the controversy as to whether the subsidiary alliance of treaty of Burhanpur was imposed on Daulat Rao in his life time. So far our information goes it was not even mentioned in the subsequent treaties of 1805 and 1807. Thus, it may be said that the treaty of Burhanpur did not come in force during the life time of Daulat Rao Sindhia,

158. B.G. Sharma's *Thesis on Malcolm*, *Kaye's Malcolm* and *Ross, Correspondence of Lord Cornwallis.*

159. Dr. B.G. Sharma "Sir John Malcolm in Madhya Bharat" (Unpublished Thesis), p. 95.

160. Dr. B.N. Mehta, Sir George Barlow in India (Unpublished Thesis) — Introduction, p. IV.

161. *Ibid.*, quoted by Dr. Mehta, p. 26, and Bengal Sec. Cons., 24th October, 1805, No. 31.

162. *Ibid.*, p. 227.

though advantage of this treaty was taken by Lord Ellenborough in 1843, after which Gwalior became a fully vassal State.

After the War

From 1806 to 1809, Daulat Rao Sindhia remained busy in realising tributes from the Rajput States, which were at daggers drawn with each other on account of Krishna Kumari, the beautiful Mewar Princess. During this period, he also planned to attack Bhopal, crushed several turbulent chiefs in Malwa, tried to make incursions into the territories of Sheo Ram Bhao of Jhansi[163] and overawe Narendra Giri, the successor of Himmat Bahadur. But nothing substantial was gained, as the British Resident warned and opposed him and Sindhia desisted.[164] Similarly, the Resident Close, prevented Daulat Rao Sindhia in April 1809, from committing any aggression in the territory of Rao Raja of Machery (Alwar) and in Agra.[165] Ranjit Singh's Vakil visited Daulat Rao Sindhia, but except for an exchange of gifts nothing materialised.[166] The death of that "double-dyed traitor"[167], Ambaji, occurred on 5th May 1809[168] and the murder of the "bold bad man",[169] Sarji Rao Chatge, occurred on 26th July. 1809. These events provided Daulat Rao an opportunity to govern his state according to his own views.

Upto 1810, Sindhia employed his own refractory officers or in Mulkgiri expeditions in Malwa, Bhopal or Rajasthan. Subsequently he pitched his camp at a short distance from the modern Gwalior city, where a new township had sprung up on the site of his encampment, known as 'Lashkar'. He made efforts to keep in touch with the Peshwa, whose Vakil Ganesh Pant called on him in 1811; with Holkar, with the Raja of Berar, other Rajput princes and Ranjit Singh, but he did not openly follow an anti-British policy upto 1813.

---

163. *Poona Residency Correspondence,* Vol, XI, No. 295.
164. *Ibid.,* No. 169.
165. *Ibid.,* No. 284, pp. 426-27.
166. *Ibid.,* No. 280 and 282.
167. Kaye, *Life of Malcolm,* p. 266.
168. Broughton States morning of 5-5-1809, p. 147 and Britiah Resident night of 4th May, 1809, *Poona Residency Correspondence,* XI, No. 286, p. 431.
169. Kaye, *Life of Malcolm,* p. 308.

Hastings and Sindhia

With the arrival of the Marquess of Hastings (1813-1823) as Governor General, British policy took a new turn, as he was determined "to render the British Government paramount" and to "hold the other states as vassals in substance, if not in name." Sindhia had now put his house in order to some extent. He kept private news writers in the British dominions[170] and tried to assess the condition of their power himself by a visit to Northern India under the pretext of taking a dip in the holy Ganga at Singhi Rampur near Farrukhabad.[171]

Sindhia and the Anglo-Nepalese War

When war broke out between the East India Company and Nepal, several Indian princes, including Sindhia, contemplated forming a confederacy against the Company. The Nepalese government first approached Ranjit Singh for this purpose,[172] but that prince was too cautious to listen to them. They then approached Sindhia.[173] In 1815, the Peshwa sent emissaries to him on the same errand.[174] The Bhonsle and Tulsi Bai Holkar also seem to have started negotiations with Sindhia for the same purpose.[175]

According to Grant Duff, reports of these activities duly reached Lord Hastings[176] and it was in the context of these moves for the revival of the Maratha confederacy under the Peshwa's leadership that the Governor General's Plans for the Pindari war were framed.[177] On 23rd March, 1816, R. Close wrote to the Governor General : "Communictions are kept up with Poona, Nagpur, Holkar and more particularly of late with Ranjit Singh, on whose part there has been evinced a reciprocal desire

---

170. *Poona Residency Correspondence,* XIV 144.

171. *Ibid.,* No. 151, p. 173.

172. *Ibid.,* XIV, No. 169, p. 193.

173. *Ibid.,* p. 270.

174. Grant Duff, *History of the Marathas,* Vol. I, p. 641 See Journal of Indian History Vol. XLIII Nepal's Relations with Indian States by Kanchanmoy Majumdar August, 1965, pp. 403-465 and C.I. Part II.

175. Malcolm, *Political History of India,* I, p. 308.

176. Duff, *History of the Marathas,* III, p. 297.

177. *Ibid.,* p. 392, I 693.

to cultivate friendship with Daulat Rao Sindhia."[178] The Vakils from the Gurkhas and Ranjit Singh visited Daulat Rao on 16th April, 1816,[179] but these negotiations did not prove fruitful, as different persons and parties failed to rise to the occasion owing to their narrow outlook and personal interests.

Holkar and even Nepal later became disinclined to any hostile measure against the British Government.[180] In the words of Sarkar, "the last hope of the trembling Indian princes vanished, when the Gurkhas of Nepal bowed down to British arms. Ranjit Singh of Lahore refused to entertain any anti-British proposal,"[181] The death of Raghuji Bhonsle on 22nd March, 1816 and the signing of the treaty for a subsidiary alliance with the British by his successor, Appa Sahib Bhonsle on 27th May, 1816 drove the last nail in the coffin of the proposed confederacy. Even the hopes of an alliance between Sindhia and Holkar were frustrated by Amir Khan and other Sardars of the Holkar Government. Thus the plan of a confederacy ended in a fiasco.

Bhopal and Sagar

In 1815, Govind Rao Nana, Chief of Sagar, and Wazir Mohammad Khan, Nawab of Bhopal, were taken under British protection with a view to provide a connected chain of military posts for crushing the Pindaris.[182] Bhopal agreed to the ingress and residence of British troops within the Nawab's territory, and to the surrender by Bhopal of a fort as a permanent depot to the Company. To support the negotiations, troops moved from all directions into Bhopal. Wazir Mohammad agreed and his alliance with the East India Company was communicated to Sindhia by Mr. Strachey, Resident in his camp.[183]

Daulat Rao Sindhia protected most vehemently against this measure, claiming Bhopal as his dependency. "The Maharaja had observed that, detaching Bhopal from him and appropriating

178. Foreign Secret Papers 1816 Sindhia.

179. *Poona Residency Correspondence,* Vol. XIV, No. 258, p. 262 and p. 307.

180. Foreign Secret Papers 1817, Nepal, p. 121.

181. *Poona Residency Correspondence,* XIV edition, J.N. Sarkar's Introduction, p. 5.

182. For British motives see *Poona Residency Correspondence,* XIV No. 201, p 234.

183. Malcolm, *Political History of India,* C.I., *A Memoir of Central India,* I, p. 412.

it to ourselves was an extraordinary sort of friendship," wrote the Resident to Hastings. Even an attack was threatened but no action was taken.[184]

The Pindari War and third-Anglo Marathawar (1817-18)

Daulat Rao Sindhia's discomfiture and immunisation were achieved completely during the course of the Pindari War. His rebellious and unsuccessful attempts to form an anti-British confederacy encouraged the British to take decisive steps against him. The extermination of the predatory Pindaris was a popular cause and necssary in the public interest. But a large number of them were believed to be attached to Daulat Rao and the need to prevent any action on his part in their support, dictated the entire strategy of the Pindari War. The four divisions of the Bengal army were to be assembled at Rewari, Agra, Sikandara near Kalpi and at Kalinjar in Bundelkhand. The two divisions in reserve were to be stationed under Brigadier General Toone on the upper Sone, and under Brigadier General Hardyman at Rewah on the upper Narmada. They were intended as detachments for observation. The division from Bundelkand under General Marshal was to advance with the southern army. Occterlony was to march from the North. The main body to be assembled at Sikandara was under the personal command of the Marquess of Hastings. It was to cross the Yamuna by a bridge of boats a little above Kalpi to march due west to occupy, in the first instance, a position south of Gwalior, while the division from Agra under General Donkin was to take up its position at Dholpur.

This was a master stroke of British Military strategy, as it placed Sindhia in such a position that it was not possible for him to oppose the British forces successfully. "The Central Division reached the Kali Sind at a point 28 miles Gwalior and nearer than Sindhia to the passes which offered communication between that capital and south...destroyed his freedom, of action" and "effectually intercepted the Pindaris."[185] Sindhia was "about 20 miles from Gwalior; there is a line of steep hills near Chhoti

---

184. Duff, *History of the Marathas*, III 392 and *Poona Residency Correspondence*, Vol. XIV, No. 218, p. 254.

185. *Private Journal of Lord Hastings and Lord Hastings Summary*, pp. 97-100.

Sindh in South...there are only two ways, by which cavalry and carts can pass, one through the Kali Sindh and another near the Chambal. Hastings occupied a position in the middle which made the arrival of Sindhia through the Sindh impossible. Therefore, there was no alternative left to Sindhia but to sign a treaty,[186] which bound him to give assistance against the Pindarics and abolished his overlordship in Rajputana.[187] The Sindhia said ruefully that "the weaker must obey the stronger."[188]

A New Treaty

Daulat Rao Sindhia was bound down to grant passports for the free ingress and egress of British troops to exterminate the Pindaris.[189] He was required to place his troops at the disposal of the British Government to be employed at its option with a British officer superintending each of the principal divisions, and any officers of Daulat Rao Sindhia's supporting or harbouring freeboters were to be dealt with as rebels.[190]

The lands recovered from the Pindaris were to be restored to the rightful owners in all cases, where they cooperated for their suppression. Where they did not, they were to be given to Sindhia. As a security for the fulfilment of the proposed terms, the forts of Handia and Asirgarh were demanded, but Daulat Rao Sindhia's flag was allowed to fly and a few of his troops were permitted to remain in each fort. The tribute due to Daulat Rao Sindhia from the Rajput principalities were not to be affected by any agreements which the British Government might make with them. On the contrary, their payment was to be guaranteed by the British Government. A treaty to this effect was signed on 5th November 1817,[191] and ratified by the Governor General the following day.

Handia was given up but Jaswant Rao Lad, the Kiledar of Asirgarh, refused to obey the order to surrender. The three

186. *Private Journal of Lord Hastings and Lord Hastings Summary*, pp. 97-100.

187. Grant Duff III and Mehta, *Lord Hastings and Indian States and Banerji* A.C. *Indian Constitutional Documents*, pp. 321-22.

188. *Ibid.*, October 11.

189. Duff, *History of the Marathas*, Vol. I, p. 643.

190. *Ibid.*, Vol. I, p. 643.

191. Private Journals of Hastings, Nov. 7 and Malcolm C.I, II.

principal divisions of Sindhia's army at the time were stationed at Ajmer under Bapuji Sindhia, at Jawad, under Jaswant Rao Bhau, and at Bahadurgarh under Col. Jean Baptiste. Thereafter, General Donkin's army marched westward, but the Marquess of Hastings contrived to move to the south of Gwalior to observe the movements of Daulat Rao Sindhia who, though compelled to accept the terms imposed, was watching the progress of events in the Deccan and intriguing with the Peshwa,[192] and endeavouring to stir up the Gurkhas of Nepal[193] to make common cause with the Marathas.[194] Col. Tod, an Assistant to the Resident in Sindhia's Camp, was sent on a political mission to the Rajput States. He went first to Zalim Singh of Kotah, who signed a treaty with the British on 6th December, 1817.

Govind Rao Nana, Subedar of Jhansi, signed a treaty on 1-11-1817, but Vinayak Rao, Chief of Sagar refused. Chitoo was harboured by Jaswant Rao Bhau, who refused to comply with the request of the Superintendent. Captain Caulfield and Colonel Bounce were sent against him. They blew up the gate of Jawad and took the town on 28th January, 1818 and captured the guns of Bhau. With enough intelligence to understand the strength of the British power, but not enough to co-operate or the energy to oppose in time, Daulat Rao Sindhia saved his state.[195]

Sindhia gave Ajmer to the East India Company and relinquished his tribute from Bundi in exchange for a part of the lands of the Jagirdar of Vinchoor, situated in Malwa, which were later forfeited by the British owing to his adherence to the cause of Baji Rao II.

Five districts were given to the Nawab of Bhopal. The fort of Islamnagar was obtained from Daulat Rao Sindhia and given to the Nawab. The fortress of Asirgarh was retained by the British under the treaty of 5th November, but the Kiledar, Jaswant Rao Lad, did not surrender it and afterwards tried to

---

192. Private Journals of Hastings, April 9, December 22, 1817.

193. *Ibid.*, October 5, 1817 mentions Sindhia's and Hindu Rao Ghatgay's letters "urging to attack the British directly" to Bhimsen Minister of Nepal.

194. *Nagpur Residency Correspondence*, Vol. III, ed. by H.N. Sinha.

195. P. Spears : *The Oxford History of India*, p. 571, ed. 1958.

harbour Appa Sahib of Nagpur and Baji Rao II, the Peshwa. This was represented to Daulat Rao Sindhia, who admitted it and justified it on grounds of friendship between him and the Peshwa, which had existed for generations. This fort was eventually taken and no additional penalty was imposed on Sindhia.

Later Events

By the treaty of 1817, Daulat Rao Sindhia had engaged to furnish a contingent of 5,000 horses, which was later reduced to 2,000. In 1823, the districts of Kunchwai, Burnwai, Poouass, Shellani and village of Dungaon, and in the following year the district of Asirgarh were handed over by Sindhia to the British Governmet. Decree was permanently ceded in exchange for Shujavalpur.[196] Daulat Rao Sindhia's subjects, Dahjee, Gopal and Ghunmurji Deshmukh tried even in 1823 to rise against the East India Company by helping Appa Sahib of Nagpur.[197] But it was an attempt to flog a dead horse and nothing came out of it.

The march of Pax Britanice was too great a blow to Daulat Rao, and partly due to this mental agony, he began to remain sick even at the age of 44. The British Government desired some arrangement which might be advantageously adopted to secure English predominance in the territories of Sindhia[198] by the stationing of a subsidiary force in Gwalior, but Sindhia vehemently opposed this, adverting to a private assurance given by Hastings to Sindhia that no subsidiary force would be imposed upon him.[199] To the end, Sindhia refused to agree to this move though his relations with the British remained more or less smooth and cordial during the last seven years of his reign. Thus, his reduction to the status of a dependent ally was really achieved in 1817, though even then he was not forced to accept a British subsidiary force stationed in his own territories.

---

196. *Treaties Engagements and Sannuds,* pp. 203-04 ed. 1864, Malcolm C.I. 250.
197. *Foreign Political Index,* 1823.
198. *Foreign Political Papers,* 1924, 22nd June 57.
199. *National Archives Foreign Secret Index,* Gwalior 1923.

6

DAULAT RAO SINDHIA AND THE CONSOLIDATION OF MALWA AND CENTRAL INDIA

Introduction

Being foiled in his attempts to secure a commanding position in Northern and Central India, as the previous Chapters have shown, Daulat Rao Sindhia turned his attention to consolidating his kingdom, by taking possession of nearby petty states and the Pindaris and annexing their territories to his dominions. It goes to the credit of Daulat Rao Sindhia that he achieved a considerable integration of his territories, that Mahadji had failed to accomplish.

Narwar was ancient state, famous for Nala and Damyanti story.

Narwar[1] was the seat of an ancient principality of Kachwaha princes situated south of the Chambal in the district of Shivpuri about 40 miles from Gwalior. The ruler of Narwar came in conflict with Daulat Rao, when he helped the Widows of Mahadji Sindhia and gave refuge to Lakhwa Dada.

Lakhwa Dada, the Viceroy of the northern territory of Daulat Rao Sindhia, made a surprise attack on Narwar and succeeded in capturing the city in October, 1795, and next invested the fort which protected the city, but it held out upto March 1976.[2] But the wheels of fortune took a strange turn and Lakhwa Dada had to seek refuge under the Raja of Narwar, after he had revolted against his master.

Ambaji Ingale was sent to crush the Raja and Lakhwa Dada. He succeeded in subduing the place and appointed his brother

1. According to Tod, The Kachwahas claim descent from Kusa, son of Shri Ram Chandra, and Nala founded the city of Narwar or classically Nishadha. Tod *Annals and Antiquities of Rajasthan*, ed. Crooke III, p. 1328.
2. *Poona Residency Correspondence,* 824 Tod, *Annals and Antiquities of Rajasthan*, p. 367, ed. 1894.

Khande Rao Ingale Subedar of Narwar. Manohar Singh, the Raja, was deposed and he took refuge with his son, Mohan Singh, in Jaipur territory.

The Raja was a man of treacherous character and maintained a troop of bandits to plunder travellers that happened to pass through his territory.[3] Khande Rao Ingale rebelled against Sindhia, after the death of Ambaji Ingale, to keep Narwar in his own possession. When Sindhia refused to tolerate this rebellion. Khande Rao offered to pay him tribute, but he did not agree.[4]

At the head of a large force, Daulat Rao Sindhia reached Narwar in the first week of 1810. Khandeji Ingale ran away and entrusted the defence of Narwar to his brother-in-law, but his troops evacuated the town on the night of 9th August, 1810, without any opposition.[5] The Fort of Narwar was well defended, but it was captured by Sindhia on 14th September 1810. Major Stewart, Resident with Sindhia, interfered on the appeal of the Raja of Narwar, and Daulat Rao Sindhia granted a Jagir containing Parone and six villages to the Ex-Raja of Narwar for his maintenance; which was subsequently withheld for some time following the depredations by the Raja, but later on it was again restored to him[6] as a feudatory of Gualior State.

Sabalgarh and Bijaipur

Sabalgarh and Bijaipur belonged to the Raja of Karaoli, a petty state of Rajasthan and now a Tehsil, having a fort and a pool. In August, 1795, Maratha forces under Lakhwa Dada attacked Sabalgarh. After a stubborn struggle, they reduced the strong fort of Sabalgarh to submission and thereafter they attacked

3. Malcolm, *Political History of India.*
4. *Poona Residency Correspondence,* XIV, No. 37, p. 61.
5. *Ibid.,* No. 39, pp. 62-63.

   Narwar remained a District Headquarter for a long time, but due to disturbances, it was very difficult to keep proper control, and so the District Headquarter was changed to Shivpuri later on by Madhav Rao Sindhia ruler of Gwalior who ruled upto 1925. Narwar being deprived of official support is in ruins and beasts of prey roam about in the fort today. It has, however, retained its old natural charms.
6. Foreign Political Index of 1820 Letter No. 2 and Foreign Political Papers 1820 under heading Gwalior No. 55.

Bijaipur and it was also captured and placed in charge of Ambaji Ingale.[7]

In 1806, Daulat Rao Sindhia imprisoned Ambaji and demanded Sabalgarh, from him but he refused, though later on he surrendered a few places in the territory to the Raja of Karaoli. The Raja thus came into the possession of Sabalgarh.[8] But these places were again taken back by Sindhia's forces and incorporated in his dominions. It was at Sabalgarh, as mentioned earlier, that Daulat Rao Sindhia and Jaswant Rao Holkar met for an alliance against the East India Company in 1805.

Bijaipur is situated on the Kunwari River. Rajasthani culture dominates Sabalgrh as well as Bijaipur. Bijaipur was also wrested by Sindhia's forces from the Raja of Karaoli, therefore, both became part of Gualior.

Rahatgarh

Rahatgarh is a town on the route from Bhopal to Sagar. It was besieged in the last week of 1807 by the forces under the command of Daulat Rao Sindhia himself. It possessed a strong fort and its ruler was a tributary of the Bhopal rulers, to whom he also did not pay tribute.[9] Rahatgarh remained under siege upto November 1807 and was finally taken by Daulat Rao[10] on 14th November, 1807.

Annexation of Raghogarh

The little state of Khichiwara, or Raghograh, was named after the Rajputs of the Khichi tribe, its capital was Raghogarh. "The Chauham Rajputs of Raghogarh have always been distinguished by the name of Kychee."[11] At a remote date, they were in possession of Gagroon[12] on the Kalee Sind, and its ruler Ghareeb Das was a favourite Amir of Akbar. Balbhadra Singh, a great grandson of Ghareeb Das, allied himself with Baji Raoji, accepted his suzerainty, and ruled over Raghogarh.

7. *Poona Residency Correspondence*, VIII, No. 24.
8. *Ibid.*, XI, No. 170, p. 270.
9. *Ibid.*, XI, Letter No. 229, p. 327.
10. *Ibid.*, Letter Nos. 229-231.
11. Malcolm, *Political History of India*, C.I.I. p. 464.
12. See Gwalior Stale Gazetteer 1908 and Tod Annals and Antiquities of Rajasthan edited by Crooke, ed. 1820.

Balbhadra Singh was succeeded by his son Balwant Singh, who paid tribute to Holkar, but later on allied himself with the British Government during the First Maratha War against Mahadji Sindhia.

Vengeance may sleep long, but never dies. So Mahadji sent a large force under Ambaji Ingale to beseige the fort in the autumn of 1785.[13] "Having captured it, he made the Raja and his young son Jai Singh prisoners and confiscated the property and territories of the family."[14] The Raja's relations took up arms against Mahadji Sindhia and committed outrages in all parts of Sindhia's territories North of the Narbada.

Being tired of these ravages and pressed by the Rajas of Jaipur and Jodhpur, who were distantly related to the Khichis, Mahadji released the Raja and his son, Jay Singh, and restored Raghogarh to them in 1785. But they were to pay a large sum as war indemnity which Balwant Singh failed to do.

Raja Jay Singh continued his depredations during the regime of Daulat Rao Sindhia also. During the Widow's War, Jay Singh allied himself with[15] them and Lakhwa Dada. During the Second Maratha war, Raja Jay Singh created great trouble for Daulat Rao Sindhia; and Durjan Sal, his maternal uncle, after the defeat of Lakhwa, usuruped "no less than 22 districts", of which Ranoud, Paucher and Gondah were the principal.

The policy of Daulat Rao Sindhia after he had made peace with the East India Company was directed to the reduction of these Rajput Tributaries of his own. He coveted Raghogarh, as it was situated at a strategic point and desired to extinguish the cruel rule of Raja Jay Singh.

On 30th December, 1811, R. Stratchery, British Resident at Gwalior, wrote that "Raghogarh is a principality belonging to Raja Jay Singh and nearly surrounded by the territories of Sindhia, of whose wish to reduce it, there is no doubt."[16]

After taking the fort of Chanderi and Garh Kota, Baptiste marched against Raghogarh. In March 1816, he attacked Bajrang

13. *Poona Residency Correspondence,* XIV.
14. *Ibid.*, p. 466 and Sardesai III, p. 150.
15. Malcolm, *Political History of India,* C.I. 475-76.
16. *Poona Residency Correspondence,* XIV, p. 107.

Garh with the utmost determination. It is said that he succeeded in tampering with some of Jay Singh's officers in the fort and this resulted in the secret introduction of some of his men and the precipitate flight of the Raja, who narrowly escaped capture. Bapiste occupied the town of Raghogarh in the first week of April, 1816, but his attempt to capture the fort by escalade failed. Jay Singh entrusted the defence of the place to his officers and he himself came out to organise reappraisals against the besiegers.

The seige of Raghogarh dragged on upto April, 1816. At last, the Pindaris under Buksh Khan and the forces of the Raja of Kotah joined the forces of Jean Baptiste. Jay Singh tried to collect troops and to disturb Baptiste's lines of communication. Later, the Raja retired to Chakowra, but the forces of Daulat Rao Sindhia attacked him there. Jai Singh made a surprise attack on Sheopur and captured the son and family of Jean Baptiste on 3rd June, 1816[17] Daulat Rao Sindhia tried to console Baptiste and sent a force to Shivpur to attack Jay Singh. Undaunted by calamity, Baptiste continued the seige of Raghogarh, and in September, 1816, Raghogarh surrendered and was occupied by the troops of Kotah.

Jay Singh then left Sheopur and tried to harass the forces of Sindhia by other means. Finally, in October, 1816, Jean Baptiste's forces occupied Raghogarh. Raja Jay Singh sent the members of his family to Jaipur and continued his activities to trouble Sindhia's forces. The British Resident, tried to effect peace between the parties, but failed to achieve anything substantial.[18]

Jay Singh was friendly to the British and used to say that "the English troops and horsemen, wherever they go, will form the good fortune of the English, be victorious, and Sindhia shall be destroyed."[19] Malcolm himself said "Had Daulat Rao Sindhia not preserved neutrality (in the Pinderi War) Jay Singh would have been an apt and popular instrument for his reduction."[20] Sindhia now pursued the Raja from place to place

17. *Poona Residency Correspondence,* p. 148.
18. *Ibid.,* XIV 348, No. 291.
19. Malcolm, *Political History of India,* C.I.I., p. 483, ed. 1832.
20. *Ibid.,* C.I.I., p. 486, ed. 1832 and Capt, Stewar to the Political Secretary to Government 20-1-1821 paragraph 14.

till Jay Singh died, disappointed and broken-hearted, in about 1818.

After the death of Raja Jay Singh, the Ranis quarrelled over the choice of a successor as the Raja had left no child. The chief Rani selected one Ajit. "An aunt of Jay Singh, a respected lady, favoured Dhokal Singh, but Sindhia's forces captured the Dhokal Singh who was hopeful of support from the British Government."[21] Later on, Dhokal Singh was released. The British Government interfered and allowed him "the fort and town of Raghogarh, with an estate of Rs. 55,000 and a few adherents to be always in Sindhia's service."[22]

In 1823, the revenue of this jagir was about Rs. 142848-8 as. and a hundred Rajputs of the Khichi tribe were in the Gwalior contingent.[23] Thus Daulat Rao Sindhia removed an obstacle that had created troubles for him for a long time and made Raghogarh a subordinate of Gualior state.

Bahadurgarh* *i.e.*, Isagarh

Raja Durjan Sal of Bahadurgarh was the maternal uncle of Raja Jay Singh of Raghogarh. He helped Lakhwa Dada against Sindhia and created many disturbances. He had subjugated Ahirwara, a territory named after the Ahirs, whose ruler Dali Singh was subdued by Durjan Sal after the battle of Seondha, in which he was defeated along with the widows and Lakhwa Dada. The name of the capital of Ahirwara, Condi, was now changed to Bahadurgarh.

After the 2nd Maratha War, Col. Jean Baptiste again employed force against Raja Durjan Sal. Bahadurgarh fell into the hands of Jean Baptiste on 11th December, 1811[24] and Col. Baptiste

21. Malcolm, *Political History of India*, C.I.I., p. 486, ed. 1832 and Capt, Stewar to the Political Secretary to Government 20-l-1821 paragraph 14.

22. Malcolm, *Political History of India*, I, p. 487.

23. Foreign and Political Papers 1823. Gwalior 21st March No. 63.

* The name of Bahadurgarh was changed by Baptiste into Isagarh meaning House of Christ or the Fort of Jesus. (Isagarh is a small place of epic fame in Guna District Old Khichi territory). In it there is a pool of Dhakuni called Dhakuni ka Talab. It is said that there Raja Nala left Damyanti in his miserable days of exile. The dense forests, small rivers, and difficult pathways lend a touch of reality to the story of Damyanti as given in the Mahabharata.

24. *Poona Residency Correspondence*, Vol. XIV, p. 104.

soon succeeded in conquering nearly the whole territory of Durjan Sal. Durjan Sal died dejected at Bheerwad.

Having left no issue, Durjan Sal was succeeded by Bhairo Lal, who continued the struggle, but Daulat Rao granted him a jagir, yielding one lac of rupees to discontinue his depredations.[25]

Sheopur

Sheopur, founded in 1537, by Gaur Rajputs, was a small principality surround by dense forests on the banks of the river Chambal and acknowledged Maratha suzerainty during the 18th century. Daulat Rao Sindhia being distressed by pecuniary difficulties, demanded 15 lakhs from the Raja of Sheopur in 1808. The Raja agreed to pay the amount on the express promise that Sindhia would shift his camp to some other place. Sindhia insisted on the payment, but the Raja expressed his inability to do so at once. Sindhia's forces had not received any pay for long and Anna Sikkanavis had to take shelter in the camp to save his neck from the wrath of the unpaid troops. Under these circumstances, Daulat Rao decided to lay seige to the fort of Sheopur and subdue it, but the Vakils of other States protested. The Raja pleaded for mercy. The representative of Jaswant Rao Holkar received instructions from their chief to get half share on completion of negotiations, but matters dragged on and the Raja failed to pay any money.

At last, Baptiste took the town of Sheopur in August 1809, The Raja, Rudra Das (or Radhika Das or Sakho Bao) made a desperate attempt to save the fort, but owing to lack of supplies, he had to surrender the fort to Baptiste on 13th October, 1809. The Raja was granted a few villages for his maintenance.

Chanderi

Chanderi* is a very old palace described in Mahabharata. It was conquered by Babar but later on it come under Rajputs. Chanderi is situated about 24 miles south of Lalitpur, in the

25. *Foreign Secret Political Index.*

* It is a place of epic fame. During the days of the Mahabharata Shishupal was the ruler of Chanderi. Medini Rai enhanced its prestige by stoutly resisting the attack of Babar. Famous proverb about it is "Shahr Chanderi Mominwara. Triya Raj Khasam Panihara."

Jhansi district and is about 3 miles from the river Betwa. It was a small Rajput state during the time of Daulat Rao Sindhia. The Raja of Chanderi, named Mor Prahlad, was a tributary of his. The principality had come under Maratha suzerainty when the Marathas conquered Malwa and Bundelkhand, but he joined Karim Khan Pindari in plundering the dominions of Daulat Rao Sindhia. Sindhia demanded five Lakhs rupees as compensation and penalty for these offences, but the Raja was unable to comply with the demand. Sindhia thereupon attacked Chanderi and desired to give possession of it to Nana Sahib, the brother of the Raja of Nagpur, in January, 1808, on payment of 5 lakhs.[26]

Vinkoji Pindara was employed by Nana Sahib Bhonsle to conquer it, but as the agreement with Daulat Rao Sindhia could not be completed, the task had to be given up.

After conquering the territory of Durjan Sal, Jean Baptiste commenced operations against Chanderi in December, 1811 and occupied the town on 11th May, 1811. The Raja fled to Jhansi, but the citadel held out upto June, 1812. The troops offered to capitulate if their arrears of pay were paid by Baptiste, but he refused. The Raja of Chanderi took asylum in Datia and negotiated for peace through Mir Asad Ali, the governor of Narwar, but the talks failed. Baptiste took possession of the citadel on 12th July, 1812 and repaired and strengthened it. It became a part of Sindhia's dominions though a minister of the family exercised considerable influence and authority in its administration.

In September, 1823, the ex-Raja of Chanderi expressed a wish to be taken under British protection, but his request was not granted.[27]

Garh Kota

The territory of Garh Kota had a strategic value and was a part of the cession made by Raja Chatrasal to Peshwa Baji Rao I. It was held under the Peshwa's suzerainty by Preeti

26. F.N. Malcolm wrote about Chanderi as a large district, producing a revenue of above five lakhs in 1820, to its Zamindar. It has a police station and Higher Sec. School. It is famous for zari saries, as place of pilgrimage of Jains.

27. *Foreign Political Papers,* no. 49 and 5 of 1823.

Singh, an illegitimate son of Chatrasal. Preeti Singh's grandson, Mardan Singh, made himself practically independent, though Sindhia for some time continued to receive some tribute from him. Mardan Singh chose to assist Amir Khan in his raids on Nagpur territory and lost his life in a skirmish with British troops. Daulat Rao Sindhia, annoyed by this hostile act, conquered most of it and only a small portion remained in the possession of Takht Singh and Arjun Singh, sons of the late Mardan Singh. Arjun Singh later on opened hostilities against Sindhia and defeated the latter's troops at Garh Kota on December 9, 1811.

In March 1813, the sons of the Raja again attacked Jean Baptiste's troops and inflicted heavy losses on them. Baptiste, who was then at Sabalgarh, immediately marched to punish them. He reached Sagar on 22nd March, 1813 and met with stubborn resistance. Sarvar Khan, an officer of Amir Khan, and the rebels of Chanderi made his task difficult, but he pressed on the siege for about two months. At last, he succeeded in taking Garh Kota, but later Arjun Singh again succeeded in regaining it. In 1818, British troops under Brigadier Watson conquered it and gave it back to Daulat Rao Sindhia and Arjun Singh was reconciled by the grant of a Jagir.

Daulat Rao annexed several other territories too unimportant to be mentioned here in detail and only a passing reference may be made to some of thcm.

Baria

Bapoo Sindhia, a commander of Daulat Rao Sindhia, took Baria which was situated near Gujarat. The Raja of Baria fought bravely, but Bapooji Sindhia succeeded in expelling him from his principality. The chiefs of neighbouring states took alarm, but were unable to achieve anything.[28]

Pauri

Pauri[29] is a Tehsil of the Shivpuri district. Originally, it was

28. *Poona Residency Correspondence,* Vol. XIV, No. 33, p. 57.

29. The Pauri Tehsil was given to Bala Bai, a daughter of Mahad Ji Sindhia, who adopted a son Lakshman Rao Deshmukh, after the death of her husband on 11th March 1810 and began to live there and led a pious life. Pauri remained under the control of the Shitole family upto the abolition op Jagirdari System by the Madhya Pradesh Government.

a Jagir of the Shitole family. It was the first Jagir of Khandoji Ingale. When Daulat Rao Sindhia marched towards Narwar, he sent a detachment to attack Pauri and secured it in 1810.[30]

Ratlam

Parbat Singh of Ratlam was also a feudatory of Daulat Rao Sindhia.[31] Bapu Sindhia attacked Ratlam for the realisation of tribute and, being assured of its payment by the British Government, he agreed through Malcolm to take Salimsahi Rs. 84,000 and undertook not to send any troops against Ratlam.

Basoda

Similarly Basoda was captured but it was restored, owing to British intervention, to Afsad Ali Khan who remained under Sindhia.[32] In 1801, Agar was overrun by Bapu Sindhia[33] but restored by Daulat Rao Sindhia.

Bagli also was under the suzerainty of Daulat Rao Sindhia, who out of grace assigned a few villages to its Raja for the maintenance of law and order in the locality.

Other Principalities

Formerly Rajgarh also paid tribute to Daulat Rao Sindhia, but it freed itself by ceding several villages to him in lieu of this payment. In the same manner, Sitamau paid him a tribute of Rs. 60,000 in 1820 through Malcolm, Amjhera agreed to pay to Sindhia Rs. 35,000 in 1819, the Raja of Bhadora agreed to pay half of his revenues to him but in 1826, 3/4th revenue was assigned to him for his maintenance. Javad, Neemuch, and Islamgarh were also overrun by Daulat Rao Sindhia; but Javad and Neemuch, which were under the control of his commander Jaswant Rao Bhau,[34] had to be given back to the Rana of Udaipur, Neemuch being assigned for the maintenance of Bhau. Sindhia had to give Islamgarh to Bhopal owing to British intervention.

Grasia Chiefs

The Grasia Chiefs of Malwa, who were Rajputs, "derived

---

30. *Poona Residency Correspondence*, Vol. XIV, No. 33, p. 57.
31. Malcolm: *Central India Memoirs*, pp. 508-09.
32. *Foreign Political Pages*, 1821, p. 9, dated 15-12-1821.
33. Grant Duff, *History of the Marathas*, p. 326, ed. 1912.
34. *Ibid.*, p. 326, ed. 1912 and *Gwalior Stale Gazetteer*, p. 192, ed. 1908.

their names from 'gras', a Sanskrit word which signifies a mouthful. Grasia has been metaphorically applied to indicate the small share of the produce of a country which these petty chiefs claimed." They created many difficulties. Their fort Sakumbari was captured, but their depredations continued. At last, Sindhia also conciliated them by allowing a small subsistence to them. The Bhils, Sondis, Grasias, Gonds, Sahrias, Meenas also created much trouble and became a standing menace to the peace and tranquility of Malwa, but Daulat Rao Sindhia crushed them and reconciled some of their chiefs by allowing petty Jagirs in land or cash to them.

The Pindaries and Sindhia

Sindhia's relations with the Pindaris merit a discussion in some detail.

The etymology of the Marathi word "Pendha" or Pendhar is doubtful. It was used for a body of stragglers, similar to the Bunga or Bazar Bunga of the regular armies.[35] The word 'Pindara' was coeval with the earliest invasion of Northern India by the Marathas,[36] and the Pindaris were a convenient ingredient of the system of warfare developed by the Marathas. In that system, ever since the days of Shivaji and Shantaji Ghorpade, there had always been a class of unpaid auxiliaries attached to each chief's fighting quota whose duty it was to step in the moment the battle ended and finish the enemy by seizing his property and camp equipage and destroying his power of recovery.[37] The word 'Pindari' occurs for such auxiliary Maratha plunderers during the reign of Aurangzeb.[38] Malcolm states that it is mentioned first in 1689.[39]

Two Afghans, Mohammad Khan and Samad Khan from Rohelkhand had joined the Peshwa, Baji Rao I, near Kalpi with 50 Afghan soldiers. They distinguished themselves in the service of the Peshwa, who placed great confidence in them. The Pindaris accompanied Holkar and Sindhia when they came to the North. They received marks of favour and encouragement from both

35. Grant Duff, *History of the Marathas*, p. 326, ed. 1912.
36. Princep, *History of Political* and *Military Transactions in India*, p. 36.
37. Sardesai, *New History of the Marathas*, III, p. 477.
38. Farista Vol. I, p. 123. Translated by Scott.
39. Malcolm, *Political History of India*, Vol. I, p. 426.

of these chiefs.[40] But they cared little for the chiefs under whose orders they served. They soon acquired the habits and the character of professional plunderers. The term 'Pindara' at length became almost proverbial as the Pindaris were mostly Afghans by nationality and military adventurers by profession.[41]

These Pindaris were named 'Sindhia Shahee' and "Holkar Shahee" Pindaris. The most famous leaders among the Sindhia Shahi Pindaris were Namdar Khan, Dost Mohammad, Wasil Mohammad, Chetoo Khan, Ranjan, Karim Khan Heroo, Kedar Buksh, Khajeh Buksh, Fazil Khan and Bheekum Khan. Their forces amounted to about thirty thousand and they also had a few guns. The Pindaris were in the regular pay of the Sindhia and Holkar Government.[42]

The Pindari leaders were granted Jagirs and ordinarily remained busy in cultivation, and accompanied the forces of their particular chief only when they were called to do so. In normal times they used to earn their livelihood by carrying grain on horses to markets.[43]

The Pindaris were not encumbered with tents or baggage. Each horseman carried a few loaves of bread for his subsistence and some grain for his horse and advanced at the rapid pace of forty or fifty miles a day.[44] Of every 1000 Pindaris, about 400 were tolerably well-mounted and armed; the remaining 600 were common plunderers. About every 15th man carried a matchlock, but they favoured the spear, which was usually 12 to 18 ft. long. Generally, the Pindaris started their operations after Dashera for plunder and exacted money mercilessly.[45]

After the Second Maratha War, when the Maratha's power received a death blow, these Pindaris had to subsist on the plunder of the territories of their own chiefs, and those of Hyderabad, Mysore and also of North India under British control. To provide them with means of livelihood, Sindhia granted them in 1794, tracts of land near the banks of the Narmada,

40. Princep : p. 35.
41. Basu, *Rise of the Christian Power in India*, p. 655.
42. *History of the British Empire in India*, p. 392.
43. Malcolm, *Political History of India*, Vol. I, p. 436.
44. Malcolm, *Report of Central India*, Vol. I, pp. 436 and 430.
45. Duff, *History of the Marathas*, III, p. 328 and Vol. I, p. 610.

which they extended by conquest, but they were too numerous and it was not possible for the Pindari leaders to meet the demands of their followers, so they were forced to have recourse to plunder.

Among the Pindaris, Karim Khan came into prominence as he acquired a considerable booty by the plunder of the Nizam's territories and became their principal leader. He acquired the district of Shujalpoor from Amir Khan. During the Second Maratha War, Karim Khan contrived to acquire several districts in Malwa, belonging to Sindhia's jagirdars and wrested some territory from the Nawab of Bhopal. His annual revenue amounted to Rs. 15 lacs. He rebelled against Daulat Rao Sindhia, and Jaggo Bapu was sent to crush him. He was defeated in the last week of December, 1811[46] and took shelter with Amir Khan, who presented him to Rani Tulsi Bai, the ruler of Indore, where he remained in confinement upto 1816, but was later on released.

The Pindaris gained in strength as the countries around them became exhausted. In April 1814, Chitoo had 10,000 followers and 17 guns, Karim Khan 6,000, Dost Mohammad, 4,000 and 7 guns.

During the year 1815-16 from October till May, the Pindaris were very active and were successful in eluding the Parties sent in pursuit of them. In November 1816, they came into clash with British forces which were determined to annihilate them. Namdar Khan, Chitoo, Wasil Mohammad and other Pindari leaders wrote pitiable letters for help to Daulat Rao Sindhia and to his officers and ministers, but were told that the 'strictest friendship subsists between the Honourable company and the presence; all that must be already known to you. It is, therefore written that you have no concern with the presence.[47]

The British Operations against the Pindaris

The British Government was determined to wipe off the Pindaris.[48] The decision to crush the Pindaris was made because

46. *Poona Residency Correspondence,* XIV, No. 228.

47. *Ibid.*, p. 354.

48. Padampani, Agent of Nepal wrote "The Pindaris amounted to 25,000...are still ready to fight, but they have no place of strength...their safety is from Daulat Roa." Journal of India History August 1965, p. 140.

Chitoo had murdered with extreme cruelty some spies of the British Government.[49] In December, 1816, Namdar Khan, Shamat Khan and Chitoo Khan tried to form an alliance, but the scheme failed. The Pindaris tried to cut the supplies of the British forces. Owing to lack of a safe refuge and the pressure of the British forces, however, they dispersed in several groups and widened their activities. James Tod, Assistant to the Resident with Sindhia, wrote to John Adam, Secretary, on 9th June, 1817, "This diminution of their means naturally lessens the control of their chiefs, and though hitherto they had contrived to keep them from extensive depredations, particularly in Sindhia's own districts. The latest account represents them as struggling over the northern parganas indiscriminately in small parties, laying violent hands on whatever property comes within their reach."[50]

The Pindari War

In July, 1817, Karim Khan tried to unite with Chitoo Khan but failed, and the British Government determined to punish them. The Governor General embarked upon a comprehensive policy to extirpate the Pindaris and, for this purpose, he wanted to rope in all the chiefs to assist him in the task. He extended a warning to all the local powers that they would be treated as enemies if they did not co-operate with the British Government. Bapuji Sindhia and Jaswant Rao Bhau tried to help them (The Pindaris[51])." But had to withdraw due to the fear of the British forces.[52] Namdar Khan surrendered on 3rd February, 1818,[53] Karim Khan on 10th February, 1818, on the promise of a jagir. Wasil Mohammad, successor of Dost Mohammad, was found in Sindhia's camp in April, 1818. He was sent to Gorakhpur for imprisonment and committed suicide there by swallowing poison.[54] Chitoo remained a fugitive and, according to Malcolm,

49. *Foreign Secret Papers*, Nos. 5 of 3-11 and 10 of 10th Nov. 1815.
50. *Poona Residency Correspondence*, Vol. XIV, p. 391.
51. *Foreign Political Pagers*, 1817, pp. 36-37.
52. Duff, *History of the Marathas*, Vol. III, p. 455.
53. *Ibid.*, p. 466.
54. C.I., *A Memoir of Central India*, p. 444.

a body killed by a tiger was identified as that of Chitoo Khan.[55] The remaining Pindaries surrendered to Zalim Singh of Kotah.[56] These were the Pindaries who harassed English forces most during the Second Anglo-Maratha War. With the destruction of Pindaris, the harassing force of Marathas disappeared, and in pitched battles the Britishers were definitely superior. Thus with the destruction of Pindaris, the dragons' tooth of Marathas was taken and their defeat was only a matter of time.

Daulat Rao Sindhia's relations with Karim Khan and his adherents were not satisfactory, but those with Chitoo Khan and Wasil Mohammad (brother of Dost Mohammad) were tolerable, but being swore of their predatory habits, he helped none of them and they had to meet with tragic consequences. According to Sardesai, "the rise of the Maratha power is closely connected with the activities of the Pindaris, a bandit cavalry which re-inforced Indian armies".[57] It is interesting to note that the fall of the Maratha empire beyond hope of recovery followed the extinction of the Pindaris.[58]

Bhopal

Relations of Mahadji with Bhopal State

The relations of the Bhopal State with Mahadji remained cordial and Mahadji was looked upon as a friendly protector by this Afghan Principality. As such considerable importance was attached to the Khilat or honorary dress annually sent from Gwalior to the Nawab Wazir Mohammad Khan, who however, procrastinated when Sindhia required him to accompany his army on its march to attack Jaswant Rao Holkar.

Relations with Daulat Rao

During the Second Maratha War the then Nawab of Bhopal got an opportunity to occupy a few tracts of the territory of Daulat Rao and of the Raja of Berar, of which Hoshangabad was the most important. Wazir Mohammad, the de facto ruler of Bhopal, allied himself with Pindari Karim Khan after the war was over. Daulat Rao Sindhia sent three battalions and some

55. *Foreign Secret Index*, 1818 April 30, No. 14, Malcolm I, p. 447.
56. Duff, *History of the Marathas*, III, p. 455.
57. Sardesai, *New History of the Marathas*, III, p. 427.
58. For details see Thesis on Pindaris submitted in Patna University.

cavalry to Bhopal to patch up differences between Nawab Ghaus Mohammad Khan and his minister Wazir Mohammad Khan and to reassert his authority in Bhopal. Sindhia laid siege to Rahat Garh and was able to capture it after a period of six month in November, 1807.

After the death of Nawab Heyat Mohammad Khan, Daulat Rao decided to achieve the conquest of Bhopal in alliance with the Raja of Nagpur.

In December 1807, Sindhia negotiated with Wazir Mohammad Khan and by promises of allowing him to retain other forts in his possession, induced him to surrender the fort of Islam Nagar near Bhopal. He hoped to fulfil his purpose of subduing Bhopal with the help of the Raja of Berar, so he sent Kishanji Hoozooree to Wazir Mohammad Khan, but he was cast into prison by Wazir Mohammad Khan. Thereafter, Daulat Rao proposed to send Appa Cundra to punish the Nawab who, after plundering the district of Astha and Shujawalpur, carried forward depredations into the Rahat Garh District, which Sindhia had taken in 1807.[59] In September, 1808, Appa Cunderao's forces marched again and got partial success against Bhopal. Wazir Mohammad Khan tried to detach Daulat Rao Sindhia from the Raja of Nagpur but failed in his attempt.

Being otherwise occupied for some time in Rajputana, Daulat Rao Sindhia was unable to pay any attention to Bhopal, but in March, 1812. Jagoo Bapu, one of Daulat Rao Sindhia's principal generals, made an attack on Bhopal, who came back after receiving a small payment and the promise of paying the rest of the arrears of tribute later on. In 1813, he had to make another attack in alliance with the troops of the Raja of Berar. In January, 1814, two separate assaults were made on Bhopal one by Saadat Ali, commander of the Nagpur forces, and the other by Dan Singh. In February, Dan Singh and Ram Lal made another desperate attack. These assaults were boldly pushed on till they advanced close to the walls of the town of Bhopal itself. Wazir Mohammad, however, forced Daulat Rao's armies to retreat. In March 1814,[60] Jagoo Bapoo died, but in April Sadiq Ali, the commander of Bhonsle, enticed Doongar Singh,

59. Malcolm, *Political History of India*, I, p. 388.

60. *Ibid.*, p. 406

an ally of Bhopal, and succeeded in entering the town. However he failed to gain a full victory. He did not pursue the seize of Bhopal on the pretext that he was urged in a dream to leave the place and not to murder the followers of Islam, his own brethern.[61]

In spite of this, Daulat Rao's forces did not lose heart and Jaswant Rao Bhau, cousin of Jagoo Bapu, again attacked Bhopal, but Jean Baptiste, who had been sent by Daulat Rao to assist him, quarrelled with Bhau over advance of money to pay his troops. He did not attack Bhopal and thus ruined the cause of Daulat Rao Sindhia. Why Baptiste did not prosecute the siege has been variously accounted for, but the real cause was the overtures made by Wazir Mohammad at this period to him.[62] Thus, the traitor who deceived Sindhia at Bharatpur once again ruined his cause at Bhopal.

In August, 1813, Baptiste was again ordered to proceed against Bhopal jointly with Samad Khan with 10 thousand troops and 5,000 Pindaris, but the British Resident, R. Stratchey did not desire that Bhopal should come under Sindhia's control. He wrote on 16th September, 1814, to John Adam, Secretary to Government : "There is no doubt that Daulat Rao Sindhia is still bent on a further extension of his territory and Bhopal is one of the first objects in view." He further stated, "The establishment of Sindhia's authority in Bhopal would be attended with mischicf not only to the interest of the British Government, but to the general tranquility of other states."[63]

He argued that "the possession of Bhopal by Sindhia would not diminish the Pindari menace, it would open the way for aggression in Bundelkhand and Nagpur for him and it would consolidate his acquisitions of Garh Kota, Chanderi, and the country seized from Durjan Sal, and would with his possessions in Malwa provide greater facility to attack the Peshwa's Jagirdars. On the other hand, by an alliance with Bhopal and Sagar, the same acquisitions should open to ourselves a range of friendly territory from the Jamuna to the Narvada". Moreover, the British Government would get the support of the Bhopal Government

61. *Poona Residency Correspondence,* Vol. XIV, No. 201, p. 234.

62. Malcolm, *Political History of India,* I, p. 412.

63. *Poona Residency Correspondence,* Vol. XIV, No. 201, p. 234.

against the Pindaris, the Marathas and the Pathans of Amir Khan.[64] Sindhia, he said was making "great efforts against Bhopal...that in its exhausted state even the heroism of Wazir Mohammad must prove unavailing."[65]

Bhopal was therefore forthwith taken under British protection. "Gopal Bhau and Annaji Bhaskar both protested that the chief of Bhopal was a dependent of the Maharaja."[66] On the views of Sindhia, Gopal Bhau commented, "The Maharaja has observed that detaching Bhopal from him and appropriating it to ourselves (the Company) was an extraordinary sort of friendship." Gopal Bhau further said, "Measures with respect to Bhopal on the part of the British Government was a step to new aggrandisement," but the Resident did not reply except by requesting Daulat Rao Sindhia to order Baptiste to respect the territory of Bhopal.[67]

Lord Hastings had determined to crush the Pindaris and for this purpose, he took Jhasi and Bhopal under his protection on February 26, 1818.

Fresh Treaty

On 5th March, 1817, a treaty[68] between Daulat Rao Sindhia and R. Close on behalf of the Company was signed, in which Daulat Rao Sindhia renounced his claims on Bhopal as well as on the Rajput States, and bound himself to give assistance against the Pindaris, he had to give the fort of Islam Nagar to Bhopal. Thus a strong state of Bhopal was created to check the possibility of any alliance between Bhonsle and Sindhia or of Sindhia with any other Maratha State. Bhopal now is capitl of Madhya Pradesh.

Review

With a view to consolidate his dominions, Daulat Rao Sindhia followed a policy of compromise and conciliation. He broke the dragon's teeth by the abridgement of the powers of

---

64. *Poona Residency Correspondence,* Vol. XIV, No. 201, p. 299 and P.R.C.
65. Duff, *History of the Marathas,* Vol. I, p. 638.
66. *Ibid.*, p. 639.
67. *Poona Residency Correspondence,* XIV, special No. 226, pp. 270-72.
68. A.C. Banerji : *Indian Constitutional Documents,* Vol. I, pp. 321-22, III pp. 519-20, ed. 1964.

the numerous turbulent chiefs in Central India, but allowed them to retain their patrimony subject to overall authority. In this way he proved wiser than his illustrious predecessor, in that he made these territories dependent upon himself. By this policy, he succeeded in wiping out the disturbing elements in his dominions and stabilizing his administration. This integration of his Kingdom reflected a sound judgement and sound grasp of British designs by Daulat Rao Sindhia. He made the best of a bad bargain and cared more for substance of power than for its shadow.

In this respect, he was more realistic than even the best of the Peshwas, Baji Rao I, who dashed to Delhi for the conquest of the north without securing a grip over the south. Nana Phadanavis and Mahadji too failed to forego the temptation of conquering the decadent territories of Mughal Empire. In the words of Sardesai, "Indeed solid possessions in Central India were more valuable to him (Mahadji) than the empty dignity conferred upon him by an insolent Emperor,"[69] which brought Mahadji in conflict with the Rajputs and other chiefs and shattered the dream of Hindu Pad Padshahi. The credit of creating a solid possession in Central India goes to Daulat Rao Sindhia. By this stroke of statesmanship, he consolidated whatever territories, he had been able to save from the jaws of the British lion. That is one reason why his state survived and the power of Baji Rao II became extinct, as the latter's jagirdars were won over by the British. In the case of Gwalior, the British found no loopholes for infiltration after 1806.

With the extinction of the Pindaris and petty states, the endemic anarchy in Malwa and Central India ended and the dominions of Daulat Rao became compact. This was the substantial and solid achievement that enabled him to survive.

Though Gwalior State was now under British supremacy, yet some degree of independence and some power remained with it upto 1843. In 1832, in the report of the Select Committee of the House of Commons of 1832 (on Political and Foreign Affairs) it was stated that "within the Peninsula, Sindhia is the only prince who preserves the semblance of independence." Before that Committee, the historian James Mill said on 16th

---

69. Sardesai, *New History of the Marathas*, Vol. III, p. 147.

February, 1832, regarding Sindia that "he neither at present has a subsidiary alliance with us nor do we include him among the protected states; in that respect he stands alone...." Before the same Committee on 27th February, 1832 Major Close in reply to a question "what is the relation in which Sindhia stood to the Company?" said, "He was independent."

Then he was asked, "Has he no treaty with the Company?" "Yes there are several treaties, but they are not such as to abrogate his independence, or to place him in acknowledged submission to the British Government."[70] Thus the Gwalior State remained the only state in India which maintained some semblance[71] of independence upto 1843.[72] It was all due to Daulat Rao's prudence and discretion, that Sindhia was able to survive with a modicum of dignity and retain some semblance of independence.

---

70. James Mill before the Select Committee of the House of Commons on Sindhia dated 16-2-1832 quoted by Sunder Lal Vol. III, p. 746.
71. *Ibid.*, 16th February 1832 quoted by Basu, p. 147 and Sunder Lal II, p. 764 Government of India Publication 1861.
72. P.E. Roberts "Gwalior was now (1843) definitely made a protected state" *History of British India*, p. 331, ed. 1943. Similarly Dr. R.C. Majumdar and others state "Gwalior, now reduced definitely to the status of a protected state." *Advanced History of India*, ed. 1948, p. 766.

    P. Spear states "Ellenborough's final exploit was the overthrow of Sindhia's army in Dec., 1843," *Oxford History of India*, p. 592, ed. 1958.

7

DAULAT RAO SINDHIA AND NORTHERN INDIA (1794-1827)

We saw in the preceding Chapter how Daulat Rao Sindhia consolidated his territories in Malwa. Now we shall study how he fared in the north where his predcccssor Mahadji and he himself had ruled in the name and on behalf of the Mughal Emperor Shah Alam.

The Punjab — Mahadji's Treaty with the Sikhs

Juridically, the Suba of the Punjab belonged to the Mughal Emperor, but half of it had been annexed by Ahmad Shah Abdali. A portion upto the Sutlej ruled over by a large number off turbulent Sikh Sardars remained in the hands of the Mughal Emperor. Mahadji Sindhia, after gaining the viceregency of the Delhi Empire, tried to come to an understanding with the Sikhs. On May 1785, a treaty was concluded with them, the negotiator being Ambaji Ingale on the Maratha side and Mohan Singh and Dada Singh for the Sikh Sardars. The terms of the treaty were :

(1) That the Sikh Sardars were to join on demand the Emperor's army with a contingent of 5,000 horse and to receive in return a jagir of 10 lacs.

(2) That they undertook not to disturb the territory outside the limits of their jagirs.[1]

But the Sikhs did not abide by the terms.[2] They even tried to form an alliance with the English on the same date.[3] They could hardly be expected to be able to do so in view of their

1. Dr. H.R. Gupta, *History of the Sikhs*, Vol. II, p. 184, 1844.
2. *Dillyyethile*, 1-35.
3. Secret Proceedings, 26th April 1785, John Gunning to Governor General 11th April 1785, 26th May. 1785. James Anderson to the G.G. 10-5-1785 Imperial Records Nos. 7.

anarchical organisation under petty chieftains with no central authority controlling their individual predatory activities. They had forgotten the noble teachings of their Gurus and became "a gang of robbers whose only law was the sword."[4]

Mahadji's Policy of Conciliation

The Sikhs opposed Mahadji in the Lalsot Campaign in June 1787; they also helped Ghulam Qadir and his father Zabita Khan. To gain their support, Zabita Khan declared himself a Sikh and this was expressed by a line. "Ek Guru Ke Do Chela, Adha Sikh Adha Rohilla."[5] In 1789, peace was made by the Marathas by legalising the Rakhi or the subsistence collected from the people by these Sardars. One thousand Sikh agents were allowed to collect the Rakhi from the villages with the help of Maratha Officers. By this course of policy, the government gave a varnish of legality to a system of exaction that could not be wholly suppressed.[6] Vithoji, brother of Ambaji, was left at Delhi to look after Maratha interests.[7] But this scheme failed. The Marathas cultivated friendship with the Maharaja of Patiala but the latter played a dubious game, in that he called for Maratha succour when he was attacked by the Sikhs and summoned the Sikhs to his rescue when the Marathas demanded tribute from him.[8]

Mahadji's policy was to win the Sikhs over by friendly treatment and by a policy of conciliation and thus establish peace and order in Northern India with their active cooperation. But the Sikhs understood only the argument of physical force[9] and so the policy failed.[10] Gopal Bhau,[11] the Viceroy of Mahadji

---

4. Dr. H.R. Gupta, *History of the Sikhs,* Vol. II, p. 16.
5. Forester, p. 315; Cunningham, p. 117 and also quoted by Dr. Gupta and Sarkar.
6. *Ibid.*, Vol. II pp. 222-23 with quotations from Calcutta Review 1875.
7. Parasnis : I 167-174, 175, 180. 168, 190; *Dilliyethil.* I 335, 355, 366, 365, 379, 380, 381, 384, 388, Mahsur II, 141-42.
8. Parasnis and Cyan Mal 958-960, Calcutta Review LXII 1875, 33, 40-43.
9. Parasnis : I 226; *Dilliyethil,* II 2, 13, 41, 47 II Additional 21, 23, 30, 35, 41, 45, 47, Mahesur, III 93-100. Muzaffernagar District Gaztt, 179-80.
10. *Ibid.*
11. For the Activities of Gopal Bhau see Parasnis 322-25, *Dilliyethil* II 89-93 Imperial Records Political Proceedings.

in the north, posted Bhairon Pant Tatya at Saharanpur, Devji Gaule and Bapa Malhar at Panipat, Jiwaji Balal and Ambaji Ingale at Sambhal and Appa Khande Rao (incharge of Delhi district) at Jhajjar, but the mutual jealousies of these officers prevented the restoration of peace and prosperity in the Punjab. Mahadji failed in the Punjab largely because of this factor of want of cooperation among his officers in the north.

Daulat Rao's Policy towards the Sikhs

The whole country lay waste and did not yield enough revenue to support the army kept for the maintenance of law and order. These conditions prevailed upto 1803, when Daulat Rao lost the Punjab after the Second Maratha War and the rise of Ranjit Singh.

In October 1794, the Sikhs took part in the dispute about the succession to the Rohila State of Rampur, on being encouraged by Bhamu Khan, brother of the notorious Ghulam Qadir.

In November 1794, Gopal Bhau was replaced as the Viceroy of the North by Lakhwa Dada, and the latter appointed Nana Rao to collect the revenues[12] of the Punjab. But Nana Rao soon grew tired of fighting with the Sikhs. He was recalled and Madho Rao Phalkey was appointed in his place.[13] In the meantime the Sikhs attacked Saharanpur in October 1795 and the Maratha garrison "Scattered like chaff before the wind." George Thomas and Appa Khande Rao, however, succeeded later in curbing the Sikhs. They also raided the Kumbh fair in 1795[14] and created havoc at Hardwar.

Being encouraged by the unstable conditions, George Thomas, an ambitious Irish General, tried to carve out a principality for himself in the Punjab, but Bourquien, a lieutenant of De Perron, defeated him on 23rd December, 1801, and George Thomas died of disappointment on 22nd August, 1802.[15] On

12. Bakht Mal 151-171 George Thomas 150.
13. *Ibid.*, 150.
14. Gupta Vol. II, pp. 262-268; Hamilton 1-450-52, Memoirs of George Thomas 44, Calcutta Review (Bound) 1875, p. 47.
15. Imperial Records Foreign Department Political Proceedings 1791 Patiala and General Perron. Proceedings of the Indian Historical Records Commission, Vol. III, pp. 34-348, Punjab Gazt. 17 and Sarkar IV, pp. 231-44.

the whole the constant changes among Sindhia's officers in the north, lack of cooperation among them and of Daulat Rao's personal supervision of them, as well as frequent changes of political interests and alignments of the Mughal court and the lawlessness of the Sikhs prevented all stabilization of the administration in the Punjab and neighbouring regions.

Relations of Daulat Rao Sindhia with Ranjit Singh

After the treaty following the Second Maratha War, Daulat Rao Sindhia ceased to control the Emperor Shah Alam, and in consequence he lost control over the territories of the East Punjab and portions of the U.P. which the Marathas had hitherto controlled on behalf of the Emperor. The trans Sutlaj parts of the Punjab had by now been consolidated by Maharja Ranjit Singh.

Ranjit Singh and Daulat Rao Sindhia were contemporaries, being born in the same year *i.e.,* in 1780. By dint of his energy, tact, zeal and daring, Ranjit Singh had made himself supreme in West Punjab and curbed the power of petty local chiefs. With the extinction of the Maratha power in the Punjab, Ranjit Singh's rise was inevitable. In 1809, the relations of Ranjit Singh with the East India Company took a turn for the worse. Ranjit Singh desired now to annex the territories of the petty Rajas in the cis-Sutlej region also, but the East India Company was determined to frustrate his plans. For a time it seemed the issue would be decided by recourse to arms. So, Ranjit Singh desired friendship with Daulat Rao Sindhia against the British Government. The British Resident at Gwalior reported to the Governor General Minto about the intrigues of Sindhia with Ranjit Singh. He also reported that[16] Sarji Rao Ghatge inspired these intrigues.[17] This was, however, a false alarm as the negotiations between the two potentates did not materialise in an alliance.

In March 1816, *i.e.,* seven years later, Sukha Singh, Ambassador of Ranjit Singh, visited Sindhia's court again and asked for a physician and Deccan horses. Daulat Rao Sindhia dismissed Sukha Singh with the assurance to send a physician

---

16. *Poona Residency Correspondence,* II No. 275, p. 407.
17. *Ibid.,* No. 280, p. 416.

and the horses as soon as these would be available. Sukha Singh departed on 15th April, 1816 from Sindhia's court. He was given some five Muslims of Chanderi, a horse, and a letter containing general expressions of regard.[18] Thus, the talks ended without any substantial result. The Resident wrote to the Secretary John Adam, that, "Private communications have passed between the two courts. The object of both parties, it would seem, is to cherish a mutual friendship and intimacy with a view to counteract any dangers which may arise to either from the British Government."[19]

There are obvious reasons for the ineffectuality of these approaches between Sindhia and Ranjit Singh. Both Ranjit Singh and Daulat Rao Sindhia did not want to take up a hostile posture against the East India Company. When Jaswant Rao Holker had visited Ranjit Singh during the Anglo-Maratha war of 1803-1805, Ranjit Singh had refused to help him against the East India Company. Daulat Rao Sindhia therefore, could not possibly ask or persuade him now to form an anti-British alliance with himself. In spite of all this a vague understanding existed upto 1843, which came to an end when the power of Gwalior was crushed and it was made a protected state.[20]

It is a pity that the last two powerful rulers of the country who could, if they would, do something to check the on rush of British imperialism were unable to do any thing and remained entangled in parochialism and petty dynastic interests.

Sindhia and the Mughal Emperor Shah Alam

When Daulat Rao succeeded to the throne, the court of Delhi was seething with interminable intrigues.[21] There was nothing that one could call a Government[22] and the country was torn into pieces.[23] At first, he did not deem it prudent to

18. R. Close to Adam 16th April 1816, P.R.C. XIV, p. 317.
19. *Ibid.*, No. 280, p. 308.
20. Sarkar, *Fall of Mughal Empire*, Vol. IV, pp. 217-244, Indian Historical Records Commission. Vol. III, 1931, pp. 4-5.
21. *Ibid.*
22. Ghulam Hussain Siyar-Ul-Mutakharin Maratha Riyasat-IV, pp. 189-220.
23. Proceedings of Indian Historical Records Commission III, 4-9 Dom. II Appendix 79-94. *The Asiatic Annual Register*, 1800, pp. 9-34.

disturb the arrangements of his predecessor. In June 1796, he appointed Jaswant Rao Sindhia, great-grandson of Ranoji, Subedar of Delhi. The person did not prove himself equal to the task and Shah Haji, a personal servant of prince Akbar Shah, was appointed in his place. He took proved incompetent and in May 1798, Shah Nizamuddin was appointed to the post and held it upto 1801. After 1801, De Perron was appointed subedar who discharged his duties through his Deputy Drudgeon upto 1803; when Delhi was captured by the British.

Daulat Rao followed the administrative policy of his predecessor of having a Subedar for administration and the realization of revenue, and another person, as kiladar, to keep military control. Mahadji generally appointed Muslims as Subedars and Hindus or foreigners as kiladars as checks upon each other.

Shah Alam had to suffer great difficulty on account of misappropriations by shah Nizamuddin.[24]

Shah Alam was a luxurious king and in the words of Sarkar neither age nor blindness had cooled the flames of passion in his blood after Ghulam Qadir's atrocities.[25] A royal family,

24. Mahadji allotted to the Emperor 32 Mahals yielding an annual revenue of Rs. 16,94,000 and fixed Rs. 1,30,000 for his personal expenses, but the times were not normal and it became difficult for the subedars to pay him the amount fixed. Misappropriation and mismanagement by Shah Nizamuddin made matters worse. With the advent of Daulat Rao Sindhia nothing was done to improve the condition (1) A friend of col. De Boigne, in a letter written from Delhi to John Murray about July 1794, states that He (Shah Nizamuddin) does not give a farthing of money to the Padshah or any of his people.... Regularly every day he furnishes the old king with two seers of pulau and 8 seers of meat; this with two leaves of bread, about the length each of a cubit, to suffice for five persons, (namely the emperor, his doctor, prince Akbar Shah, a little favourite daughter and one of his two hundred Begums in turn). The rest of the royal household, without distinction, princes, and princesses, nay Queens and all eunuchs and female slaves, have two seers a day of barley flour for every three persons, which they are to bake for themselves. De Bougne also testifies to the same and writes that the province (*i.e.,* Jagir) in Shahji's possession intended for the support of the Royal family may produce 7 lakhs per annum.... Shahji takes the greatest part of it for himself.

(1) Sarkar, *Fall of the Mughal Empire*, Vol. IV, pp. 221-224.

(2) Dr. Gupta : II, Hingane Daftar II, 42.

25. *Ibid.*, of I.

which bred with the fecundity of rabbits, needed an ever-increasing supply of money.[26] Shah Alam desired same amenities of life which his predecessors had enjoyed and he applied to the British Resident, the Peshwa and Sindhia himself. He even invited an attack by Ahmad Shah Durrani and wrote to the king of Afghanistan to relieve him of misery.[27]

It goes to the credit of Daulat Rao that he carried on the burden that was Shah Alam and his family against heavy odds. When Lord lake attacked Delhi and defeated Sindhia's forces in the battle of Paharganj on 11th September, 1803, he took the person of Shah Alam under British protection and all the northern possessions of Daulat Rao passed into British hands under the treaty of Sarji Arjungaon of 30th December, 1803. This treaty Sir, J.N. Sarkar thinks, sounded the death knell of the Mughal Empire too[28] and of the Maratha overlordship of Hindustan.[29]

Agra

Another important province in the north under the control of Sindhia was Agra. Mahadji had acquired it in March 1785, and had established a permanent camp at Mathura to control it. Except for a short duration during the temporary usurpation of Ghulam Qadir, this province remained in the hands of Sindhia all this time.

It was also one of the most prosperous provinces of the Empire, but soon it became a cockpit of war and suffered untold miseries brought about by the tornado of Ahmad Shah

26. Crompton 83-86 and also quoted by Sarkar, Vol. IV, p. 224.

27. The French Administrator, the Compete De Modava, who visited Shah Alam in 1775, writes "He is marvellously devout and very much given to women. He passes his life in their midst having no less than 500 in his seraglio." The Bad Shah at present has 27 male children, all alive and swarming. It is reckoned that today in the fortress of Delhi there are more than 80 Shahzada prisoners, who are all provided with wives and most of them with children. (1) Modava Tr. by Sarkar in Islamic Culture, July 1937.

Swiss Engineer Polliar also supports this, Polliar in Gupta's Shah Alam II and his court 69-70, Delhi Distt. Gazt. p. 22 Wellesley dated 2 Jan. 1805.

28. J.N. Sarkar, *Fall of the Mughal Empire*, IV, p. 337, ed. 1950.

29. *Ibid.*, p. 343.

Abdali's invasion and numerous other clashes between the Jats, the Rohilas and the Marathas for the control of Delhi. These totally deprived the province of its former prosperity. Agra also was captured by the British forces on 17th October 1803 and its possession along with Delhi passed from Daulat Rao Sindhia to the East India Company.

Nepal

Daulat Rao Sindhia came in contact with the northern Kingdom of Nepal, as already pointed out, when a war broke out between it and the East India Company in 1814 and Priti Ram Bilas, an envoy from Nepal, came to Sindhia's court, but nothing came out of the mission.[30] In 1817, again proposals for an alliance between Nepal and Daulat Rao Sindhia were reopened. Padampani, an ambassador of Nepal, visited Sindhia's court but this effort also failed owing to the disinclination of Nepal to any hostile measures against the British Government.[31] "Astreak of hesitancy ascribable to a lurking doubt as to the sincerity of Nepal restrained Sindhia from committing himself completely to Nepal's plans.[32]

"Thus, the last hope of the trembling Indian Princes vanished," writes Sarkar, "When the Gurkhas of Nepal bowed down to British arms."[33] The relation between the Nepal Government and Sindhia's Government were cordial, but they failed to make a common cause against the British. Relations of ruling family of Nepal with Sindhia family of Nepal remained good.

The Jats

During the last years of the Mughal rule, the Jats also rose like the Sikhs and carved out a small kingdom of their own between Agra and Jaipur, with Bharatpur as its capital and a revenue of about two million sterling.[34] Churaman led the Jats

---

30. *History of Nepal* by Deniel Wreight, and *Poona Residency Correspondence*, Vol. XIV, No. 265, p. 310.
31. *Foreign Secret Paper Nepal*, 1817, p. 121 and No. 148 of 19-12-1817.
32. Article of Sri Kanchanmoy Majumdar "Nepal's relations with Indian States," p. 409 of Journal of Indian History, Vol. XLIII, August 1965 and Nepal and the East India Company by B.D. Sanwal (Asia Publications) 1965.
33. Sarkar, *Fall of the Mughal Empire*, Introduction to *Poona Residency Correspondence*, Vol. XIV.
34. H.R. Gupta, *History of Sikhs*.

against the Mughals, and, though he was defeated by the Mughal Emperor, Suraj Mal succeeded him and under his banner, the Jats reached the pinnacle of their glory. He was present at Panipat in 1761, but did not take part in the battle, though he helped the Marathas after their defect. He was killed in a battle with Najib Khan, the regent of the Mughal Emperor, and under his successors, the state narrowly escaped extinction at the hands of Najib.

The Jats helped Mahadji after the battle of Lalsot and in his war with Ghulam Quadir and Ismail Beg. The Sindhia family considered the state as a tributary of the Marathas as over since the expansion of the Maratha Empire to the North, the Jats had been paying tribute to them.

During Daulat Rao Sindhia's rule, Bharatpur was ruled by Ranjit Singh. He followed a pro-Maratha policy in the beginning but when Lord Lake came to Agra (4th October 1802), after his victory at Mathura, the Raja concluded a treaty with him. According to Sardesai, he was the first Hindu chief in northern India to seek an alliance with the British Government.[35]

But soon this marriage of convenience came to naught. When Jaswant Rao Holkar came to Deeg, after his defeat at Khudaiganj near Farrukhabad, Lake[36] though of occupying Bharatpur himself. Wellesley also wrote : "The entire reduction of the power and resources of the Raja of Bharatpur has now become indispensably necessary."

The Raja of Bharatpur as feared, now openly espoused Holkar's cause, repudiating the treaty of alliance which he had signed one year before with the British Government. Wellesley therefore desired the complete annihilation of Bharatpur which, as is well known, accomplished though with unexpectedly heavy losses, later on at the time of Lord Ahmursk.

Daulat Rao Sindhia now proceeded towards Bharatpur. This move of Sindhia made Lord Lake nervous and he concluded on 10th April, 1804, a treaty with Ranjit Singh before the arrival

35. For details see K.R. Qanungo, *History of the Jats*; Lake's letter dated 27.11.1804.

36. G.G. Wellesley to Lake, 24 December 1804 Secret and official papers.

of Daulat Rao Sindhia. The Raja hastily entered into a treaty with the Company. Daulat Rao Sindhia, therefore, came to a halt at Sabalgarh on account of this change of face by the Raja, and the treachery of Bapuji Sindhia, who delayed meeting him owing to him (Bapuji Sindhia's) alliance with the British Government.[37] The Jats severed all connections with Daulat Rao Sindhia after the treaty of Surji Arjungaon.

Jat Raja of Gohad

The eclipse of the Jat state of Bharatpur produced another small principality nearby under the Rana of Gohad, comprising the district of Gohad and the fort of Gwalior. The Rana employed European officers and De Perron in his service, who later on joined Mahadji. In the First Maratha War, the Rana helped Captain Popham to capture the fort of Gwalior from the Sindhia. Mahadji, however, defeated the Rana and got back Gwalior[38] on 27th July, 1783 and Gohad in I784.[39]

During Daulat Rao Sindhia's regime, these places remained under him and the Rana of Gohad looked for an opportunity to regain them. During the second Maratha War the Rana again helped the British and got back all the territory in 1803, though the fort of Gwalior remained in British hands. An English Officer was appointed as Qiladar of the Fort. Gwalior was not restored to Sindhia under the treaty of Surji Arjungaon and Gohad was given back to the Rana. This annoyed Daulat Rao Sindhia. But, later in Nov. 1805, according to the next treaty of Mustafapur, Gwalior with the Gohad territory was restored to Sindhia. The people of Gohad, however, refused to surrender their independence. Ambaji attacked the Rana in December 1804 and finally Gohad was taken on 24th February 1806 with the help of British forces. The Rana of Gohad was given Dholpur, Baree, and Raj-Kirrah and came to be known subsequently as the Rana of Dholpur. Daulat Rao Sindhia's relations with the Dholpur State afterwards were those of mutual watchful jealousy. Marriage of Vasundhra Raje Sindhia later on in Jat ruling family made relations cordial.

---

37. General Lake's private letter to Wellesley dated 22-9-1804.
38. Sardesai, *New History of the Marathas*, Vol. III, p. 140.
39. *Ibid.*

Hathras and Mursan

During the disintegration of the Mughal empire, the Jats became dominant over the area between the Ganga and the Jamuna. They set up a small principality around Hathras, ruled over by one Daya Ram, who was one of the relatives of Raja Ranjit Singh of Bharatpur. It is said that a petty dispute took place between some English officers and Raja Daya Ram, because the latter refused to surrender a few British subjects in his custody and to give permission to English officers to see the fort. The main cause of British hostility to the petty stage, however, was that Daya Ram was sympathetic to the Marathas, particularly to Daulat Rao Sindhia, and Hastings was not prepared to have a thorn in his guts in the middle of the company's possessions.

British forces attacked the fort of Hathras on 11th February 1817. For some time, the Jaths fought bravely, but in the end they had to surrender to superior arms.[40]

Mursan, another Jat principality nearby, about seven miles from Hathras towards Mathura, was at this time ruled by one Raja Bhagwant Singh. With the defeat of Daya Ram, Raja Bhagwant Singh lost heart and surrendered his state and fort to the British forces without fighting.[41]

The position of these places was of strategic importance, as Hathras is only a few miles from Aligarh and Mursan is about 20 miles from Mathura, which was under Daulat Rao Sindhia.

Zebunnisa Begum or Begum Samroo

Zebunnisa Begum, popularly known Begum Samroo, ruled over Sardhana, a small jagir near Meerut, granted by Mahadji to his German commander, Sombree or Samroo, the husband of the Begum. Four battalions of her troops accompanied Daulat Rao Sindhia in the Assaye campaign, but took no part in the battle. On 18th July, Marquess Wellesley sent orders to Colonel Scott to see that means might be contrived to enable four of Begum Samroo's battalions then with Sindhia in the Deccan to

40. *Princep,* Vol. I, p. 418 Mill and Wilson VIII, pp. 93-94.

41. *Ibid.*, No. 419-420.

join General Wellesley.[42] The move was successful and Begum Samroo's troops defected to the British side.[43] She then entered into a treaty with the East India Company and was allowed to retain the Jagir for the whole life.

Mahadji Sindhia and the Rajput States

The Marathas had maintained political relations with the Rajput States ever since Shivaji's times. These became strained when with the assistance of Mahadji, Shah Alam returned to Delhi and again began to demand tribute from the Rajput states. Up to the regime of Najaf Khan, these demands were enforced very casually, but during the regency of Mahadji, particularly after 1783, they were enforced more rigidly. He demanded Rs. 60 lakhs from Jaipur but got only a part of it. Mohammad Beg Hemdani, and his nephew Ismail Beg, encouraged the Rajputs not to make any payment to Mahadji. A battle took place at Lalsot in 1787[44] in which Mohammad Beg Hamdani died, and Mahadji suffered a serious reverse owing to the desertion of his Mohammadan troops. In 1790-91, Mahadji again marched against the Rajputs and defeated Ismail Beg and Pratap Singh at Patan on June 20, 1790; captured Ajmer on 21st August, 1790, defeated Bijay Singh of Jodhpur at Merta on September 10, 1790 and concluded a treaty with him on 6th January 1791. He intervened in the domestic feuds of Mewar, restored Chitor to the Rana of Udaipur (17th Nov., 1791), and thus established his authority over the Rajput chiefs. But this was a wrong move as "instead of becoming the arbiter of India, he left only the reputation of being the Nestor of Rajputana."[45]

Daulat Rao and the Rajput States

On Daulat Rao Sindhia's accession in 1794, Ambaji, who had been the Maratha *charged affairs* in Udaipur, was continued in that office, but he was found to be a very corrupt officer. Tributes of Jodhpur and Jaipur began to be collected through De Boigne and De Berron, and they were found to be more

---

42. M.M. III, p. 192.
43. Gulgule D. and Khare XIV, 6720 A.W. in Gur. II, 434 and 456.
44. Col. Tod, *Annals and Antiquities of Rajasthan*, p. 513, ed. 1920.
45. *Ibid.*, p. 517 ed. 1920 and 353, ed. 1950.

honest and efficient. During the Widow's War, Mewar became the arena on which Ambaji and Lakhwa contested with each other for power.

After the Second Anglo-Maratha War, Daulat Rao had to give up his right to tributes from the Rajput States, but by the treaty of Mustafapur, he regained them. This was really a master stroke of British diplomacy. Daulat Rao Sindhia was deprived of a very considerable territory by the loss of the Punjab, Delhi and Agra. But he had still large armies to maintain, and needed large revenues to retain them in his service and the only way open to him was to collect the tributes from the Rajputs more zealously. This was bound to create bad blood between him and the Rajputs and the company could now exploit the situation to its own advantage.

As Colonel Tod states, "Deprived of all power in Hindustan and of the choicest territory in the north and south of the Narmada, with numerous discontented armies now let loose on these devastated countries, their passions inflamed by defeat and blind to every sentiment of humanity, they had no alternative to pacify the soldiery and replenish their own resources but indiscriminate pillage."[46] The touching episode of Krishna Kumari's marriage involved the rulers of Jaipur, Jodhpur and Udaipur, Sindhia and Holkar, and had a direct bearing on the fortunes of Daulat Rao. A representative of Raja Jagat Singh of Jaipur reached Udaipur with a proposal for the hand of the princess (Krishna Kumari) for Raja Jagat Singh. The Maharana consented to the proposal. Man Singh who succeeded to the throne of Jodhpur after Bhim Singh, demanded the hand of the princess for himself as being legal successor to the dominions and claims of Jodhpur, like Sir Anthony Absolute in 'The Rivals' by Sheridan, who said, "I have taken over the State with stock in it." It thus became a dispute of honour between the Rathore and Kachwaha royal houses. The Raja of Jaipur also conspired with Dhokal Singh, who pretended to be the heir to the throne of Jodhpur.[47]

---

46. Tod, *Annals & Antiquities of Rajasthan*, pp. 353-55, ed. 1950.

47. *Ibid.*, 535-542, ed. 1920 edited by Crooke and P.C. Mehta "The Relations between Mewar and the Marathas" (Unpublished thesis) p. 182.

Interference of Daulat Rao

Raja Man Singh solicited the mediation of Daulat Rao Sindhia in these conflicting claims for the hand of Krishna Kumari. Daulat Rao Sindhia, in the hope of realising his tribute from Jodhpur and getting some money from Jaipur marched into Mewar, sending in advance Bapuji Sindhia to the Maharana at Udaipur.[48] The Sindhia further advised the Maharana to give in marriage to Jagat Singh and Man Singh each, one of his numerous daughters, and if the two Rajas declined to accept that proposal the Maharaja should get the question decided with the help of the rulers of neighbouring states.[49] But the Maharana, ignoring the advice, refused to dismiss the Jaipur troops till Sindhia withdrew to Ujjain. It is said that Daulat Rao desired "to obtain the hand of the princess (Krishna Kumari himself)"[50] but later on withdrew his proposal to marry Krishna Kumari.[51]

Jaswant Rao Holkar also wanted to fish in troubled waters. He too demanded tribute from the Rajputs. It stiffened the Rana's attitude, who now decided not to pay any pecuniary contribution to Sindhia either.[52] When Sindhia's deputies at Ajmer and Nagaur failed to collect tributes from the Rajputs, they were ordered to be replaced by others, but these too did not comply with the orders and this indiscipline in the camp of Rao Sindhia worsened his position.

In the meanwhile, Sawai Singh, chief of Pokran, induced the Raja of Jaipur to fight Man Singh in favour of Dhokul Singh, the posthumous son of Raja Bhim Singh. Jagat Singh, the Raja of Jaipur, got help from the Raja of Bikaner (Surat Singh) and Amir Khan. He also lured Daulat Rao Sindhia to his side by an offer of Rupees ten lakhs.[53]

In March 1807, Rajasthan was in flames. The Raja of Jodhpur marched to face Jaipur and allied troops at Parbat Sar, but they

---

48. P.C. Mehta, *The Relations Between Mewar and the Marathas* (Unpublished thesis) p. 183.
49. *Poona Residency Correspondence,* XI, No. 102 and also quoted by Mehta, *Ibid.*, 184.
50. *Ibid.* No. 172 and 173, pp. 204, 265, Tod First Edited by Crooke K.N. p. 536, ed. 1920 and Mehta, p. 185.
51. *Ibid.*, letters 163, 172 and 178 and Mehta, p. 185.
52. *Ibid.*
53. *Ibid.*, Vol. XI, p. 315.

had to abandon the place. Jaipur troops pushed forward and in May they captured the city of Jodhpur.[54]

Ambaji Ingle's army reached Jaipur in the middle of May to help that State and he found a changed tone and temper in Jaipur. Ambaji urged Daulat Rao Sindhia to come for subduing Jaipur, but the party opposed to him at court did not favour the suggestion, and Daulat Rao remained busy at Rahat Gargh in Bhopal. Ambaji's mission to Jaipur thus came to nothing.[55]

Sindhia now ordered Ghatge to attack Jaipur, but his lieutenant Hira Singh was defeated. Bapu Sindhia and Sharze Rao ravaged the territory of Jaipur, but in January 1808, Chaturbhuj Haldia came into power at Jaipur and established the influence of Holkar at the Jaipur Darbar. He bluntly refused making any pecuniary contributions to Sindhia and adopted measures for vigorous resistance. Daulat Rao Sindhia's commander, Bapu Sindhia, won fortress after fortress, but the Raja of Jaipur refused to yield. At last in May 1809, Jaipur's representative, Khushali Ram Bora, agreed to pay a sum of Rs. 15 lakhs and also presented many other gifts.[56]

Amir Khan also advanced his claims on the Rajput states in the name of Jaswant Rao Holkar and devastated Rajasthan from 1810 to 1817. Sindhia chose to follow a temporizing policy towards the Rajputs.[57] He decided to adhere to his agreement with Jaipur, but the Raja of Jodhpur solicited the aid of Holkar and Amir Khan. Dhokul Singh's Vakeels urged Daulat Rao Sindhia for help, but the latter paid no need to them. He received Rs. 3 lakhs and 70 thousand from Raja Jagat Singh.[58] Jaipur Vakeels left Sindhia's court in December, 1809 and attempted reconciliation with the Raja of Jodhpur, who had come under the influence of Mohemmad Shah Khan, an adherent of Amir Khan.

Here we need a pause to relate the episode of Krishna Kumari. All these manoeuvres and counter-manoeuvres could not solve the problem of Rajasthan. The question of Krishna

54. *Poona Residency Correspondence,* No. 225, 228, 230 and Tod I, p. 637, ed. 1920.

55. *Ibid.*, letters 230, 231.

56. *Ibid.*, II, No. 287, p. 433.

57. *Ibid.*, XIV, No. 1, p. 2.

58. *Ibid.*, No. IV, p. 9.

Kumari's marriage was still there like a running sore. Her removal from the earth might ease the situation and this was now done. Who brought it about is a controversial question. Colonel Tod reports that for this foul deed only Amir Khan was responsible,[59] but the Resident C.T. Metcalfe, gave a non-committal report[60] about it he said "The daughter of the Rana of Udaipur, the innocent cause of the war between Jaipur and Jodhpur has been poisoned." It is supposed that the tragedy was enacted by the Raja himself to avert further trouble on the advice of Amir Khan.[61]

Relations with Udaipur

Bapu Sindhia was appointed the new Governor of Mewar and remained there from 1811-17. Ambaji Ingle...who harboured ill-will against the Maharana, once proposed that the two chiefs (Holkar and Sindhia) should divide between themselves the kingdom of Mewar, but Jaswant Rao Holkar rejected the proposal.[62] According to col. Tod.* Sardar Singh Chundawat, the Maharana's envoy in the Sindhia's camp and Baiza Bai, the Sindhia's wife, advised against Ambaji's proposal and so the proposal was dropped. Bapuji Sindhia could do nothing to strengthen his position owing to opposition of Amir Khan, and his deputy Jamshed Khan and the other General of Sindhia, named Jaswant Rao Bhau, so all efforts of Sindhia proved fruitless.

Desire for British Alliance

According to Dr. Mehta "The Maharana in June 1805, sent his emissary Bhairon Baksh to Lord Lake at Mathura, offering to co-operate with the British against the Marathas and later on the Maharana applied for an[63] alliance with the British, and a treaty[64] was concluded and in Delhi on 13th January 1818."

---

59. Tod, *Annals and Antiquities of Rajasthan,* I pp. 539-543, ed. 1920 and *Poona Residency Correspondence,* XIV, No. 51, p. 71.
60. *Ibid.,* No. 39 dated 10-8-1810 Metcalfe to Minto.
61. Mehta P.C., p. 200 and N.B Roy (vide modern review April 1942 thinks murder of Krishna Kumari "the result of a sordid bargain".
62. *Ibid.,* p. 179.

* Tod, *Annals and Antiquities of Rajasthan,* p. 534, F. Note ed. 1920.

63. Quoted by Mehta, p. 179 and also see Tod, *Annals and Antiquities of Rajasthan,* Vol. I, p. 537.
64. *Ibid.,* p. 215, For treaty see Banerjee A.C.

At last, tired of all these happenings the Raja of Jaipur proposed to despatch Deena Ram Bohra and Seth Sawar Das for negotiations with the British. In January 1812, the Raja of Jodhpur also desired a British alliance. In March 1814 Maharaj Kumar Umed Singh, regent of Banswara, also sent Ratan Jeo to solicit the protection of the British Government.

Torn by dissensions among themselves and by internecine fighting among their jagirdars and Sindhia's helplessness to give them any protection, the Rajput princes had now come to the conclusion that they could secure protection from the British alone. In April 1816, Lord Hastings himself wrote to J. Duncan Governor of Bombay, "we entertain a confident expectation that the permanent establishment of a British subsidiary force in the territories of Jaipur would terminate all these quarrels." He urged upon the Governor of Bombay and Henry Russel, Resident at Hyderabad, and Elphinstone, Resident at Poona, to keep an army ready to meet any opposition or hostility from Sindhia.[65] "Sindhia preserved his state at the price of his supremacy in Rajputana and lands around Ajmer."[66]

Kotah

Kotah was the only state in which the administration was efficient. Zalim Singh, the *De facto* ruler of the state was respected both by Amir Khan and Daulat Rao Sindhia and Sindhia's relations with Zalim Singh were cordial. But Zalim Singh was now the first to enter into a treaty with the East India Company.

The Policy of Daulat Rao Sindhia

To conciliate Sindhia, Amir Khan wrote that his only object was to find means to maintain his troops and that this ought not to excite His Highness, jealousy, as they might one day be of service to himself.[67] Sindhia urged him to retire from Rajput states and to serve Holkar faithfully. He further wrote to Bapu Sindhia "to conciliate the Rajputs by every means in his power, and not to discourage them by any conduct which may interrupt the harmony that Sindhia wishes to preserve with them."[68] He

65. *Poona Residency Correspondence,* Vol. XIV.
66. *Oxford History of India,* p. 571, ed. 1958.
67. *Poona Residency Correspondence,* Vol. XIV, No. 270, p. 328 and Malcolm p. 493.
68. *Ibid.,* No. 270, p. 328.

also tried to act with some vigour against Amir Khan, short of actually going to war with him. Daulat Rao succeeded in impressing the British Resident that his policy was only to conciliate the Rajputs and to maintain the status quo and not to form any anti-British coalition.[69]

On 5th November 1817, as we have mentioned in a previous chapter, Daulat Rao Sindhia was obliged to sign a treaty by which he accepted British overlordship over Rajasthan and abandoned all his claims on the Rajput States. Thus, the policy of Daulat Rao Sindhia in respect of the Rajputs was a total failure and the Rajputs came under British control.

Lord Hastings' Policy

With the arrival of Lord Hastings, British Policy towards Indian states took a new turn, namely to detach the Rajput states from the Marathas. Colonel Tod succeeded in winning the Rajputs to the side of the British Government. He proceeded with a right psychological approach to the Rajput States and played upon their sentimental nature.[70] He succeeded where Ambaji Ingle, Bapu Sindhia and Jaswant Rao Bhau had failed. Daulat Rao tried to conciliate the Rajput states, when he discerned the British game, but the depredations of Amir Khan. Shah Mohammad Khan and other mercenaries worked up hatred in the hearts of the Rajputs against the Marathas, and this was exploited by the British diplomats to their advantage.

Cases of the Failure of Daulat Rao Sindhia

The real cause of dissatisfaction of the Rajputs was the inability of Sindhia to protect them against Amir Khan and Holkar and the dishonesty and quarrels of Ambaji, Jaswant Rao Bhau, Bapu Sindhia and Jaggoo Bapu, who had worked as Sindhia's subadars in Rajasthan. Their functions were like those of the British Residents, but they used to interfere constantly in the internal affairs of the states. No special spheres of influence were demarcated between Holkar and Sindhia. The Maratha officers habitually used to misappropriate the tribute money also.

---

69. *Poona Residency Correspondence*, No. 275, p. 353.

70. Crooke writes "He was held in affection and respect by all the upper and middling classes of society." Introduction to Tod I, p. 28, ed. 1920.

It is interesting to trace the cases of this animus between the Marathas and Rajputs. After Baji Rao I, Maratha-Rajput relations were seldom cordial. Constant Maratha interference in Rajput affairs was responsible for the non-co-operation of the Rajputs in the third battle of Panipat. That battle gave a rude shock to the idea of Hindu Pad Padshahi and seriously affected Maratha Rajput amity. Realisation of forced tributes from the Rajputs by Mahadji as regent of the Emperor was a blunder of the first magnitude. Moreover, the battles of Lalsot, Patan, Merta and Nagore exhausted the energies of both the antagonists and brought untold sufferings to Rajasthan and Malwa. They worsened the relations between the two beyond any hope of reconciliation. Daulat Rao Sindhia tried to conciliate the Rajputs in 1816, when it was too late, and in 1818 all the Rajput states accepted the suzerainty of the East India Company.

The consequences of Maratha control over the Rajput states may now be considered. In the words of Sarkar, "Mahadji Sindhia found that he was called upon to play the part of a British Residen governing a protected native State. But unlike the British in the days of their paramountcy, Sindhia had neither the civil service nor the subsidiary force nor even a capable agent from outside at his disposal for getting the work done."[71] Colonel Tod who was sent to enlist the sympathies of the Rajputs for the English, states "Nothing but ruin met the eye-deserted town, roofless houses, and uncultured plains. Wherever the Maratha encamped, annihilation was ensured, it was a habit; and twenty-four hours sufficed to give the most flourishing spot the aspect of a desert."[72]

It is not quite fair to fasten the blame for the decline of the Rajputs decline in this period on the Marathas alone Rot had set in the in most narrow of these gallant people. Their administration was appalling. In fact, all Rajasthan except Kotah, was ruled by the most incompetent Rajas. The policy of the Rajputs themselves was to keep the Sindhia-Holkar feud alive by hook or by crook to play the one against the other and thus evade payment of tribute to either. The absence of any ruler

71. Sarkar, *Fall of the Mughal Empire*, IV, p. 63, ed. 1950.

72. Tod, *Annals and Antiquities of Rajasthan*, I, p. 372, ed. 1950.

of outstanding administrative and military capacity among the Rajput rulers of this period added to their weakness and helplessness. According to Dr. P.C. Mehta, the Marathas failed owing to uncapable officers, factions of nobles, Holkar-Sindhia rivalry and lack of proper checking of accounts.[73]

According to Dr. Raghubir Singh, the Marathas failed to make their establishment permanent on account of the weakness caused by the death of Mahadji, and the exit of foreign generals in 1803 made their position still weaker as the new Maratha Generals were undisciplined and untrained. Amir Khan and other semi-independent soldier chiefs made the task of Sindhia still more difficult. The personal jealousies of the Maratha Generals in Rajasthan and the policy of the Rajputs to keep them burning; and the absence of Sindhia from Rajasthan weakened the position of the Marathas still more, and there was no alternative before Daulat Rao Sindhia except to look helplessly on the disappearance of his power in Rajasthan.[74] Commenting on the condition of Rajasthan, the same writer says, "There was unlimited luxury; and unabashed lust, polygamy and corruption was rampant. Sunk in luxury, wine and opium the Rajputs were like the proverbial frogs in the well. Not to speak of foreign countries, they were even ignorant of the changing politics of their own region.[75] "This was the age of never-ending civil wars and unlimited sexual immorality. Rajasthan and Rajputs lost the sterling qualities of their character and became utterly imbecile and lifeless."[76]

Sarkar has also said "Unfortunately after the death of Ishwari Singh of Jaipur in 1750 and of Bakht Singh of Jodhpur in 1752, the line of warrior Rajas ended."[77] The old Indian method of warfare in which the Rajputs charged in a tumultuous body and engaged in a desperate hand to hand fight with their swords, had proved futile before fire arms.[78] The Rajputs came to be cooped up within their small sterile districts; they had no

73. Mehta P.C. "The Relations between Mewar and the Marathas," p. 204.
74. Dr. Raghubir Singh "Purva Adhunin Rajasthan" p. 201, ed. 1951.
75. *Ibid.*, p. 215.
76. *Ibid.*, p. 262-263 translated from Hindi.
77. Sarkar, *Fall of the Mughal Empire*, Vol. IV, p. 69.

means of advancement left to them except by devouring each other.[79] Concubinage and opium eating contributed to their downfall. "The tragedy of Rajputana in the period embraced in this history was only the result of the modern age bursting upon a sleepy, inert, mediaeval society that could make no attempt to adjust to the necessary change."[80]

CONCLUSION

Further comment on the matter is unnecessary after stating the views of the two eminent historians. J.N. Sarkar and Dr. Raghubir Singh, but even these two historians seem to have based their conclusions largely on the reports of Col. Tod, who painted the Marathas, particularly Daulat Rao Sindhia, in the blackest dye.[81] They seemed to underrate the fact that the mission of col. Tod was to win over the Rajputs to the British side by fanning their vanity and presenting imaginary Maratha atrocities in most exaggerated terms, so that the Marathas and Rajputs might always remain at daggers drawn with each other. It is astonishing that they themselves have highlighted the defects of the Rajputs, but still they regard Daulat Rao as the sole cause of the ruin of the Rajputs. This certainly needs some further comment.

Daulat Rao Sindhia saw the signs of the changing times and began to follow a policy of conciliation with other states even in 1809, as the Resident himself confirmed : "His Highness now appears returning to that temporising policy with regard to foreign states which has for some time characterised this Government."[82] He sent orders to Bapu Sindhia in May 1816 "to conciliate the Rajputs by every means in his power."[83] His attempts to conciliate Amir khan to enter into an alliance with Holkar and to establish diplomatic relations with Nepal, Ranjit Singh and other states have already been mentioned.

---

78. Sarkar, *Fall of the Mughal Empire*, Vol. IV, p. 81.
79. *Ibid.*, p. 71.
80. *Ibid.*, pp. 73-74.
81. Crooke Editor of Tod's book states "He (Tod) was notoriously a partisan of Rajput Princes" (Introduction I, p. 27, ed. 1920) and Dr. Mehta says "Tod...had a...dislike for the doing of the Marathas" p. 218.
82. *Poona Residency Correspondence*, XIV.
83. *Ibid.*, No. 270, p. 329.

Thus, Daulat Rao Sindhia seems to have been fully aware that peace and consolidation were the pressing needs of the time, but there was no positive response from his contemporaries, with the result that all his efforts came to naught. Even his kith and kin and commanders did not co-operate with him. Sarkar asserts, "they (Daulat Rao and his advisers) had whispered conference without finding any remedy."[84] He thought, and perhaps rightly too, that discretion was the better part of valour. There was no wisdom in rushing out like a moth into a burning flame and inviting immediate destruction by having recourse to arms single-handed against the mighty British power. In a joint effort of all the states to resist the company lay unmistakably the surest remedy, which he tried to achieve but found it beyond his reach. He then wisely inclined to the less heroic but securer path of compromise. The policy of the British of setting one power against another defied all attempts at unity. Besides, the outlook of the rulers of the age was not yet inspired by nationalism. They were still wallowing in the slough of parochialism and self-centred intrigues. Thus, ended Maratha control over Delhi and Rajasthan and therewith also went the honour and distinction of Sindhia as the Vicegerent of the Mughal Empire.

84. *Poona Residency Correspondence*, Introduction, Editor (Sarkar's Note), p. V.

8

Daulat Rao Sindhia's Civil and Military Administration

We have gone through the relations of Daulat Rao Sindhia with other Indian States in the previous chapters. A civilized Government, however, ought to be judged not so much by its territorial extent or its diplomatic record, as by its administrative achievements of value for the people.

The first thing to note in this connection is that the dominions over which Sindhia ruled were a congeries of territories, not a geographically or politically unified state.

First, there were the tributary Rajput States of Rajputana, namely Jaipur, Jodhpur and Udaipur, which necessitated the employment of a large army to coerce them when necessary and to employ suitable persons to deal with them in ordinary times. Ambaji, De Boigne and De Perron functioned during Daulat Rao Sindhia's reign as military and civil agents of Sindhia in Rajasthan.

Another class of territories subordinate to Sindhia and bound to help him in emergency consisted of such states as those of Begum Samroo and the Jat States and the State of Kotah. Apart from a small nucleus of lands around Ujjain, which had been held by his family ever since Baji Rao I commissioned Ranoji Sindhia to collect the revenues of a part of Malwa on his behalf, the rest of the lands under his control were acquired at different times and sprawled disjointedly all over Malwa and Central India. The later capital of this territorial complex has upto our own days been known as 'Lashker' or 'Cantonment.'

A Military Hegemony

This name for the capital provides a clue to the nature of the Government of Sindhia's State, for it was primarily a military hegemony rather than a regular civil state. Apart from the small internal of the home territories in Malwa, the other lands over which Daulat Rao ruled were some dependent principalities like Bhopal, Raghogarh and Chanderi, Sardana, Hathras and Mursan.

"Mulkgiri"

The Marathas acted on the principle of "Mulkgiri," which might be described as military overlordship of territories from which they had collected "Chauth and sardesmukhi, since Shivaji's days, but took no part in their civil administration. To realise these exactions and tributes, officers combining civil and military functions were appointed in or near all such states.

In Delhi and Agra, alone where Daulat Rao Sindhia functioned as vicegerent of the Mughal Emperor, he had to maintain the traditional Mughal administration. Mathura had been the northern headquarters of Mahadji and being surrounded by Jat States, a considerable army was kept there. Agra was ruled by a Qiladar or Governor of the fort with a contingent of troops to help the local civil authorities in civil administration.

The civil administration of Delhi remained in the hands of Maratha Subedars and the Military administration was entrusted to a Qiladar who was independent of the Subedar of Delhi, but his rank was inferior to that of the Subedar.

Mahadji was friendly to Sikhs, but he had to keep a large force to guard the frontiers and had to post the best of his Generals in the Punjab for this purpose. Under such circumstances armies marched and counter-marched as often to collect revenue as to curb disturbances.

Principal Divisions

Thus, surrounded by refractory chiefs and hereditary jagirdars, it was very difficult for Daulat Rao to keep up a high standard of administration. After the Second Maratha War when he lost the Punjab and Delhi and Agra Provinces, his territories were still divided in three Subas of Gwalior and Gohad, Malwa and Rajasthan (Ajmer and Mewar), but after 1818, he surrendered Rajasthan and Ajmer to the East India Company. Thereafter only two provinces Gwalior and Gohad and Malwa remained under his control. In Malwa the chief of the Suba was called Sar-Subah.[1] His duty was to supervise the work, of Subas, *i.e.*, District Magistrates. Only a part of Malwa however, was under Sindhia, and there too there were numerous petty Rajput States differing in race, rank and antiquity and creating constant trouble in the administration. The States of Raghogarh, Narwar, Chanderi and Shivpur were, as has been shown already, a constant headache. In addition to these recalcitrant chiefs, the Pindaris were a permanent menace to the maintenance of law order. In practice, however, Daulat Rao Sindhia exercised little control over these feudatories. In cities like Ujjain, Gwalior, Mandsaur and Bhilsa administrative control was more real, but the interiors of these districts were in a state of endemic anarchy owing to the internecine quarrels of his Rajput, Bhil, Gond and Afghan feudatories and the depredations of the Pindaris.

Nobility

Whatever regular civil administration existed was in the hands of a feudal nobility, and a brief review of this class will not be out of place here.

At the apex of the social ladder, stood this nobility or the jagirdars, from among whom were recruited the bureaucratic personnel of Sindhia's Government, both on the civil and military side. Appointed by the chief to administer various territories, they usually misappropriated large sums from the local revenues. Ambaji was richer than his master. He is said to have amassed a fortune of more than one crore of rupees. The sme was the case with De Boigne, who amassed £4 lacs.[2] De Perron made a personal fortune of 50 million francs.[3] Louis Bourquien and Lesteantau misappropriated the treasure found with the Mughal Emperor and Ghulam Kadir respectively. Besides, these nobles were addicted to wine and women and were ruthless tyrants in their dealings with the people.[4] Persons

1. *Gwalior State Gaztt.* Vol. I, 1908, Heading Administration, pp. 89-100.
2. Crompton 92, 68.
3. Martin, Wellesley's Despatches III, XXXI, Martineau : General Perron and Crompton.
4. Quite a few old persons detailed the miseries of their fore-fathers at the hands of the jagirdars. In the words of one of my peons, named Dhanraj, "these jagirdars used to catch (my parents) for the purpose of forced labour. My parents used to hide under the trees, bushes

at the top were immersed in the pleasures of life, while the poor spent their lives in tears and tribulations.

Incompetent Civil Service

It is, therefore, obvious that the most serious defect of Sindhia's Government in Gwalior and Malwa was that he did not possess an honest, public-spirited and competent civil service. The feudatory chiefs were illiterate or almost so, and so they were incapable of checking the accounts of their civil servants, though in Gwalior state accounts were kept in Marathi. Nor would they undergo the drudgery of calling their collectors to account. The result was that their entire revenue administration was left to the Brahman Diwans and Prabhu clerks, who were notorious for their love of illegal gains and ignorant of the economic law that the revenue cannot be increased simply by squeezing the peasantry. De Boigne wrote "The Pundits who have the management of all business of Sindhia's court will never put aside old way of embezzling the half of what is to pass their hands."

The Sindhia Government had to pay dearly for the incompetence and inefficiency of the Maratha civil officers.[5] The actual collections were really one-tenth of the standard revenue in many places.[6]

Absence of a Middle Class

Eighteenth century society in India had one great lacuna in its collective structure; namely, the absence of a middle class between the feudal nobility at the top and the common people at the bottom, over which the former tyrannised Maratha polity in general, suffered from this defect.

Daulat Rao Sindhia's Civil Administration

Like other Maratha princes, Daulat Rao Sindhia was theoretically subordinate to the Raja of Satara as well as to the Peshwa, and to the Mughal Emperor, but the Mughal Emperor Shah Alam II, was as subordinate to Daulat Rao as were the

---

and cows and to run away as soon as they heard about the arrival of horseman. If they were caught they were forced to work for two or three days on scanty meals to keep them alive."

5. De Boigne quoted by Sarkar Vol. IV, pp. 113-14.
6. Historical Papers of Gwalior, 607.

Wadiar Rajas of Mysore to Haider Ali, and Ram Raja and his successors at Satara to successive Peshwas at Poona. Thus this state of affairs involved no obvious and violent break with traditions and the supposed overlordship of the Chhatrapati and the Peshwa gave a varnish of legality to what might be regarded otherwise as usurpation of authority by Sindhia and other Maratha chiefs at the expense of the former.

Sindhia's Powers

Like that of Mughal Emperor, Daulat Rao's authority knew no bounds in his own territories. He was an all-powerful autocrat. He had, of course, made no innovations or set up any new institutions. He generally followed the established practices and also respected the local customs and laws of each region under his sway. All ministers were his creatures and he was the fountain head of justice, honour and executive authority. His administration was modelled on that of the Poona court.

The Ministers

Next to Maharaja, ranked his chief minister, called Karbari. The Diwan was the principal executive officer and controlled other officials. He was assisted by the Phadnavis or chief accountant the financial officer (the 'Potnis' or treasurer) the Chitnis or political secretary, and the Sabnis or Daftardar, who kept records, and some other subordinate officers.[7] Owing to the vacillating policy of the Maharaja, no minister was able to work under him for a considerable time. Maratha Govt. being a semi-military institution, all officers of the state, including the Ministers, were under an obligation to perform military service also. The Viceroys and Subedars in the provinces also functioned both as civil as well as military officers.

Other Central Ministers

There were several other minor ministers at the centre designated as :

(1) The Mazumdar, who ranked next to the chief minister, and used to check all orders issued and acts done under the authority of the ruler.

(2) The Shikkanavis, who kept the royal seal and state documents.

---

7. *Gwalior State Gaztt.* pp. 89-92, ed. 1908.

(3) The Phadnavis, who signed the grants and deeds issued.

(4) The Pagnis who kept the state accounts of pay.

(5) The Peshawar or the Bakshi, who like the Mughal officer of that time, was the paymaster of the forces.

Household Officers

Apart from these officers, there were other officers, who ministered to the needs of the royal household. They were:

1. The Steward or officer holding charge of the royal ward robe and jewellery.

2. The Havildar Khasgi Paga or commander of Household troops.

3. The Jamadar Dak in charge of intelligence.

4. The Faujdar Khas (Elephants)	Incharge of the Maharaja's animals
5. The Faujdar (Camels)	
6. The Faujdar (Horses)	

Besides, there used to be a host of minor officials like Munshies, clerks, Harkaras, etc.

The Diwans

The first Diwan of Daulat Rao was Jeoba Dada Bakshi, who died in 1796 and was succeeded by Aba Chitnis, who was dismissed owing to the influence of the Bais. Balloba Pagnis became minister thereafter.[8] Soon after the marriage of Daualt Rao with Baiza Bai, Surji Rao Ghatge became supreme. But he had to be dismissed, owing to the intrigues of the Widows. To conciliate them Balloba was again installed as minister, but was finally dismissed in 1800.[9]

Anna Vithal Mahadeo thereafter came to power.[10] For a few years Anna worked as minister and after a short time Mahadeo and Jaggoo Bapu again secured the favour of Daulat Rao Sindhia. Sarji Rao regained influence, but British diplomats hated him, and Ambaji was restored to favour in 1805, as the result of a compromise between Ambaji and Surji Rao. Both died in 1809,[11]

---

8. *Poona Residency Correspondence,* XI 234, 238 Khare X, p. 4814.
9. *Ibid.,* IV no. 239.
10. *Ibid.,* XI no. 2 and 5.
11. *Ibid.,* no. 55, no. 286, p. 431.

and Devji Gaule became Minister. He was succeeded by Gokul Parokh, who remained in office for a long time. Babaji Patankar and Hindu Rao Ghatge came to power after 1818, but they remained obscure figures, because British power became supreme after the debacle of the Maratha power in 1818.

Criticism

One of the main causes of the weakness of Sindhia's administration was the lack of any continuity of policy and stability of its personnel. The frequent change of ministers reflected the shifting and indolent temperament of Daulat Rao Sindhia. Malcolm accounts for this in this way : "He continues as devoted as ever to his amusements and seems willing to give the fullest powers and the most implicit confidence to any minister, who will take the burden from his shoulders, and leaves him to the uninterrupted pursuit of his favourite occupations, among which the chase is the principal. There is, however, a boldness and resolution in his character which has the effect of making those in whose hands he trusts the administration act in a very guarded manner, as they are perfectly aware that the fact of their conduct being exempt from scrutiny arises from the indolence and not from the weakness of their chief, who has, in more instances than one, shown he can assert himself and punish those whom he conceives to have abused his confidence."[12] Daulat Rao's administration possessed neither the vigour of that of Haider Ali — "a vigour hitherto unexampled in India"[13] nor that of Ranjit Singh. Generally, only one person at a time among the Ministers was prominent but occasionally, as in 1809, Babu Rao Angaria, S.R. Ghatge and Ambaji jointly looked after the ministerial functions.[14]

The Viceroys of Daulat Rao Sindhia

Daulat Rao Sindhia continued the system of his predecessor of appointing a Deputy or a Viceroy in each region of his principal territories. During Mahadji's regime, Gopal Rao Bhau was his Deputy or Viceroy and De Boigne his Supreme

12. *Poona Residency Correspondence,* XI no. I, Malcolm to Wellesley 1-5, 1804.
13. N.K. Sinha : Haider Ali, p. 235.
14. *Poona Residency Correspondence,* XI no. 276, p. 409.

commander in northern India. This practice seems to have been borrowed from the Peshwa, who appointed Sar Subadars to look after their possessions in the north. These Viceroys had full powers to transfer the local officers and to assign different posts to the commanders, subedars and local officers. To realise tribute, to maintain peace and order and to fight battles were also their functions. Gopal Bhau and his army fought at Lakheri against Holkar in the absence of Mahadji and appointed commanders in the Punjab to check Sikh raids. Subject to the control of the Maharaja, these Viceroys were supreme in all local affairs. After the Second Maratha War Sindhia lost his northern possessions. However, Bapu Sindhia and Jaswant Rao Bhau, functioned as his viceroys in his dominions in Malwa and Rajasthan, Devji Gauli at Gwalior, and Babu Rao at Ujjain. Though their powers were as ample as those of the Viceroys of earlier times, their Jurisdiction was smaller in comparison.

Subedars

Subedars and Sar-Subedars were appointed by Daulat Rao Sindhia from among his most reliable and trusted officers. But they occasionally acted contrary the orders of the Central Government, and sometime they had to be severally punished. Devji Gauli was sentenced to death and Babu Rao Angria, later Subedar of Ujjain, was dismissed. The functions of a Subedar were to maintain peace and order in their Jurisdictions, to realise revenue or tribute therefrom and to punish persons who defied the central Government.

Kiladars

Most large towns and places of strategic importance had forts and the army used to be garrisoned under a Kiladar, who used to help the civil authorities in times of any danger or uprising. These Kiladars were usually very reliable persons. Lakhwa Dada worked as Kiladar of Agra, Ambaji of Gwalior and Jaswant Lad Asirgah; and the first two achieved high political positions by their devotion to their duties.

Village Administration

The basic territorial unit was the self-contained village. Munroe wrote that "every village is a kind of little republic with the Patel as the head of it." Each village had a headman, called the Patel, who combines in himself the functions of a revenue officer. Magistrate, Judge and representative of the village vis-a-vis the Central Government. His office was generally hereditary and he used to get a fixed percentage of the revenue from the village. He was responsible for the peace and welfare of the village and generally used to take pride in its progress and prosperity. Another local officer was the Kulkarni or village clerk and record keeper but in some villages there used to be no separate Kulkarni, want of village were supplied by 12 artisans called 12 Boaluts and 12 servants called 12 allotes.

These were helped by Mahar who functioned as a watchman and chaguas who acted like Patwari.

Village Officers

The Registrar, called the Qanoongo, used to keep the records of a large village and was allowed a percentage of usually 1 or 2% on the revenue and also a small charge on the cultivator and tradesman. The surveyor, called 'Mirdha', was generally a Muslim. The Patel or Headman was responsible to the Darbar for good cultivation and enjoyed some land according to the size of the village and a fee on cultivable land. He was also entitled to impose fines according to local customs. He collected land revenue and was a medium between the villagers and the Government. The Patwari kept the records of a small village and generally enjoyed land revenue. The Bullai kept information about all persons and transactions and worked as the Patel's spy. He worked as a guide to travellers and was a government witness in Police cases. The parsee or priest of the village possessed some land and got Dakshina on the occasion of sanskar. The Chowkidar worked as the village watchman and was paid small sums as gifts and a charge on travellers and cattle. There were paggees whose business was to trace thieves. They were provided with a small plot of land and some dues on cultivators. There were some villages reserved personally for the king and his relations, as for instance, Paury was allotted to Bala Bai, Shahajahanpur to Maina Bai and later on to Baiza Bai.

Sukhbasis were farmers, who resided and cultivated land for a limited period.[15]

---

15. *Gwalior district Gaz.* Heading Administration, by C.E. Luard ed. 1908 and Gwalior State Records and Shivpuri Distt. Records.

Administration at the District Level

The entire territory of the state was divided in Sarkars or Governments each, Sarkar comprising ten to forty districts, each district having 50 to 300 villages. The district or Zila was in charge of a Suba who was the chief administrative officer, and a Paragna or sub-division was in charge of a Kamvisdar, who was the highest authority in all departments of the Pargana and was assisted by a Naib Kamvisdar. Gwalior, Bhind, Shivpur, Tomargarh, Bhilsa, Narwar, Isagarh, Ujjain, Mandsor, Shahjahanpur or Shahjapur and Amjhera were the main districts.[16] Bhilsa district had about 750 villages, but this was an extraordinary case.

A district was divided into Taluqas or Tappas. The lands in each Tappa were measured, including the space occupied by tanks, wells and houses, and the whole record was prepared in the district office as well as in the Phadnavis' office at the centre. The taluk officer, called Chaudhary, Mandloe or Zamindar was also hereditary. His duty was to preserve law and order in his Jurisdiction and to help Government officers in the realization of state dues. He received a petty commission of one or two rupees from every village in the district and a trifling levy in kind from the traders such as a blanket from the weaver, oil from the oil man and so forth.[17]

Jagirs

The feudal basis of the entire structure of the Maratha State involved permanent or temporary alienation of large areas as jagirs, saranjams and Inam or Nankar grants to private persons. Jagirs were assigned to nobles and hereditary Rajput Rajas for their maintenance. Saranjams (temporary land grants) were granted to military personnel. Inam or Nankar (free gifts) lands were assigned to persons, who had rendered official or personal service to the ruler, and khairat or lands revenue was assigned for charitable purpose to temples, pathshalas or religious

---

16. *Gwalior district Gaz.* Heading Administration, by C.E. Luard ed. 1908 and Gwalior State Records and Shivpuri Distt. Records.
17. For details see Gwalior State papers and Jankins Report 1827 about Nagpur also quoted in *Journal of Indian History,* Vol. XLIII, Part II August 1965 serial no. 128 Article by Dr. R.M. Sinha, pp. 633-645 and Elphinstone report p. 59, *Selections from the records at the East India House,* Vol. IV (1826).

persons. Feudalization weakened the financial position of Daulat Rao Sindhia.[18]

Land Revenues

Land tax was usually realised in cash and only exceptionally in kind. It was realised generally in three instalments, keeping in view the yield of a crop and some days of grace were allowed to the farmer for payment.

Taxation in Cities

There were no fixed taxes in the cities and sometimes rich persons had to pay the officers and the prince according to their demands. But the Bankers were very powerful and the tyranny of the officers and princes was checked by the collective influence and strength of the wealthy citizens.

Sources of Revenue

The sources of revenue of the Sindhia Government were similar to those of the Maratha Government at Poona or of the Mughal Government at Delhi and Agra, since the Marathas followed the Marathi adage : "Do nothing new, do not change the old". So the shell of the government remained Mughal, though the core underwent some changes in the latter period.

The most important item of the Maratha revenue was the Chauth. The chauth from earliest days was sub-divided into the following shares :

(a) Babati or 25% reserved for the Raja or ruler.

(b) Moksha or 60% granted to Maratha Sardars and chiefs for the maintenance of their troops.

(c) 6% Sahotra granted to the pant Sachiv.

(d) Nadgunda or 3% awarded to various persons at the ruler's pleasure.

Originally, the Marathas used to collect Chauth only from dependent states, but it was continued even when these states were incorporated in the Maratha State. Three quarters of the chauth continued to be given in specified proportions to different individuals, as for instance, in the case of the Raja of Narwar, Chanderi and Sheopur etc.

---

18. For its effect on Marathas see Rajiwade, Marathaohen Ithasanchis Sadhen Vol. II.

Land Revenue

The second important head of state revenue was the assessment upon village lands. Theoretically, the assessment was supposed to be based on a careful survey of the cultivated area, the lands themselves being divided into three main classes. Allowance was also made for the nature and quality of the crop and the facilities existing for irrigation. The assessment was payable either in cash or in kind, and it was generally recognised that remission of the assessment and the advances of money and grain (Tagai or Toqavi) were to be granted to the peasantry in seasons of draught and distress. "Theoretically indeed, the Maratha land revenue was favourable to the interest of the cultivator."[19]

Method of Assessment

The assessment varied according to the soil and the crop and whether it was irrigated or unirrigated land, but generally the land tax was not less than one-fourth and not more than one-half of the yield. In Shahjahanpur land tax varied from Rs. 1.50 to Rs. 4.50 per bigha, according to unirrigated or irrigated land respectively. Land which produced sugarcane was taxed from Rs. 4/- to Rs. 7 per bigha and the tax on opium was a bit higher.

Realisation of Taxes

The collectors of revenue used to be transferred every year. The expenses of collection generally did not exceed 20% of the revenue.[20]

Miscellaneous Taxes

The third item of Maratha revenues consisted of miscellaneous taxes such as a tax equal to one years' rent in ten years on the lands held by the Deshmukh and Deshpande, a triennial cess on occupants of land reserved for the village Maharas, a tax on land irrigated from wells, a house tax on all except Brahmans and village officers, an annual fee for testing of weights and measures, a tax on marriages and remarriages of widows, taxes on sheep and she-buffaloes, a pasture fee, a tax on cultivation on river beds, a succession duty, a town duty

19. *Cambridge History of India*, Vol. V, p. 398, ed. 1929.
20. Malcolm, *Political History of India*, C.I. 11, p. 51, ed. 1832.

and duty on sale of houses, etc, Chhapai *i.e.*, a fee for the stamping of cloth and other merchandise was also realised.

Karja Patti or Jasti Patti, which was equivalent to one year's income of the individual tax-payer, was also realised when necessary from all land holders owing to financial stringency of the government.

Customs

The fourth source of revenue was customs duties divided into two classes. "Mohatarfa" or tax on trades and professions and 'zakat' or duty on purchase and sale, octroi and ferry charges. At every place, for taxes there were outposts called Nakas and Nakedars who collected the toll on behalf of the State.

Other Sources of Revenue

A small revenue was derived from forests by the sale of permits to cut timber for building purposes or fuel; by the sale of grass, bamboos, fuel and will honey, and by fees for pastures in reserved areas and on materials used for industrial purposes. Licences for private mints to bankers, and coining of money at central mints also brought profit to the treasury.

Expenditure

The main items of expenditure were defence, *i.e.*, maintenance of military forces, the Maharaja's personal household expenses, religious expenses, such as sadabrat or alms, festivals, maintenance of police and construction of roads and buildings, etc. Education expenditure was considered as religious expenditure and only alms were provided for that purposes.

The revenue of Daulat Rao Sindhia showed improvement. In 1819, his income was Rs. 1,27,68,459 and in 1824, it was Rs. 1,43,20,227.

Law and Justice

Justice was administered in much simple ways the community was left to its own resources to get the disputes settled.[21]

---

21. Dr. V.G. Dighe article Maratha Political System, *Theory and Practical. Studies in Indian History,* ed. 1668 Kolhapur India.

Civil cases used to be compromised in the village through influential persons or matters were settled by arbitration or through Panchayats. For the local Panchayat, both parties used to select two persons each and the fifth person was co-opted by these four persons. The greatest advantage of the Maratha system of justice was that usually cases were decided in a very short time. Cases did not linger on for years, as was the case under the British regime or as it is even now. It was also free, impartial, non-technical, easily available and cheap. Civil cases, when men of ranks were the suitors, or which involved a large property, were generally referred to the ministers and submitted to their arbitration, or tried by special Panchayats. Petty crimes and disputes were referred to the Patel, who possessed the power of sentencing offenders to whipping. Disputes of greater importance or concerning different villages were referred to the revenue officers, who either settled them themselves or constituted a Panchayat for their disposal. The Sardars adjusted the disputes of their own servants. Seths and Mahajans used to decide their mutual disputes through their own caste Panchayats. The Panchayat was thus a highly respected institution. "The Panchayats" writes Elphinstone "were more frequently named by the parties. The members of the Panchayats received no fee, but the winner of the suit made them openly a present for their pains."[22]

More emphasis was laid on rendering equitable justice than on technicalities of the law. There were no lawyers to complicate matters. In both civil and criminal matters, decisions were based upon custom and upon injunctions of the Hindu Shastras and the Muslim Shariat. In civil cases, the main object aimed at was amicable settlement and usually cases were either decided by compromise or through arbitration or through the Panchayats. The most important cases used to go to the Maharaja himself in appeal. In doing justice, the traditions of Vikramaditya and Jahangir were considered as the ideal, and it was believed that if any injustice, was done by the Raja he would surely be punished by God. The current legal adage was "Raja Kare so Nayaya," which means that the king's decree was infallible. The king, too, always took care to follow the principles of

22. Kincaid and Parsnis, *History of Maratha People*, p. 243.

justice except in political cases or in those cases in which he himself was interested. Daulat Rao Sindhia punished even his maternal uncle, Babu Rao Angria, and removed him from Subadarship, when a complaint was made against him.

Torture was usually applied to force criminals to their guilt. Flogging was the common punishment for petty crimes, but theft and immorality was considered as great crimes, and a sentence of mutilation was awarded in such cases. Imprisonment was awarded in comparatively few cases. Prisoners used to be kept in forts, and particularly dangerous criminals like Karim Khan were kept in dungeons. Sometimes, prisoners were freed on the occasion of festivals, etc. Capital punishment could be given by Maharaja only, but this rigid rule was usually not followed. Brahmins were punished with fine only.[23] It is refreshing to point out that Maratha justice has been praised by English writers themselves. "The fact must be admitted that among themselves, within the confines of the self-contend ancestral village, the peasantry did obtain a fair medium of rude justice from the village Panchayat."[24] This arrangement survived well violent crimes were rare.

Comparison of the British and Indian judicial system

It will be interesting to state the opinion of some writers about the British and Maratha judicial system. According to Kincaid "There were two innovations that Elphinstone especially dreaded, the establishment of English law courts, and the attempts to spread Christianity." He adds "the English lawyers had evolved so intricate and unintelligible system that Bentham compared law of England to a poisonous parasite fastened to on OAK and asserted that it was stifling the very life of country to which it clings."[25] They add "The Indian who was unfortunate as to get entangled in a law suit might dream himself lucky, if he escaped with a single rag to cover his nakedness or he lived long enough to see its conclusion."[26] Colebroke states "a traveller riding through a village, saw its population fleeing panic stricken

---

23. *Gwalior State Gaztt,* Vol. I, Heading Administration, ed. 1908.
24. *Cambridge* V; p. 390, ed. 1929 and Kincaid pp. 233-34.
25. Kincaid and Parasnis, *History of the Maratha People,* Oxford Press. p. 233. 1925 XI, p. 233.
26. *Ibid.,* 234.

through a jungle. He assumed that they dreaded the expected arrival of Lake's forces. The peasants assured him that it was not so. It was something much worse. It was the 'Adalat' that was coming. They could have born with stoic resignation the approach of British arms; but they were fleesing, sickling and unmannered at the rumoured advent of British justice."[27] The religious danger proved illusory...the legal peril proved more real."[28] According to Tone "British Government destroyed the most ancient institution of the country, the village community, the miniature republics of Munroe and introduced "new" British system within the reach only of those, who had the longest purse to pay for the stamp dues, the court process and the unending principle of legal advice."[29] It can be safely asserted that if the maxim "Justice delayed, is justice denied" is true and if cheapness, simplicity is also virtue of the system, Maratha justice can be rated superior to the British justice. There were no arrears of cases while now in 2004, more than 3 crores are pending and are in arrears from many years.

Police Arrangement

Under Maratha rule, the village Patel was the unit of the Police force also, as being responsible for law and order in the village. He was helped by the Chaughula, the Kulkarni and generally by the villagers themselves. But his chief assistant was the watchman or Mahar. It was the latter's duty to keep watch at night, scrutinise strangers, and report suspicious characters to the Patel. When a theft was committed, it was the Mahar's duty to detect the thief.

Over the headman was the Subadar, who kept a corps of 'Sibandies' or irregular infantry and a small body of regular horse. There were also 'Tapasnavis'[30] or C.I.D. men whose duty was not only to detect crime but to prevent it by super-vigilance. "This system, rudimentary though it seems, worked admirably."[31]

---

27. Kincaid and Parasnis, *History of the Maratha People,* Oxford Press, p. 234.
28. Colebroke : *Elpihnstone,* Vol. II p. 131.
29. Tone, *Institutions of the Maratha People,* p. 75.
30. Forest, pp. 305-6 and Tone, *Institution of the Maratha People,* p. 76.
31. Kincaid and Parasnis, *History of the Maratha People,* p. 237.

Under Daulat Rao, the Police system reflected a mixture of Mughal and Maratha practices. Police arrangements were based on the doctrine of "setting a thief to catch a thief." The village watchman was assisted in the detection of crime by groups or gangs of hereditary criminal tribesman like the Grasias and Bhils, etc. Aboriginal tribes, like Saharies and Bhils, were notorious thieves but their leaders had to answer to the Patel, if any untoward event happened in the village. Watchmen and heads of these tribes were held responsible for tracing criminals or to compensate the sufferer. Whenever dacoities or serious crimes took place, the villagers were helped by Sihbandies, or irregular infantry, from the neighbouring hill forts.

The kotwal's duties were based on the model of the Kotwal of the Mughal days. The urban police was composed of foot police, mounted police, watchmen and trackers and spies from the criminal tribes, who were very efficient in this task. Night rounds were a usual feature of the routine of the police officers. People were not allowed to go outside their houses after 10 P.M. Special care was taken to keep a watch on gambling houses and brothels, as these were considered to be the strongholds of criminals. A strict watch was kept on new arrivals in sarais and Dharmshalas also, for the purpose.[32] With these police arrangements, Daulat Rao Sindhia's dominions ordinarily enjoyed greater peace in comparison to other states.

Military Administration

Since Shivaji's time, the character of Maratha armies had changed considerably. The cavalry had become its main arm and the infantry had come to be manned almost wholly by the 'Purvias,' *i.e.*, persons living in Oudh (U.P.). The artillery was manned mostly by Europeans.

The highest military commander was, of course, the Maharaja himself, and on critical and decisive occasions, he personally led the army to the battle-field. Daulat Rao Sindhia was personally brave, but he was not such a great general as Jaswant Rao Holkar or Ranjit Singh. Next to the Maharaja was the Bakshi, who was both Commander-in-chief and Paymaster of the forces.[33]

32. Tone, Sen, *Gwalior State Records and Shivpuri Court Records*, Malcolm C.I.

33. *Gwalior State Gaztt*, pp. 89-100.

The Viceroy of the North, or the Deputy, was next higher in command of the armies Gopal Bhau and Lakhwa Dada, Ambaji and De Perron all often functioned as such, as under the Mansabdari system of Akbar, the commanders were responsible for maintenance of their armies. Usually particular lands or districts were assigned to commanders for this purpose. This was a fatal mistake, as it made the commanders semi-independent, and if they happened to be dishonest, they revolted against their chief, as for instance Lakhwa Dada rebelled against Sindhia, and Ambaji and De Perron proved treacherous. Sometimes these commanders used to clash with one another[34] and the armies of the respective commanders used to fight with one another. Jean Baptiste and Jaswant Rao Bhau fought with one another.

Besides the regular army, there were small contingents under the petty local Rajas also. Sometimes they also accompanied Daulat Rao Sindhia on his campaigns.

The Pindaris, of whom Karim Khan, Wasil Mohd and Cheetu were the most famous, served, as has been pointed out earlier, rather as irregular auxiliaries. They were very useful for guerilla warfare. In addition to the Pindaris, the Bhils, the Grasia chiefs and other abori-ginal tribes used to help the regular armies in wars.

The Army[35]

The Army of Daulat Rao Sindhia was classified into four divisions. (1) Cavalry, (2) Infantry, (3) Artillery and (4) Navy. Both Marathas and Musselmans were employed in the cavalry. The Infantry was in the main manned by the Purvias, a few Rajputs and the Jats. The Artillery was under the command of European officers like De Boigne and De Perron. Daulat Rao Sindhia got his victories largely with its help and that of the European officers, though they deceived him on several crucial occasions. Lord Lake wrote after the victory of Loswari in 1803: "All the sepoys of the enemy fought exceedingly well, and if they had been commanded by French officers, the event would have been extremely doubtful."

Sindhia's army, like other contemporary Indian armies,

---

34. *Poona Residency Correspondence,* XI no. 264, Reports Fight between S.R. Ghatge and Bala Rao Ingle, Similarly Baptiste and Bhau also fought with one another.

35. *Ibid.,* XIV Duff III 256 Pearse 249.

had no engineering service. According to Dr. Sen, "even for crossing rivers, they had to remain at the mercy of the local low caste boatsmen." This proved to be a serious handicap. Arthur Wellesley chose the rainy season for his war against Sindhia, because he had coracles made to carry his army across rivers, while Daulat Rao Sindhia had no such means of transport. Sindhia's armies were normally garrisoned in forts under the qiladars, as already pointed out.

The total strength of Daulat Rao Sindhia's army was about 45,000 before the Second Maratha War. In the battle of Hadapsor, his army numbered about 84,000 men, 68,000 cavalry and 1,000 artillery.[36] There is some difference of opinion about the actual strength of his army at the battle of Assaye. Arthur Wellesley estimated that it numbered about 50,000 and P.E. Roberts corroborates the statement.[37] It is variously estimated at Laswari by writers like Grant Duff, Skinner, Khare, and in the narratives of Hindu clerks, but the report of John Poster's diary, who was lord Lake's Quarter Master General that their strength was of 13 battalions seems reliable.[38] There is doubt about the actual strength of the Deccani troopers. Khare in his despatches[39] records it to be about 2,000 Deccani troopers and fifteen battalions. In 1817, the army consisted of 14,250 horses, 15,750 foot, 140 guns, 1,500 gunners, *i.e.*, 31,500 men.

At Sabalgarh, Daulat Rao Sindhia's army was about 9,000 besides 20,000 Pindaries and 18 battalions with 140 guns, and Baptiste had 10 battalions and 64 guns.[40] In 1814 Sindhia's forces consisted of 14,280 horses, 16,260 foot and 140 guns.[41]

---

36. Sarkar, *Fall of the Mughal Empire*, Vol. IV, p. 307. Dr. Sen administrative...and Military system of the Marathas, Asiatic Annual Register for 1803, Cromton pp. 979-281, Mohan S.F. 109-110, Khare XIV nos. 6465-6471, Holkar Kaifyat, pp. 94-95.

37. Roberts P. *History of British India*, p. 257, ed. 1945.

38. *Elphinstone,* I 80, Khare XIV 679. Gulgule, 15th October, *Gurwood Second,* 527, No. X.

39. Khare no 7931, XVI.

    Not Resident Collins gives a total of 16,360 Siladar 1725 Paigah, 10,000 pindaris. The entire army in Malwa and Hindustan consisted of 15,000 men. He has also given the names of chief officers of the army, see *Poona Residency Correspondence,* XI No. 94, pp. 150.

40. *Poona Residency Correspondence,* XI, No. 94, pp. 150-51.

41. Capt. Sydenham Political Agent of Berar in 1814 Memoirs.

Forts

Much reliance was placed on forts, though they have lost their importance in modern warfare. Daulat Rao Sindhia's cavalry was divided as usual between Bargiras and Silledars. All soldiers had to furnish their own weapons except the Pagahsor Household troops of the Maharaja who were supplied everything by the State.

Arms

The Marathas horsemen generally used to wear a pair of tight breeches covering the knee, a turban, a frock of quilted cotton and a piece of cloth round the waist with which they generally girded their swords. Usually, horsemen were also armed with shields and swords, but their favourite and national weapon was the long spear. A certain of each cavalry regiment used to carry matchlocks.

Maratha soliders used to wear ornaments like gold rings, earrings and even necklaces and used to keep long moustaches, which was considered as a mark of distinction. They were experts in fighting with the spear and used the sword only when the spear broke, but these weapons proved of no value when they had to face an adversary equipped with fire arms.

General character of the Army

Sindhia's army had now assumed a professional instead of national character. A huge army founded on internal strife and dissensions was not calculated to give stability to the state; and ultimately lack of cohesion induced by this policy contributed largely to the downfall of the Maratha confederacy.[42] The same view has been put forward by R.D. Bannerjee.[43]

Discipline and Payment

Shivaji always maintained strict discipline in the army and did not permit anything which might weaken its morales, but Sindhia's forces were ill-disciplined, not well paid and inefficient. Daulat Rao Sindhia had lost the best part of his dominions and best commanders in the Second Maratha War, and was unable

---

42. Cambridge V, p. 394.
43. R.P. Bannerjee, *History of Orissa,* Vol. II p. 265, ed. 1921 and also British Relations with Nagpur State in 18th Century, p. 197.

to pay his forces regularly. On account of this, he had to face dharna, and some times even revolts as in 1822 at Isagarh,[44] and at Chanderi.[45]

Defects of Sindhia's Military System and cause of his defeat

It seems strange that the Maratha military system so efficiently organised by Shivaji, which proved superior to the Mughal armies, should have failed so miserably under Daulat Rao against the British forces.

In the first place, Daulat Rao's army failed to keep pace with the times, and proved a failure against the musketeers of the British forces, even in guerilla warfare.

Europeanisation of the Army

Again, Europeanisation of the army also did not help Daulat Rao, because his European Generals proved traitors.[46] They were also generally no match in training and capacity for British officers like Lord Lake and General Arthur Wellesley.

De Boigne did open a factory for the manufacture of muskets and canon balls at Gwalior and for guns at Mathura and Ujjain, but the products of these factories were inferior to British equipment and there was further deterioration after him.

Maratha officers adopted habits, like those of the Mughal officers, of keeping seraglios and heavy and cumbersome luggage. Daulat Rao Sindhia, who also moved with heavy luggage was unable to adopt mobile tactics. The same luxury, dances and songs, prevailed in his camp as used to resound in the Mughal camps.[47]

Sivaji's system of intelligence was the greatest check on every abuse.[48] But during later days, the Marathas failed to pay proper attentions to an intelligence system and were often unware, until the last moment of traitors in their own camps. Not that they had no intelligence officers. S.R. Chatgey and

44. Foreign Political Papers Resident with Sindhia 1822.
45. *Ibid.*, Under Gwalior 17-5-1822, no. 53.
46. See Rajwade, Sardesai Vol. III, pp. 515-16, and Prof. Limaya Misc. Writings, p. 354, Holkar Kaifiat 62-63.
47. Broughton's description of Sindhia's Camp and Bazar and *Poona Residency Correspondence*, VIII, IX Mohan 136 Sarkar IV, p. 108.
48. Grant Duff, *History of Marathas*, Vol. I, p. 108.

Trimbackji Dingalia began their careers as intelligence officers (Jasus).

Lastly, there was disparity between the old world Indian weapons and mode of warfare and scientific military training, strategy and firearms of the company. And, above all, it lacked loyalty and patriotism among the commanders and officers as well as in the rank and file due to its heterogeneous composition.

REVIEW

The administrative and military system of Daulat Rao Sindhia reveals the inherent weaknesses of Maratha rule. Every government to be stable and effective needs honest and devoted officers, sound sources of revenue and an efficient soldiery. Daulat Rao Sindhia had semblance to all these requirements but not the substance. His officers were mostly disloyal and looked to their own interests rather than to those of the state. His sources of revenue were undependable and uncertain. The Marathas depended more on extortion than on a regular fiscal system for their revenues. Chauth, Sardesmukhi and other local taxes, although regularly levied, were hated by the peasantry and a discontented peasantry is a constant menace to the stability of an empire. They failed to accord to the ruling class their willing co-operation which is the very sine qua non of any stable government.

Though there was no lack of individual chivalry and deeds of heroism among Sindhia's commanders and armies, yet as a national army it was a failure. Unfortunately it had to face an army which was national to the marrow of its backbone. Better equipped, commanded and by more efficient and patriotic officers, inspired with a mission and fired with the hope of establishing an empire, the British army was more than a match for Daulat Rao Sindhia's army.

9

Social and Economic Conditions in The Gwalior State

The People

The territories ruled over by Daulat Rao Sindhia were in compact and far flung, hilly and heavily forested and lacked good roads and bridges to facilitate inter-communication between the several parts. The population of his state was not homogeneous. Hindus formed the bulk of the population and were divided, as now, into various castes. Brahmins were universally respected and enjoyed social privileges, they were broadly divided into two categories — Northerners and Deccanis. Malcolm hints that Deccani Brahmins were favoured under the Maharaja (Daulat Rao) and five hundred Deccani Brahmin families resided with Sindhia at Gwalior (Lashkar) alone, and 3,000 Deccani Brahmins were in his pay. They occupied important posts in the Civil and accounts services and looked down upon Brahmins from Northern India, as the latter were mostly engaged in trade or as priests. The Deccanis called them 'Rangray' or rustic.

Next in the social hierarchy were the Marathas, who were generally employed in the army. Daulat Rao Sindhia preferred to employ north Indian soldiers in his army in preference to Marathas, but about four thousand Maratha soldiers were so employed. The Rajputs formed a large element amongst Sindhia's subjects and many of them held petty states, with their caste fellows forming the bulk of their armies. High Rajput families remained involved in unending family quarrels, arising from polygamous marriages and claims of rival Ranis and their children. According to Malcolm "Maratha chiefs themselves encouraged such quarrels among the Rajputs and Daulat Rao Sindhia and his nobles were no exception to this practice."

THE MERCHANTILE CLASS

Trade and commerce were the monopoly of Banias. In the words of Broughton, Banias, were a general term for all description of merchants, (they) are generally either from the province of Mewar or from Delhi. The former are the most numerous; as a body they are one of the principal supporters of the Maratha state.[1] The Jains were very rich and lend money at exorbitant rates of interest. Shudras and farmers were the lowest class in the social hierarchy. Different castes followed different customs and worshipped different deities, Karas Dev was the God of the Gujars and Ahirs and Baba Khubat of the dhobies.

The condition of the untouchables and aboriginal was simply deplorable. Mistaking them for a representative Hindu, Lord Hastings once remarked, "The Hindu appears a being merely limited to mere animal existence."[2] The Bhils, Saharies and Gonds mostly lived in the forests unaffected by change of Government. Daulat Rao Sindhia's rule affected them in one respect they were encouraged to settle in regular villages. Then, as now, they were a poor wandering people, very fond of song and dance. The folk songs and folk dances were patronised by the Maharaja and the Maratha nobility.

The artisan class, particularly goldsmiths and silversmiths, were prosperous, as wearing of ornaments was common both among men and women. The richer class habitually wore gold chains, necklaces and rings. This gave a great impetus to the manufacture of ornaments of artistic designs and of fine textile goods. There is reason to believe that it was in Daulat Rao Sindhia's reign that zari saries and embroidery work of Chanderi caught the fancy of rich Maratha ladies.

Toleration

Daulat Rao respected the traditional policy of toleration towards Muslims. There was no bar to any office or post in society or government for them. Some of them occupied posts of honour and responsibility. The bohras among the Muslims carried on Commerce on a large scale. Malcolm however, points

1. Broughton, *Letters written in a Maratha Camp*. p. 149, ed. 1809, 1892.
2. Lord Hastings Private Journal, p. 17.

out that Daulat Rao had comparatively fewer Muslim soldiers in his army. Among the artisan classes, many crafts were pursued by Muslims and special mention may be made here of printers and musicians who were generally Muslims. There were about 5,000 musicians in the Gwalior area. Daulat Rao was a lover music and so the public following the maxim of "Yatha Raja thatha praja" gave encouragement to music. Criminal tribes like the Minas, Bungaries, Mughers, Bhils, etc. lived by stealing and selling birds and animals. It was from this class largely that the thugs and Pindaris were recruited.

Position of Women

The position of women was deplorable during the regime of Daulat Rao Sindhia. He did but little to put a stop to the trade of women and children. Women were sold for slavery and immoral purposes, common in the Chambal or Kunwari river valleys. The Rajputs used to keep Golias, *i.e.* maid slaves. Keeping of a maid servant or a female slave was the fashion. Beggary was also widely prevalent. Polygamy, Sati, early marriages, infanticide of girls - an ancient evil, continued as before. There was strange custom among lodhies that no one can be Chaudhary without having two wives. Early marriages were common. It is common to see woman of 12 with child in her arms, at 18 their beauty in on decline.[3]

Malcolm states : "If married to a man of rank, they (Maratha women) have usually a distinct provision and estate of their own, enjoy as much liberty as they desire, seldom, if ever, wear a veil. Females were devout religious and superstitious."[4] Rajput and Maratha ladies were proud, war-like, quarrelsome, but brave. Brahmins and Maratha ladies exercised great influence in state affairs. Kesara Bai, the adoptive mother, and Bala Bai, the sister of Daulat Rao and daughter of Mahadji, used to advice Daulat Rao Sindhia in political matters. All the wives of Mahadji Sindhia were famous for administrative capacity and horse riding. Bhima Bai daughter of Jaswant Rao Holkar was a famous spear woman and Baiza Bai was a famous horse rider.

---

3. Asiatic Annual Register 1800.
4. Malcolm C.I. *Memoirs*, Vol. II.

The practice of keeping women in military camps was an evil acquired from the Mughals. The ladies of the royal family used to accompany Daulat Rao in camps. In 1803, Lakshmi Bai and Yamuna Bai, two of Mahadji's widows, Bala Bai and Chima Bai, the two daughters of Mahadji, Maina Bai, the mother of Daulat Rao and his three wives, all accompanied him on his tours and campaigns. Broughton states Maratha ladies have a bold look, which is to observed in no other woman of Hindustan.[5]

Dress and Ornaments

In articles of dress and ornaments, the spell of Mughal influence was further discernible. The Sindhias used to attire themselves in gorgeous and bright costumes surmounted by a turban decorated with jewels. Daulat Rao used a tilak on his forehead and wore ornaments round his neck, arms and fingers. He was punctilious in his toilet and prayers. He held in great reverence Ganga-jal (water of the river Ganga) and it was obtained for his use, even while he was out on fighting campaigns.

Personality

Broughton writes about the appearance of Daulat Rao in 1809 that "He is turned of 30; about five feet and five inches in height; and inclined to be fat, but not largely made. His complexion is rather dark, and his features agreeable, but his whole appearance strongly indicates a debauche, and in showing does not most certainly belie him.... He was dressed very plainly in a purple turban and yellow-silk robe, called Acchkan or Acchkan, a long quilted garment with sleeves fastened with buttons and not strings and a folded silk shawl thrown carelessly over his shoulders. He wore several strings of valuable pearls and uncut emeralds round his neck. Of the former he is particularly vain and even affects to be styled as Motiwala or the man of pearls."[6]

As a Builder

Daulat Rao was a great builder. Ujjain, also known as Amravati, Avanti and Padmawati, was the capital of Mahadji. Daulat Rao changed it to Gwalior, but his mother Maina Bai

---

5. Malcolm C.I. *Memoirs*, Vol. II., p. 152.
6. Broughton, *Letters written in a Maratha Camp*, p. 280.

and maternal uncle continued to live at Ujjain. Ujjain contained the Chhatri of Ranoji Sindhia and the old palace of the Sindhia's, famous for its splendour and artistic merit. Daulat Rao, granted the right of the management of the Mahakal temple to Ram Bhatji, a Telinga Brahman, and his heirs. Many buildings were constructed by him, of which the Gopal Krishna temple is prominent. It was built by Baiza Bai, his wife. It is a large square block flanked by two massive towers and crowned by an enormous dome. There is a lot of sculpture and decoration both on the facade and the inner walls. The entire structure has an imposing grandeur. Malet wrote in 1785 that "Ujjain is as extensive as Surat.[7] Until 1810, when Daulat Rao Sindhia founded his new capital at Lashkar, it was the largest town of his dominions."

Gwalior or Lashkar called Gopadri or Gopagiri or Gowalgarh or Gopachaldurg, was named by Suraj Sen, prince of Kutwar in the name of Gwaliapa, who cured him, of which the present name is a corruption, and was the capital of the Gwalior state thereafter. It is said that it was founded in Koliyog 3101 B.C. In 1810, Daulat Rao Sindhia wrested it from Ambaji, fixed up Lashkar from which the name is derived and a year later erected the Maharajawara palace. In 1818, it was still a village,[8] but in 1829, the city had assumed a more settled appearance, the main street having many large houses built of stone.[9] The earlier Moti Mahal palace is a copy of the Peshwa's palace at Poona. It contains a considerable amount of mosaic marble work, two large paintings represent the Dashera procession and different rags. He built a market, which is still called "Daulat Ganj" after him. After the fashion of the Mughal Emperors, he too had a passion for constructing beautiful buildings. So the monuments constructed under his behests bear his nickname Moti Mahal of Gwalior or Moti Jheel and bear the name stamp of the mixed Hindu-Muslim style of architecture. Moti Mahal is a fine piece of architecture.

The forts of Chanderi (captured in 1811), Narwar captured in 1809 and Gwalior were most famous. Another old and well-

7. Melot's *Diary*, p. 418.
8. *Gwalior State Gaztt*, p. 256, ed. 1908.
9. *Ibid.*, 267.

known city in the state was Bhlisa or Vidisha. Daulat Rao founded mints at Sipri or Shivpuri captured in 1804-5 from the Raja of Narwar. It issued coins known as 'Top Shahi'. Vidisha, Sheopur and Guna were developed by Daulat Rao Sindhia, Narwar, Chanderi, Sabalgarh, Asirgarh, Shivpuri, Bijaipur, Bajrangarh and Isagarh were the towns conquered by him and developed into flourishing centres.[10]

Religion

It is heartening to note that Daulat Rao kept the spirit of religious revival alive by his policy of liberalism and moderation. Speaking of the religious upheaval among the Marathas, Ranade avers, "the religious revival was the work also of the people, of the masses, and not of the classes. At its head were saints, poets and philosophers, who sprang chiefly from the lower orders of society, tailors, carpenters, potters, gardeners, barbers, and even scavengers more often than Brahmins."[11]

Tuka Ram tried to reconcile Hindu and Muslim faiths, "The followers of Sheikh Mohammad, who became Bhaktas observe both the Ramzan and the Ekadashi fast, and make pilgrimages both to Mecca and Pandharpur."[12]

This eclectic spirit inspired Daulat Rao Sindhia, who observed both the Moharram and the Dashera and had a Muslim Pir and a Hindu Guru as his religious preceptors. Bapu Sindhia and Amir Khan desired marriages among the children of their concubines.

Economic Conditions

Sadashiv Dinkar an agent of Nana Phadnavis, a contemporary of Mahadji has given an account of the economic conditions of Sindhia's dominions in a despatch to Nana Phadnavis :

"Mahadji had just obtained ten lakhs, but you will be surprised to know how many have been spent. As for his army

---

10. For details *Gwalior state Gaztt.*, part IV, Erakin, Tata Chand, p. 256, Cole Preservatian of National Monuments p. 2, Cunniaghan or Archaeological Survey Vol. I; Gwalior and Briffle the Monuments of Central India.
11. Ranade : *The Rise of the Maratha Power*, p. 10.
12. Tara Chand, *Influence of Islam on Indian Culture*, p. 224, ed. 1946.

expenditure, the Maratha forces from the Deccan have been suffering appalling miseries, which I am unable to describe in words. They are not able to pay of their debts by selling horses. Mahadji never enquires, if all men put down on paper in the roll of the infantry regiments are really present or not. There is no inspection, no roll call, and the vast amounts spent on them do not reach the hands of men to whom they are due, but the money is pocketed by unscrupulous middle men...." He ended his letter by remarking "I know what I am writing; it is the naked truth. A healthy administration is that in which the master is never in want and in which the army is contented and the Ryots are happy."[13]

Sardesai remarks :

> "If this was the condition of the finances of one of our best and famous chiefs in his palmy days, we can easily imagine what Maratha rule was like in its declining period."[14]

Thomas Twining, European traveller, also has left a sad picture of the ruin of agriculture, etc.[15]

In the words of J.N. Sarkar :

> "In the year 1796, the dark clouds of anarchy, rapine and popular sufferings descended on the unhappy land. The peasant and the artisan lost the fruit of their labour and perished from brigandage or famine." He further adds: "The desolation of fields, the degradation of the women to servile concubinage, and the ruin of trade and industry, turned the most fruitful part of Aryavarta into a wilderness."[16]

Improvements under Daulat Rao Sindhia

Now we are in a position to state that, if any, improvement was effected by Daulat Rao Sindhia in the week and structureless administration that he had inherited. There is no denying the fact that from 1796 to 1803, the economic condition of the

---

13. Various Letters, *Poona Residency Correspondence*, XII.
14. Quoted by R.D. Choksey in his book "A History of British Diplomacy at the Court of the Peshwas" pp. 93-94 and Sardesai : Main Currents of the Maratha History, pp. 146-50.
15. Sarkar, *Fall of the Mughal Empire*, IV, p. 113.
16. *Ibid.*, IV, p. 157.

people hardly shows any sign of improvement. It was scarcely possible, because of the war of the Widows, the rebellion of Lakhwa Dada, and of the wars with Jaswant Rao Holkar and the East India Company.

With the restoration of peace, the condition of the common man improved slightly, as is testified by the increase in revenue and increase of population. In the least disturbed districts, the revenue registered at the end of three years an increase of 10 to 15 per cent; in Bhilsa district alone, from 40,000 in 1817 it rose to 2.5 lakhs in 1821. On the whole, Sindhia's territory showed a rise of 25% in revenue as soldiers and refractory persons returned to their former occupation as cultivators.[17] The revenue of Rs. 1,27,68,429 in 1819 rose to Rs. 1,43,20,227 in 1824.[18] In addition to this, Daulat Rao after the Second Maratha War, built up a private treasure of his own, which according to Broughton "amounted to fifty lakhs in 1809."[19]

Subsequently, Daulat Rao Sindhia made considerable financial improvements and succeeded in restoring peace and prosperity to his dominions. Economic prosperity prevailed during the last days of his regime, as Malcolm informed the Governor General "Sindhia had a rise of about 25% and a deduction of 15% in the expenses of its collection."[20] He improved his financial condition so much that a British diplomat jealously remarked "Sindhia felt that the fullness of his treasury was the test of successful administration."[21]

The Nobles and officers were paid very high salaries, and they spent lavishly on articles of luxury and display. They were fond of sumptuous dinners, costly dresses, precious jewellery, elephants and horses and music and dance. The middle class people, consisting of professional classes and ordinary state employees, were fairly well off. Skilled workman earned enough to lead a decent life, but the condition of unskilled workers, peons and shopkeepers was not good.

---

17. Malcolm, *Political History of India*, p. 153, and C.I.II.
18. *Ibid.*, Vol. II, p. 375.
19. Broughton, *Letters written in a Maratha Camp*. p. 106.
20. Dr. Sharma B.G., "Malcolm in Madhya Bharat", p. 228.
21. *Correspondence regarding the comparative merits of British and native administration in India*, pp. 114-17, Printed by the order of the Government of India.

Crops and Prices

The chief Kharif crops were millets and maize and of the Rabi wheat and gram. Cotton, Sugarcane and opium were also common. The prices of wheat and gram fluctuated from 50 or 60 seers a rupee to a hundred or 120 seers a rupee. Things of daily use, such as corn, vegetables, fruits, milk, ghee, oil, meat and fish and articles of clothing were very cheap, except in times of famine or war.

Imports and Exports

Exports from the state consisted of Opium, Grain, Coarse Cotton Cloth, Chanderi Saris, Zari Saris, Linseed and Tobacco. The tobacco of Bhilsa was famous for its high flavour. Clothes of very superior quality were produced at Chanderi and exported to every part of India.

Silk, Chint and gold cloth were main imports. Dry goods such as coconuts, betel nuts, and spices were imported from Gujarat; diamond and pearls from Bundelkhand and Gujarat, and gold, silver, and copper from Bombay and Mewar.

Coinage

It is interesting to find that coinage was not a state monopoly in the Sindhia state. The right of coining was allowed to bankers or merchants of Ganj Basuda, Ujjain and Bhilsa, guaranteeing to maintain a regular standard. Government used to test these coins through a Superintendent, Assay Master, an accountant and some refiners. The Ujjain coin maintained a sufficient degree of purity. A mint generally used to coin Rs. 8000 to Rs. 10,000 of coins a day with the help of about 50 silver smiths, 10 or 12 stampers, 6 or 8 refiners and to minters. Copper coins consisted of half pice, pice and the two pice copper coins of Ujjain.

AGRICULTURE

Agriculture was the main occupation of the bulk of the population in the state. The agricultural crops of the time were much the same as those of today. There were also localised as well as commercial crops. Indigo was developed by De Boigne in the northern territories during the regime of the Sindhias. Cotton was grown in the Malwa area.

Communication and Transport

There was no lack of means of communications in the shape of kachha roads and of rivers in northern India, for the purpose of mercantile traffic, though they compare unfavourably with present day improvements. Horses, bullock-carts, and polanquins were used for the purpose of transport.

Industry and Crafts

Daulat Rao Sindhia's rule was marked by extensive and varied industrial activity which, besides, supplying the needs of the local aristocacy and merchants could meet the demands of other lands.

By far the most important industry was the manufacture of cotton cloth. The whole country produced cotton cloth, but Chanderi was the most reputed centre of the textile industry. Sheopur was famous for wood work and is still famous for making chess and sport goods. The dyeing industry, too, was in a flourishing condition. Silk fabrics were also manufactured at Chanderi. Toy making was also revived at Gwalior during the days of Daulat Rao Sindhia. Preparation of catechu and gur were common cottage industries. Other important industries were oil making, basket making, Biri making and many articles of decoration. Cotton goods, toys and Biris were exported outside the Gwalior territories. Indigo and saltpeter were the most important items of export during the days of De Boigne. The condition of the weavers and artisans was probably better than that of their counterparts during the British period.

Cultural Aspects

There was nothing like the modern system of education established and maintained by the government in the Maratha states. But primary and secondary education of some sort existed. Daulat Rao Sindhia himself, as well as many of his grandees, encouraged such education by grants of land or money to temples, monasteries and individual saints and scholars.

At Ujjain, there were scholars who used to teach astronomy. Due to the patronage of Daulat Rao Sindhia, Gwalior became a famous centre of cultural activities, especially dance and music, and education in Music of highest standard was imparted there.

The greater part of literature was religious, marked by the exposition of either the Krishna or the Rama cult, Krishnaji took shape of a profound lover of music and dance and verses were composed to celebrate his skill in flute playing and The Rasleela. Literary activity thrived even the midst of wars. Female education, both among the Hindus and the Muslims, was not unknown to the age, as Malcolm states : "Rajput ladies have sufficient learning to carry on their correspondences."[22]

His Literary Activities

Daulat Rao was a great patron of art and literature. A number of renowned poets lived at his court. Padmakar, a renouned poet of Hindi, flourished under the sunshine of his patronage. He was born at Banda in 1753 and died at Kanpur in 1833. He wrote the *Aalijah Prakash* in praise of Daulat Rao Sindhia in 1821 A.D., and translated the *Hitopadesh*, the famous Sanskrit book of fables, into Hindi verse at the request of Udaji, a court noble of Sindhia. Pandit Ram Chandra Shukla, the famous critic of Hindi says that no poet other than Bihari attained so much popularity in this age. The versatility of his genious is nowhere found except in Tulsidas. In his *Aalijah Prakash* he wrote about his patron in 1821 :

मीना गढ़ बम्बह समंद मंदराज बंग,
बम्दर को बद करि बन्दर बसाबैगौ ।
कहै पद्माकर बसुधि कासमीर हू कौ,
पिंजर सो घेरि के कालिंजर छुढ़ाबैगौ ।
बांका नृप दौलत अलीजा महाराज कबाँ,
साजि दल पकरि फिरंगिन दबाबैगौ ।
दिल्ली दहपहि पटना हे को झटपट्टि करि,
कबहूक लत्ता क्लकेता को उड़ाबैगौ ।

Translation of poet Padmakar's poem is given in Hindi :

Padmakar wrote book on Daulat Rao with the title of *Alijah Prakash* as Daulat Rao Sindhia was called Alijah *i.e.*, most

---

22. "King Daulat Rao Aalijah, will win Minagarh, Bombay, Madras and Bengal, etc. He will imprison the English monkeys and will gain victory over Kashmir and Kalinjar. Brave king Daulat Rao will prepare his army and will defeat the Britishers. He will not only capture Delhi and Patna with a lightning speed, but will also conquer Calcutta."

superior Maharaja. He wrote poem in praise of his patron Daulat Rao Sindhia which has been given here in original. In English briefly it means that Daulat Rao Sindhia will conquer Minagarh, Bombay, Madras ports (in Hindi called Bandergah) and Bengali poet Padmakar says that after surrounding Kashmir, he will get kalinjar fort freed from Britishers. Superior King Daulat will organise military to attack British forces and will conquer Delhi, Patna and even capital place Calcutta of (East India Co.). Thus, this poem depicts inner ambition of Daulat Rao Sindhia in exaggerated terms.

A free library was also started at Maharajwara by Daulat Rao Sindhia in Gwalior.

Art and Architecture

Daulat Rao was a lover of painting, as is proved by pictures of the Mysore War collected by him. Not only this, even houses of the common people were decorated with exquisite paintings. Calligraphy, Decorative carving, Mosaics, too, were, profusely used. Gwalior was a ruined fort, used for the incarceration of notorious and dangerous prisoners, when Daulat Rao Sindhia settled there. It was Daulat Rao, who beautified the town with fine buildings and laid the beginnings of what Laskhar looks like today. He also erected many buildings at Ujjain and Bhilsa. Budhist structures were at Bagh Udaygiri, Gyaraspur, Marod. Udaipur and Chanderi were famous for Hindu and Jain architecture.

In Gwalior houses were of stone but in Malwa bricks were used for the construction of houses. He had a cultured heart and did not spare any pains to patronise poets, musicians, dancers, artists and skilled architects and designers. He left behind certain traditions in Gwalior, which inspired his successors until recent times.

Cultural Synthesis

Mahadji always laboured to bring about amity between the two major communities and Daulat Rao, too, made no distinction between the two. As Vicegerent of the Delhi Empire and as Subedar of the Peshwa, he achieved a singular synthesis of the two cultures in the Gwalior State. This synthesis is discernible in the times of Daulat Rao Sindhia also, who, as pointed out earlier, made no distinction between Hindu and Muslim festivals. Sometimes Moharram and Dashera fell on the same day and the Maharaja and all his officers and courtiers used to participate in both after changing their dresses. "Daulat Rao Sindhia and his officers joined Moharram processions in green dress like Mahammadans."[23]

Daulat Rao encouraged people by his example and precept to participate in both Hindu and Muslim festivals, consequently Id and Shabharat of the Muslims and Holi and Dashera of the Hindus were celebrated with great eclat by him and his court along with the people. These were gala festivals and there was a lot of feasting and merry-making. The festives were so impressive that even foreigners took part in them with the same zeal and eclat as the sons of the soil.

Holi was celebrated with great pomp and show even amidst the wars. "I am to deliver the treaty today" wrote Malcolm to Arthur Wellesley, "and after that ceremony is over, to play Holi, for which I am prepared with an old coat and an old hat. Sindhia is furnished with an engine of great power by which, he can play upon a fellow at 50 years distance. He has besides, a medium of syringes, so I expect to be well squirted." Malcolm wrote to Shaw "The cursed Holi play has given him a sharp attack of fever."[24]

Broughton, an eyewitness of these festivals, has also given vivid and graphic descriptions and he translated some of the Maratha songs.

Kanhaiya : (Kanhaiya-Krishna).

Again my fair one? — Hast thou purchased me? —
— Ah see me —
The Gopi : Think'st Thou uncalled I boldly came?
The gathering clouds, dear youth invite to love.

Kanhaiya

How could a frame so soft, such dangers prove?
While e'ven thy pretty self was lost in night,
How see thy way?

---

23. Broughton also quoted by Dr. R.C. Majumdar and others in *An Advanced History of India*, p. 569, ed. 1948.

24. Keye, *Life of Malcolm*, Vol. I, p. 270.

The Gopi

The lightning gleamed so bright,
Kanhiaya : O'er broken routes, through mire, and tangling thorn,
Thy tender limbs ache, thy feet be torn?

The Gopi

Steps light and firm will weariest way o'ercome.

Kanhaiya

Yet dark is the night; and thou wert alone;

The Gopi

No my soul's Lord; for love was with me still,
Pointed my path; and warded every ill;

In the same way, Broughton has translated another :

A Basant Song

The lively drum is heard around,
The tomborine and cymbals sound
But I of lengthened absence plaint
And perish by a parching flame,
The women all round me sing
And own the inspiring joys of spring;
While I, from darts of ruthless love,
Never ending torments prove.
The amorous koil strains his throat and
Poems a plaintive pleasing note;
My breast responsive heaves with grief,
Hopeless and reckless of relief,
When he again shall glad my hours.
Then, girl, I will take thy blooming flowers,
But now my love is far away.
Where should I place thy Basant gay?

Dashera also was celebrated with great pomp and show. A durbar attended by all concerned was held and Daulat Rao used to lead the procession, followed by the nobles and prominent persons. Gangoor or Ganesh Chaturthi was also celebrated with great pomp.

Anna Maharaj, a saint from the Deccan was granted land and an annuity by Daulat Rao. His successors held the saint's

Bhandara in February every year. Similarly, Daulat Rao invited Mahipatina, who was granted the gift of Rs. 100 per mensem by Sindhia. He died in 1823, and thereafter his chela Kashi Nath Maharaj held Bhandara in phagun and built the temple of Dholi-Bulama Math in honour of his Guru.

Daulat Rao instituted the Urs in honour of a Muslim saint, who had blessed Mahadji. The poor were given food and clothes. Several such Urs as of Ghaus Abdul Ghaffar and Khwaja Sahib were started under the patronage of Daulat Rao.

Gwalior became a famous centre of dance and music. During the Jat rule these were neglected arts. Under Daulat Rao classical music and dances became so popular that most Maratha women picked up this fine art. Malwa has been famous for its folk dances from time immemorial, but these were revived during the days of Daulat Rao and the war ravaged territory once more echoed with songs and jhankars of payals. Folk dances of Malwa, Maharashtra, Bundelkhand and of the aboriginals in which both men and women took part, were a notable feature of life, which lent colour to these barren lands.

10

Last Years

Between 1803 and 1818 Daulat Rao Sindhia was preoccupied mainly with disciplining his tributary principalities to consolidate his kingdom. In 1818, the outcome of the Pindari war of Lord Hastings proved a serious blow to his power, and his tributaries, though not so disturbed as those of Holkar, were worse off than ever before. His army, too, was disorganised and it was imperative that some reformative means should be adopted to improve conditions in his state all round.[1]

By 1818, as pointed out in an earlier chapter of this thesis, he came to an understanding with the Raja of Narwar,[2] settled disputes with Raghogarh,[3] Khichipur, the Grassia chiefs and others.[4] He accepted the British decision in the case of Rajput Rajas and about Ratlam, Sitamau, Amjhera, Sailana, Bhatgarh and Deoree.[5]

The British Government was able to confirm his authority in his own state proper, but he seldom gave them a chance to make British influence unquestioned in Central India. British Residents tried to interfere even in the cases of Grassia chiefs[6], Gopal Rau Bhau,[7] Raghogarh and Deoree. He relinquished his rights of tribute from Ratlam and Sailana to the British Government[8], perhaps because the states were outside the

1. Malcolm, *Political History of India.* C.I.I., p. 153.
2. *Foreign Political Index,* 1818, 20th January, no. 55.
3. *Ibid.*, Under Head Gwalior, p. 56.
4. *Ibid.*, Foreign Political Papers 1822.
5. *Ibid.*, 10th February 1821; no. 27 of 1821.
6. *Foreign Political Papers,* 1827, 18th December, p. 161.
7. *Ibid.*, no. 27 of 1821.
8. *Ibid.*

area which he claimed to be his own. In 1822, disturbances took place at Chanderi, but these were successfully curbed.[9]

Friction with the East India Company

Anna Ram Chandra Bhaskar died on 13th September 1822 and Hoozaria died the same year on 11th April.[10] The Ghatge family now came to have over-whelming importance in Sindhia's Government, as all important business passed through the hands of Baba Rao Patankar, uncle of Baiza Bai and later on her brother Hindu Rao Ghatge. Friction with the British Government in such a context of policy and affairs was inevitable. Further, the British authorities refused to continue the Jagir granted to Jija Bai with reversion to a daughter after her death.[11] The Governor General even refused to receive the envoy of Daulat Rao Sindhia, named Khwaja Hussain All khan, in the open Darbar at Calcutta on 22nd June 1824.[12] They also interfered on behalf of Nawab of Afsand Ali khan to compel Daulat Rao to grant the Jagir of Basoda to him.[13]

On 13th February, 1824, Major Josiah Stewart succeeded Captain Close as British Resident with Sindhia. He freely recruited the Khichies, arch enemies of the Sindhia, for the British army. In October 1824, the Resident demanded reforms in the Gwalior currency.[14] During these last years of his reign from 1824 to 1827, Daulat Rao was constantly ill, so Major Close, the Resident, desired fresh treaty arrangements, to place a subsidiary force in the state as a precautionary measure. Sindhia, however, referred to a private assurance given to him by Lord Hastings that no subsidiary force would be imposed upon him.[15] Stewart, in a letter of 4th December, 1826, conveyed the reluctance of Daulat Rao, to adopt a son, and this reluctance on his part prevailed till his death.[16] During 1827, his health was rapidly deteriorating and at last on 21st March 1827, he breathed his

9. *Foreign Political Papers,* 17th May, 1822, no 53.
10. *Ibid.*, no. 50, 1822.
11. *Ibid.*, 17th May no. 53.
12. *Ibid.,* 1824 no. 57.
13. *Foreign Political Papers,* 1821, p. 9 of Index.
14. *Ibid.*, 1824 no. 19.
15. *Foreign Secret Index Gwalior,* 1823 dated 12th September, no. 1.
16. *Ibid.*, 1824 no. 109, 110, p. 114.

last. Daulat Rao's last hours have been described thus by Resident J. Stewart, to which he was an eye witness.[17]

The mission from Sindhia was headed by Hindu Rao, brother of his favourite wife, Baiza Bai. The Raja himself had been suffering from illness and his early dissolution was expected. The representation of his ministers, to adopt a son, as he had no son of his own, were of no avail, in overcoming his reluctance to a measure which was considered essential to perpetuate the existence of Gwalior State. He declared that he had no relation in whom, he was interested, or from whom he could select an eligible object of adoption and he was satisfied to leave the future to the determination of the British government, which might make whatever disposition they thought best. The real cause of his reluctance, however, was his attachment to Baiza Bai, who had long exercised an imperious influence over his mind, and to whom he wishes to bequeath the full authority of the state, although the opposition of the principal persons of his court and probably some misgivings of the result deterred him from declaring her a successor.

"Sindhia, in a conference with the Resident intimated another although, not altogether dissimilar motive. If a son was adopted by him, Maratha custom required that the senior of the Bais should function as a Regent. Rukma Bai, and not Baiza Bai, was the senior most Rani, and she was notoriously unfit for the office of Regent, which should have devolved on her as the legal mother of the minor Raja.

Later, the Resident Stated :

At about 9 O'clock yesterday morning, a horseman came at full speed from the Maharaja's camp to the Residency with a message from Hindu Rao that the Maharaja had expressed an anxious wish to see me and begging that I would as soon as possible proceed to the place. Conceiving that the Maharaja must be in his last moment, I instantly mounted a horse, and accompanied by Capt. Dyke alone, I reached the place in a very short time after I had received the message. I found an anxious crowd outside and all chiefs and people of respectability assembled in different apartments of the palace. As soon as I met Hindu Rao, I anxiously inquired after the Maharaja.

17. *Gwalior State Papers.*

Hindu Rao said that he was very ill and that I should see him immediately...during his conversation from the interior apartments, where the Maharaja was. It was found that his Highness was ready to receive me. I proceeded to his apartment, accompanied by Hindu Rao, Raoji Khasgiwala, Atma Ram Pandit, and perhaps there were one or two more. Captain Dyke also accompanied me. His Highness lay or rather reclined on a coach, supported by pillows, the number of female servants were in attendance around him. Behind a purdah close to him were Baiza Bai, Rukma Bai and Bala Bai and their attendants. I was shocked to observe such change that had taken place in the Maharaja's appearance; his arms and upper part of his body had become quite emaciated; his belly and lower extremities were greatly swelled.

I went upto him, took his hand in mine and went over him so as to hear what he might say.... He remained silent for some time apparently unable to speak. At last, he said, in a distinct and audible voice, so as to be heard by every one present and even I believe behind the purdah : "I wish you to do whatever you think proper (Jo tum Munasib Jano So Karo). I replied that everything would be arranged according to His Highness' wishes; and I added some words of consolation and said I trusted by the blessings of God he would yet recover. He appeared affected and said, "By the side of you and your friendship" (Ap Ke Dekhne Se Aur Ap Ki is Mohabbat Se) but he could not finish the sentence. A long pause now ensued and I at last said, "is there anything else that your Highness would wish to say to me," he replied "he had a great deal to say" (Bahut Sa Kahna Hai)" but after waiting a considerable time, he could add no more. I then proposed to retire to another room for a short time and to return when His Highness might recover a little and be able to speak. This was agreed to by all present. When I was about to retire, I heard the voice of Baiza Bai suggesting that Doctor Pawtou should be sent for. I asked the Maharaja whether it was his wish that the gentleman should be called. Then His Highness made a faint sign of assent. I have been thus particular in giving expression used by the Maharaja on this occasion, as they were probably the last words he uttered. I had not retired above an hour to an upper apartment when the screams of females mourned that Maharaja's life had fled.

"It would be difficult for me to give adequate notion of the scene that ensued; the cries of women and lamentations of men, the uproar and tumult were beyond all description....

Shortly afterwards a memorandum of seven articles was brought to me purporting to be the Maharaja's last will, but not bearing his signature, the principle of which were that the Maharaja declared his intention to adopt a son, the appointment of Hindu Rao to be the Superintendent and...the adopted son shall be obedient to orders of the Maharaja and Baiza Bai as long as they live. For the fulfilment of all intentions, he appears to the British Government."

"It was a singularly melancholy sight to see the Maharaja in his last apparel, decorated with jewels and pearls, seated in his palankeen, and accompanied by all the state elephants set out on his last procession. He was accompanied to the funeral by almost every man in camp, and the tears of the multitude showed that, however deficient in many of the qualities of a good prince, he was neither a cruel nor a tyrannical sovereign."

Character

Stewart's judgement of Daulat Rao's character given below is interesting :

"The Maharaja was by no means deficient in understanding to which he owed the salvation of his state amid the wreck of the Maratha empire. In conversation, the comparisons and illustrations he used were frequently striking and happy. His temper was mild and gentle in the extreme, though his courage was never doubted. Whatever may have been the vices and crimes of his youth, and this I believe all were to be ascribed to the evil counsellors than to himself, his latter years have been unmarked by any gross violation of morality".

Robert Close while depicting Daulat Rao Sindhia's character, stated :

"Whilst it continued to be His Highness' policy to move himself at the head of his army and to be always in the field, he let loose those habits of dissipation which a long residence in a camp was often bound to produce. He was excessively negligent of public affairs, so that his ministers could seldom prevail on him to give any attention to them, but on the other hand, he was fond of personal exertion, which he showed in indulging in field sports to a degree of activity seldom found amongst the natives. In private hours, he used to be attended by a set of abandoned favourites, who employed every art of low and contemptible buffoonery for his amusement, and the scenes that were reported to be exhibited at such times are not fit to be described. Since had changed his mode of life, however, by remaining in a fixed station and in consequence of satiety and the change which was brought by time (Sindhia being now nearly forty years of age) a great alteration had taken place in his manners and habits. He attended much more to public business than he used to be and sometimes complained in his turn of the want of industry and application in his ministers. Many of his low companions had been obliged to leave him, and although from the turn of his mind he sometimes indulged in a levity that was unbecoming his station, he did not pass his hours in their society as formerly, nor do those who remained, presume as they used to do upon the familiarity to which he admitted them. As his character had thus acquired a greater degree of steadiness than before, his love of pleasure and personal activity had diminished when I was formerly in this camp."[18]

This long citation from the Resident brings out in bold relief the change in Daulat Rao's character in the latter part of his life. There is a ring of sympathy and truth and appreciation in the words of the Resident.

There is, however, another side to the picture Sindhia has been severely castigated by other writers. Broughton wrote of him that "a tiger or a pretty face, an elephant fight or a new supply of paper kites have each sufficient attraction to divest his chagrin, and restore him to his wonted thoughtlessness and good humour." Prof. Choksey states: "Women and low company were his bane, and appeared to have quite corrupted a heart and mind originally meant for good things. Virgin charms were deliberately sought for and almost daily sacrificed on the altar of his lust."[19] According to Uthoff : "He

---

18. Resident Close to Hastings dated 7-9-1816 no. 288 *Poona Residency Correspondence,* Vol. XIV, p. 344. Similarly Malcolm says Daulat Rao Sindhia who is personally of good disposition. C.I.I. p. 141.
19. Choksey, *A History of British Diplomacy at the Court of the Peshwas,* p. 132, ed. 1951.

(Daulat Rao) was of an imperial bent of mind and activity of body, displaying but little of either greatness or goodness, and was said to have been of late addicted to debaucheries which have already afflicted his constitution."[20]

The verdict of Sarkar and Sardesai, the two eminent historians of the period, is also not in his favour. This is clear from the quotations from their writings included in the foregoing pages of this book. Some writers have painted him as a worthless wretch, while others acclaimed him as a fighter for Maratha freedom. He was neither of the two. He was a man of ordinary calibre. He had some serious faults. He was addicted to unsavoury habits when young, as he was nursed in north India among Mohammadan and Rajput Sardars, where luxury was a common feature. He learnt kite-flying, hunting and other sports[21] instead of learning state business as a cadet in some territory or province, keeping of nautch girls, concubines and debauchery were a common feature of high life during those days, and Daulat Rao Sindhia fell into these evil habits.

He was a man of mild disposition. He never desired the extinction of Holkar's rule. He first supported Kashi Rao and tried to conciliate Jaswant Rao Holkar and desired an alliance with him even after the latter's defeat. He was never vindictive. The widows rebelled against him but he treated them with all respect. Jaggo Bapu, in alliance with Lakhwa Dada, rose against him, but Sindhia kept him in his service until his death. In the same way, in spite of the treachery of Ambaji, he always respected him and kept him in his service till the last days of his life, and expressed grief over the latter's death. He wrote to Amir Khan to serve Holkar faithfully, when he tried to usurp all the power of the state. The British Resident also wrote that he never entertained a spirit of revenge against the British Government.[22]

Daulat Rao Sindhia has not been accused by any body of lack of courage. He tried to lead his armies in person during the Second Maratha War and against Holkar, and the various

---

20. *Poona Residency Correspondence,* I, Letter of May 1797.
21. Sarkar, *Fall of the Mughal Empire,* Vol. IV, p. 150 and *Poona Residency Correspondence,* Vol. XIV introduction.
22. Resident J. Stewart on the occasion of his death in 1827.

Residents have testified openly to the fact that Daulat Rao Sindhia was not a coward.

J.N. Sarkar has affirmed that even in the proud race of the Rajputs, queens have to hear the taunts of concubines,[23] but this never happened in Sindhia's household, and he never allowed any of his female favourites to behave pertinently. After the murder of Sarji Rao Ghatge, Daulat Rao Sindhia himself shared the grief of Baiza Bai, wiped her tears and tried to console her in every possible manner, as has been described by Broughton. Never the less with all his consideration for her, there is only one instance of Udaipur in which Baiza Bai influenced his political decision.

Daulat Rao Sindhia was a little too credulous and probably that was why he failed to match British diplomacy and was so often deceived by his Generals and officers. He did not realise that Collins was sent by the East India Company to while away the time, so the British forces might prepare themselves and in the meantime to seduce his officers by gold and other allurements. Little did he know, that the war between him and the British Government was inevitable, as this was a war for political supremacy in India. Daulat Rao Sindhia was not a good general. Jaswant Rao Holker and Ranjit Singh were far superior to him in generalship. Lord Lake and Arthur Wellesley also out-matched him in this respect. This was certainly a serious defect in him. Had he possessed the capacity for military organisation like Ranjit Singh or military ability like Jaswant Rao Holkar, the sequel might have been different.

Daulat Rao Sindhia was an administrator of average calibre. The army became indisciplined, though its condition was actually not so bad as has been represented by foreign writers. But it cannot be denied that it was indisciplined in comparison to British forces. His generals were semi-independent and they often quarreled with one another. For this indiscipline, foreign generals and his financial difficulties were also responsible. After the Second Maratha War, Daulat Rao Sindhia lost the best portions of his kingdom and it was difficult to maintain the army without having sufficient and productive territory. Gwalior

23. Sarkar, *Fall of Mughal Empire*, Vol. IV, p. 72.

and Narwar were in the hands of Ambaji and Devji Gaole, who did not pay the tribute regularly. The Pindaris usurped various territories and realization of tribute from them was nearly impossible. The Rajas of Raghogarh, Sivpur and Chanderi were semi-independent and instead of paying tribute, they used to plunder, Sindia's own territory. Even after 1805, he needed a large military establishment to enforce his rights of tribute from the Rajput states but the dishonest Deccani administrators, who looked after his finance, habitually mulcted him of half the revenue and there were always arrears of pay owing to the troops. No wonder, therefore, that they were always sullen, disloyal and mutinous.

Daulat Rao was not by any means a person of heroic mould, but that he could learn wisdom from his mistakes and failures is clear from the fact that he never again entered into a direct conflict with the East India Company after 1805, and always tried to maintain friendly relations whenever and as far as possible, with all persons including the Peshwa, Holkar and the Rajput princes. He lacked that quality of instinctive judgement of character and ability, that sense of wise opportunism, in the best sense of the word, that marks the great generals and rulers of history, but he did possess a prudent realism, which enabled him to save his state from annihilation in the cataclysmic progress of British imperialism in India.

Various Testimonies

Various opinions have been expressed about Daulat Rao Sindhia's character and achievements. "It was the good fortune of the British" Elphistone said "that neither Baji Rao nor Daulat Rao Sindhia possessed the requisite strength and the spirit to stand forth boldly at a critical moment...the Marathas had at their command ample means of waging a successful war, armies, money, arms and ammunitions. Everything was ready. They had men but not the man. Both Baji Rao in the south and Daulat Rao in the north became traitors to their nation and lost the game."[24] Thus according to Elphinstone, it was Daulat Rao Sindhia, who failed the cause of the Maratha Empire and paved the way for British imperialism.

24. Elphinstone quoted by Colbrroke in his *Life of Elphinstone*, Vol. I, p. 372.

Sardesai seems to have been influenced by the same point of view. He writes, "A fatal conjecture certainly occurred in the fortunes of the Maratha states, at the end of the 18th and the commencement of the 19th century, when the Government of Poona fell into the hands of two raw wicked youths, the Peshwa Baji Rao II and Daulat Rao Sindhia both equally incompetent."[25]

Sardesai castigates Daulat Rao in strong language. He deplores that "both in character and capacity, Baji Rao was utterly worthless and he courted the support of an equally incompetent young lad, Daulat Rao Sindhia, the successor of Mahadji. The strong battalions of Sindhia trained under French officers were of no avail to him, as he had not the skill to keep them under proper control."[26]

He further writes, "I can unhesitatingly attribute the Maratha downfall primarily to the incapacity of the two frivolous youths, Peshwa Baji Rao II and Daulat Rao Sindhia, who owing to a fortuitous coincidence came into possession of express power in the Maratha state."[27] Sardesai argues that if the state had a proper organisation and good constitution, even these two incapable youths could have been set aside to make room for a more competent agency. He admits that the Maratha Government lacked this strength. But he strongly feels that in all human affairs, one individual alone can do or undo any good great work.[20]

According to N.B. Roy, "Sindhia's vision of a new order thus faded away. Revolution, pillage, insecurity stalked across Central India and threw various kingdoms, small and big into indescribable confusion. All classes of people were involved in a deepening misery and suffering."[29] He further asserts "They were, however, the destined precursors of a new order, an order that would be set up by no Indian king or potentate, but by the new power that had come from across the seas, with a

25. Sardesai, *New History of the Marathas*, III, p. 517.
26. Sardesai, *Main Currents of Maratha History*, p. 158.
27. *Ibid.*, p. 161.
28. *Ibid.*, p. 162.
29. N.B. Roy Introduction to *Poona Residency Correspondence*, XI, p. 20.

new strategy of war, new principles of Government and new ideas of life."[30]

Grant Duff expresses his opinion in the following words : "Had Sindhia possessed power of organisation, then he might have controlled Holkar and after Jaswant Rao Holkar, other Maratha states."[31]

Malcolm says that after the defeat of Jaswant Rao Holkar, had Sindhia followed up his blow, the power of Jaswant Rao would have by this victory been annihilated.[32]

According to Sarkar, "The incredibly rapid success of British arms in driving Tipu Sultan into his capital and their annihilating him (4th May 1799), coming after their enslavement of the Nizam 8 months earlier, fell like a thunderclap on the Indian Princes that still remained independent. Henceforth, the Peshwa and Sindhia seem to act like birds fascinated by the blazing eyes of a python and walking unresisting into his open jaws."[33]

In the opinion of Dr. Raghubir Singh, "Daulat Rao was an immature lad of thirteen, dull of intellect, without education and so prone to self-indulgence; to his lack of the power of chosing worthy servants, he added an obstinate persistence in one course and the truly oriental habit of letting matters drift without coming to any decision."[34]

According to Col. G.B Malleson, "there was a laxity of principles about Daulat Rao, which manifested itself, in all the transaction of his life. The death of the Peshwa's able minister, Nana Phadnavis, in the year 1800 showed him again in the light of a man, who would scruple at nothing to seize the property of others." In his view, Daulat Rao never throughout his life "showed any of the great qualities of a general."[35]

According to C.E. Luerd, "Daulat Rao was neither a general nor an administrator, while his training made him impatient of

30. N.B. Roy Introduction to *Poona Residency Correspondence,* XI, p. 20.
31. Duff, *History of the Marathas,* Vol. I, p. 555.
32. Malcolm C.I., *Political History of India.*
33. Sarkar, *Fall of the Mughal Empire,* IV, p. 156.
34. Dr. Raghubir Singh, *Poona Residency Correspondence,* Vol. VIII, Introduction.
35. G.B. Malleson, *The Native States of India,* Chapter "Gwalior" ed. 1876.

failure and opposition and unable to wait for the proper moment to strike. He was undoubtedly unequal to the task of controlling the vast possessions to which he had succeeded or maintaining the political ascendancy created by his predecessors. He took no pains to behave with courtesy with the Peshwa, interfered most want only in the affairs of Holkar's family with almost unconceivable blindness, proceeded to extremities with the British and wrecked the great name of his house."[36]

Munroe states, "Daulat Rao Sindhia was never formidable even at the height of his power. The great means which he possessed were lost in his feeble hands. The exertions of Holkar against Lord Lake were still weaker than those of Sindhia."[37]

Let us analyse the views of another school of thought. Dr. Basu in his work "Rise of the Christian Power in India" is definitely of the view that Daulat Rao Sindhia was the person who did his utmost to save the Maratha empire. Sunder Lal, the author of "Bharat Men Angrezi Rajya" is also of the opinion that it was Daulat Rao Sindhia, who genuinely fought for his motherland and never came completely into the clutches of British diplomacy.[38] It was the power of Sindhia and the Sikhs which the British dreaded upto 1843, when finally Gwalior forces were subdued due to civil war, by Sir Hough Gough at the battle of Maharajpur and Paniar.

Thus, the verdict of History on Daulat Rao Sindhia remains inconclusive and obscure. Another unfortunate element, which hinders us in making a correct appraisal of Daulat Rao, is that he was the successor of a more renowned person and so he fails to get the careful assessment that he deserves.

Yet another cause of adverse opinions about Daulat Rao Sindhia is that most writers have taken into their consideration only Marathi records of the Poona Daftar, or those of the British Residents, who were alike, hostile to Sindhia, or of Broughton who has painted a lurid picture of Daulat Rao Sindhia.

---

36. Luerd, *Gwalior State Gaztt.* p. 28, ed. 1908.

37. Munroe quote by Sardesai in the *Main Currents of Maratha History,* p. 163.

38. Sunder Lal : *Bharat Men Angrezi Rajya,* ed. 1938, Vol. II, p. 575.

British Aims

The main policy of British diplomats between 1800 to 1818, was to glorify the deeds of the persons who supported them and denounced those who put a spoke in the wheels of British imperialism. That is why Col. Tod glorified those Rajputs, who fell an easy prey to British diplomacy. Even Ranjit Singh was highly praised by English writers, because he was always friendly to the East India Company.

Daulat Rao Sindhia's achievements can be studied under several heads — territorial, cultural, administrative, financial and diplomatic. In the territorial sphere, he achieved compactness of his kingdom, increased his direct authority over it by wresting Narwar, Sabalgarh, Pauri and other places from minor Rajas and his own semi-independent chiefs like the chiefs of Shivpur, Chanderi, Garghkotah, Bahadurgarh, Raghogarh. With the destruction of the power of the Pindaris, he succeeded in bringing a large part of their territories under his direct control.

With the consolidation of these territories, his revenue also increased, and it increased to twice what it was before 1805, and, as Malcolm testified, "he utilised his increased revenues to the restoration and maintenance of internal tranquility."[39]

In the sphere of administration, the encouragement of the Panchayats was Daulat Rao's outstanding achievement. He revived the Panchayat system, and in his territories it received special impetus and survived continuously until the merger of Madhya Bharat in the Madhya Pradesh of today. His management of the revenue system was favourable to the farmers. In the judicial sphere, his system was also superior to what the British set up in their own territories.

He founded the modern town of Lashkar and beautified it with many palaces, lakes, gardens and markets, and constructed many buildings at Ujjain. He was a munificent patron of art and learning, and music and dance flourished at Gwalior under his patronage. As pointed out in an earlier chapter, the famous Hindi poet Padmakar lived at his court. Above all no commercial distinctions were observed either in his administration or in the general life of his state, and his practice in this respect

39. Malcolm, *Political History of India*, C.I. I., p. 141.

gives the lie to the false accusation that the Marathas were hostile to the Muslims.

He first made Gokul Parikh his Finance Minister. Dishonest persons who did not make punctual payments were dismissed. He remained conscious of the need to replenish his resources, maintained a private treasury and this appeared to have increased after the Second Maratha War. On 30-9-1809, the Resident estimated his cash treasure at 50 or 60 lakhs in 1809 which rose, according to the same authority to 1½ crore in 1817. This speaks of his administrative efficiency m financial administration. He has been praised even by Malcolm and envied by others.

In the diplomatic sphere, Daulat Rao Sindhia was no match for British diplomacy, and it was the superiority of the latter that caused the defeat of the Marathas in the struggle for supremacy in India. In the world of P.M. Joshi, the period of Daulat Ras Sindhia was "a period during which the British wrested the sovereignty of India from the Marathas. Its main theme naturally is the rivalry between these two powers for the dominion of India, which...ended with the former's triumph."[40]

Daulat Rao Sindia and the Fall of the Maratha Confederacy

Daulat Rao Sindhia's reign was contemporaneous with the Anglo-Maratha conflict for supremacy. S.J. Owan writes that the control of entire India was indirectly in the hands of Daulat Rao Sindhia. We must need come to some conclusion as to how far Daulat Rao Sindhia was responsible for the dissipation of that power during the period under review. He was certainly overwhelmed by British diplomacy in all phases of the conflict. They created internal feuds among the Maratha nobles and seduced many of Daulat Rao Sindhia's officers from their allegiance to him. But the record would go to show that eventually he was able to survive with a large measure of independence, though he could not save the confederacy. He reacted with prompt vigour to the implications of the treaty of Bassein but he failed to establish a consolidated front against the British due largely to the blind and weak factiousness of other Maratha chiefs. Sarkar and Sardesai's indictment that he alone was responsible for the defeat of the Marathas thus appears to be exaggerated.

40. *Poona Residency Correspondence*, XIV, Foreword by P.M. Joshi.

After the Second Maratha War, Daulat Rao Sindhia made the best of a bad bargain. He consolidated his truncated kingdom and thwarted as far as was possible consistent with his own survival all British designs. He even succeeded in controlling the Pindaries to some extent, a task in which even British diplomacy had failed.

In the last Maratha War, by following a dubious policy, he saved his kingdom even after the defeat of Holkar and the Peshwa. In 1816, he seems to have been favourable to the formation of a confederacy of all Maratha rulers, the Sikhs, Nepal, and the Rajputs against the British. He received Govind Rao the ambassador of Poona. He instructed Bapu Sindhia to conciliate the Rajputs by every means in his power and not to discourage them by any conduct which might interrupt the harmony that he (Sindhia) wished[41] to preserve with them.[42] He encouraged the misunderstanding between the Peshwa and the British. The Resident writes : "Remarks were thrown out obviously with a view to raise distrust between us (the British) and the Peshwa."[43]

Daulat Rao Sindhia expected a joint effort to oppose the British challenge, but when he failed to secure such collaboration, he changed his policy to save his kingdom. The Resident wrote to J. Adams, Secretary to Governor General : "He (is) not likely, therefore, to change the line of policy by which he (has) retained it or risk the total loss of it by any rash act."[44] Similarly, Malcolm remarked that "he preferred the path of safety."[45] He knew when to accept the inevitable and how to make the best bargain in the worst circumstances, as is testified by his policy after the Second Maratha War. He regained Gwalior and Gohad and gained some more territories after the extermination of the Pindaries. Thus, it was his temporising policy after 1806 that

41. *Poona Residency Correspondence,* Vol. XIV, No. 270, p. 338.

42. Malcolm, *Political History of India,* C.I., *A Memoir of Central India,* 1st, p. 140.

43. *Poona Residency Correspondence,* Vol. XIV No. 269, p. 325 also see Private Journal of Lord Hastings letter 23-3-1827.

44. *Ibid.*, p. 407 dated 24-4-1817 J. Stewert to J. Adams, Secretary to Government.

45. Malcolm, *Political History of India,* C.I., *A Memoir of Central India,* IInd.

saved his kingdom from a fate like that of the Peshwa or the Bhonsle.

Relations with the Company

An interesting point that needs to be discussed at this stage is the relation in which Daulat Rao Sindhia stood to the East India Company at the end of his reign. Answering a question on this subject in the Parliamentary Committee on Sindhia in 1832 (Feb. 16, 1832), the well known historian, Mill, replied that "he was independent" and then he was asked "has he no treaty with the Company?" and he replied : "Yes, there are several treaties but they are not such as to abrogate his independence or to place him in acknowledged submission to the British Government."[46] This Committee finally reported to Parliament that "within the Peninsula, Sindhia is the only prince who preserves the semblance of independence...he neither at present has a subsidiary alliance with us, nor do we include him among the protected states. In that respect, he stands alone."[47] How the status of the successors of Daulat Rao changed later is another story with which we are not concerned here.

Further proof of this singular status of Daulat Rao Sindhia even after the fall of the Peshwa can be sought in the very treaties of Surji Arjungaon and Burhanpur between the East India Company and Sindhia which, it may be noted, was treated almost as a dead letter after new engagements were entered into between these powers in 1805 and 1817. Further, it is essential to remember that the essence of Wellesley's Subsidiary Alliance system was that British forces, paid for by the subordinate partner to such a treaty, were stationed within the territories of the protected state. The provisions of the Treaty of 1804 itself do not show that alliance was in any technical or substantial sense, a subsidiary alliance. Relevant Articles of the treaty run as follows :

Article 3 : The Maharaja agrees to receive, and the Hon'ble East India Company agrees to furnish a subsidiary force.... This force is to be stationed at such place near

46. James Mill before the Select Committee of the House of Commons on Sindhia dated 16-2-1832 quoted by Sunder Lal Vol. III, p. 746.
47. Quoted by Basu, p. 147 and Sunder Lal II, p. 764, *Govt. of India Publication*, ed. 1961.

the frontier of Daulat Rao Sindhia, as may hereafter be deemed most eligible by the British Government.

Article 6 : Explains the function of this force as follows : "The subsidiary force will, at all times, be ready, on the requisition of the Maharaja, to execute services of importance, such as the care of the person of the Maharaja, his heirs and successors, the protection of the country from attack and invasion, the overawing and chastisement of rebels or exciters of disturbance in the Maharaja's dominions, but it is not to be employed on trifling occasions."

It is true that Sindhia had to abandon Delhi, Agra, the Doab, and in 1817, his claims to tribute from the Rajputana States in return for this protection by the Company, so the lost revenue from these territories may be considered as payment for the subsidiary forces maintained by the Company near his frontiers for the purpose. But, on the other hand, since Sindhia's claim to the ceded territories was only one by conquest, it was only natural that he lost them by military defeat. Further, other articles of this superceded treaty, also deserve a glance :

Article 8 : The Maharaja engages neither to commence nor to pursue in future any negotiations with any principal states or powers, without giving previous notice and entering into mutual consultation with the Hon'ble East India Company's Government. They on their part declare that they will have no manner of concern with any of the Maharaja's relations, dependents, Military chiefs or servants, with respect to whom the Maharaja is absolute : and they will, on no occasion, ever afford encouragement, support or protection to any of the Maharaja's relations, dependents, chiefs or servants, who may eventually act in opposition to the Maharaja's authority, but, on the contrary, at the requisition of the Maharaja they would aid and assist to punish and reduce all such offenders to obedience, and it is further agreed that no officer of the Hon'ble Company shall ever interfere in the internal affairs of the Maharaja's Government,

Article 9 : The Maharaja Daulat Rao Sindhia engages never to commit any act of hostility or aggression against any state or chief in alliance with the Hon'ble Co., or against any other principal state or power; and in the event of differences arising, whatever adjustment the Company's Government; weighing matters in the scale of truth and justice, may determine shall meet with his full approbation and acquiescence.

Article 14: Neither of the two contracting parties shall enter into alliance, or have any concern with the tributaries or chiefs of the other; and in order to support the independent authority of both Governments, it is agreed and declared, that hereafter neither of the contracting parties will give protection or countenance to the rebellious tributaries and subjects of the other, but they will use their utmost endeavours for the apprehension of such rebels....

Thus, it is clear that, even this superceded treaty gave no right to the Company to interfere in the internal administration of his territories, determine the successor to his state or limit the number of his armed forces. It only promised aid at the Maharaja's own request and not at the discretion of the Company. It was an alliance different in spirit from those with the Nizam or Oudh and, at the worst, gave Sindhia the status of a "Protected" prince within the sphere of British influence. Indeed, it was Ellenborngh's treaty of 1843,[48] when the states' army was cut down to 9,000 men, a British contingent of 10,000 men was stationed within the state, and the British Government took power to administer the state during an interregnum, that the state of Gwalior became totally dependent on British goodwill for its existence, and lost that 'semblance of independence' which it enjoyed between 1803 and 1843.

It is thus a tribute to Daulat Rao Sindhia's diplomatic and political clear-sightedness that he was able to preserve even such a status for his state during his reign and was indeed even able to survive the storms that beset him from the beginning. He faced the intrigues of Nana Phadnavis, Baji Rao II, and the widows against him successfully, when he was still in his teens. They joined with Holkar, Lakhwa Dada and Balloba Pagnis

48. "Gwalior was now definitely made a protected state" P.E. Peluets, p. 331, ed. 1745.

against him; they seduced his officers into mutiny against him; and all the time, the East India Company was unresistingly planning to undermine the power of the Maratha confederacy and its individual members. Even after the treaty of Bassein, as Arthur Wellesley reported : "Raghoji Bhonsle was sincerely in favour of Daulal Rao Sindhia." Jaswant Rao Holkar throughout remained aloof from and hostile to him. Against this powerful combination of hostile forces, Daulat Rao was not only able to survive but also able to maintain a "semblance of independence." This is a notable achievement, indeed, for which he legitimately deserves Political credit.[49] Daulat Rao Sindhia saved him and his family fortune by hair's breadth.

Tipu has been called a martyr to the national cause; but Daulat Rao Sindhia proved wiser than Tipu in this respect. He challenged British power when he thought that the time was opportune. His calculations cannot be said to have been exaggerated. After the battle of Laswari, Lord Lake remarked that the issue would have been doubtful, if Sindhia's armies had been led by French officers.[50] According to Basu and Sunder Lal, the history of India might have been written differently had the armies been led by Daulat Rao Sindhia himself at Assaye, and had his generals not deceived him.[51] Daulat Rao Sindhia tried his best to oppose British expansion, when there was the proper opportunity to do so, but when he found himself faced with non-cooperation from Holkar, the Peswa, the Bhonsle, the Gaikwar and the treachery of Ambaji, De Perron, Bouroquien, Shah Alam and Begum Samroo. Padampani, a tried ambassador of Nepal reported "the Maharaja's (Sindhia's) ministers have leagued with the English, this alarms and prevents him from quarrelling with them,"[52] then he saved his kingdom from complete extinction by coming to terms with his formidable

49. P. Shear : *Oxford History of India*, p. 571 Ed. 1958.

50. Sarkar, *Fall of the Mughal Empire*, Vol. IV, pp. 304-07.

51. Sunder Lal, *Bharat Men Angrezi Rajya*, Vol. II, p. 567, ed. 1938 and p. 446, Ed. July 1960.

52. Padmpani to Raja of Nepal 12.6.1817 enclosed in Despatch of Govt. to Gardener on 7.7.1817, *Nepal Residency Records* (N.R.) Vol. II quoted by Ranchan Moy Mojumdar in *Journal of Indian History*, Vol. XLIII August 1965, p. 409.

adversary. "In acting thus, he showed the truest political wisdom and preserved such part of his state for his successors."[53]

ABANDONMENT OF GUERILLA TACTICS

The abandonment of guerilla tactics, according to Alfred Lyall and Munroe, was the principal cause of the failure of the Marathas. Dr. Sen in his famous book "Military System of the Marathas", says that Maratha armies were like an eagle and British armies were like a lion, the eagle always harasses the lion if it attacks and flies away, but if it fights face to face, it is bound to be defeated by the lion. The same was the case with the Marathas and the British forces. Abandonment of guerilla tactics brought the Maratha eagle face to face with the British lion and it was routed. Dr. Banerji also attributes the downfall of the Marathas to change in the tactics of the Maratha army and the replacement of Marathas by northern Pathans and Thakurs in its ranks.

Conclusions

The true cause of Daulat Rao's defeat and discomfiture should rather be sought in the general factors which were responsible for the downfall of the Maratha Empire as a whole. To blame him exclusively for that colossal catastrophe is to mistake the effect for the cause. It is clear that to attribute the entire failure of the Marathas to Daulat Rao is unfair. Treachery was the main cause for the failure of Daulat Rao Sindhia[54] in the Second Anglo-Maratha War. Not only this, but Bhonsle did not co-operate with him whole-heartedly. Jaswant Rao Holkar did not join him and Baji Rao II, instead of helping him, helped the East India Company. Under these circumstances, it was very difficult for him to wage a successful war.

It is true Daulat Rao lacked the genius of Shivaji and Baji Rao I and the political dexterity of Mahadji Sindhia. So far as British diplomats were concerned, it cannot be denied that whatever might be the ethical aspect of the means they employed, their achievements were unmistakable, Sindhia's failure was the failure of a person who fought against heavy odds.

53. Kincaid and Parasnis, pp. 223-24, ed. 1925.

54. An notable instance of desertion was that of a high officer in the service of Sindhia of Gwalior who had secretly come to terms with the British, Nehru, p. 295.

Daulat Rao Sindhia had to fight against some of the most competent persons — Like Lord Wellesley, the Duke of willington, Lord Lake, Malcolm, Elphinstone and Metcalf who ever came to rule India from the British Islands. It goes to the credit of Daulal Rao Sindhia that he was able to save his kingdom in the face of such heavy odds. He failed to check the advancement of British imperialism, but to damn him as the sole cause of British expansion is unjust and apocryphal.

To quote Sarkar : "The Mughal Empire and with it the Maratha overlordship of Hindustan fell because of the rottenness at the core of Indian Society. This rottenness showed itself in many directions. The country could not defend itself, royalty was hopelessly deprived and imbecile; the nobles were selfish and short-sighted; corruption, inefficiency and treachery disgraced all branches of public service. In the midst of this decay and confusion, our literature and even true religion had perished."[55]

These remarks of Sir J.N. Sarkar, mutatis mutandis depict through the characters of Balloba Tantia, Lakhwa Dada, Ambaji Ingale and the widows of Mahadji Sindhia the tragedy of the Maratha empire. There was no school for higher learning or military training and consequently India failed to produce men of strong character, integrity and honesty. Baji Rao II, Asafuddola, Saadat Ali Khan, Bijay Singh of Jodhpur, Jagat Singh of Jaipur, Ratna Bhim Singh of Udaipur, and old Shah Alam gave themselves up completely to wine and women. When it is remembered that the Indian powers never were united the success of the British ceases to seem either extraordinary or unaccountable.[56]

No effort was made to check the disintegrating forces. The system of granting jagirs and of granting offices on hereditary bases brought disastrous consequences. Even Nana Phadnavis encouraged the Holkar family as a counterpoise to the influence of Mahaji Sindhia. In fact, the Marathas never learnt the value of a single unified authority.

The Marathas believed in mulkgiri, that is, in realising chauth and tributes. This policy was followed even by Mahadji, and his successor had to face constant warfare with semi-

55. Sarkar, *Fall of the Mughal Empire*, IV, pp. 343-44, Khare Vol; XIV, 6710.
56. P. Spear : *The Oxford History of India*, p. 499, ed. 1958.

independent chiefs. Armies marched and counter-marched and to collect the revenue as to defeat the foe.[57]

The basic cause of the disintegration of the Maratha Empire was the lack of a strong Central Government that could keep the Governors of different Subas in check and maintained unimpaired the basic conception of a national Government.[58]

The Maratha armies were generally composed of men of various communities and religions and consequently presented a very motley combination. They wore no regular uniforms and they lacked discipline.

Mahadji's policy of introducing foreign generals proved disastrous. Leaders of the armies of the same chief fought with one another. The rapidity of movement, the power to strike swiftly and disappear, that is, guerilla tactics, were given up even before the third battle of Panipat. They modelled their army on European or Mughal lines. Major Diroham writes, "It (Maratha Camp) had the appearance of a large irregular town". Broughton also confirms this opinion. The Marathas sought ease, comfort and even luxury on the field of battle. Orme, in his 'History of the Military Transactions of the British Nation in Hindustan' says, "Every common soldier in any Indian army is accompanied either by a wife or a concubine, the officers have several, and the generals have seraglios, the armies are encumbered by a number of attendants and servants exceeding the number of fighting men." So in the period under review here, the Maratha army was neither the army of Shivaji's days when the taking of women to the war was prohibited with on pain of death[59], nor of Baji Rao I, who fought as a common trooper and ate Joo-naree.[60] The introduction of Pindaries in to the armed forces made confusion worse confounded.

Above all, the Marathas failed to compete with the British army on account of the latters' improved and superior methods

57. P. Spear : *The Oxford History of India*, p. 449.

58. Foreword by Sir Shafat Ahmed Khan to V.V. Joshi's *Clash of Three Empires*.

59. Grant Duff, *History of the Marathas*, Vol. I, p. 103 says "No soldier in the service of Shivaji was permitted to carry any female follower with him in the field on pain of death".

60. *Ibid.*, p. 252.

of warfare. This view is supported by Khare, Rajwade and Sardesai. The tragedy of the Marathas was only the result of the modern age bursting upon a sleepy inert medieval society, that could make no attempt to adjust itself to the necessary changes. They lost the art of guerilla tactics and failed also to adapt themselves to scientific warfare.

Another drawback of the Maratha State was its lack of a sound economic policy and satisfactory financial arrangements, without which the political development of nation becomes impossible. The result was that even in the hey-day of its glory, person like Mahadji had to suffer from financial stringency.[61]

The Marathas failed to build up a stable administrative machinery based upon a trained bureaucracy. They lacked the broad vision of the British. In the words of Sardesai, "Malet proved himself superior to the shrewdest Maratha dipilomat Nana Phadnavis." The 15 volumes of the Poona Residency correspondence clearly establish the superiority of British diplomacy over Maratha diplomacy. Baji Rao II told Malcolm that "Elphinstone knew the very dishes that were served at his meals,"[62] because he purchased traitors who supplied all information to him. It was such secret information which enabled Arthur Wellesley to attack the Marathas at Assaye, when the latter were not ready for battle.

The organisation of the Maratha State was defective also in this that it was not based on common tradition or rules. In the words of J.N. Sarkar, "The cohesion of the people in the Maratha State was not organic but artificial, accidental and, therefore, precarious.[63]

The growth of patriotism among the Marathas was hindered by the infinite sub-divisions of the society which made the formations of one nation or a compact body of men moved by a feeling of community of thought and interest, impossible and even inconceivable. In the words of J.N. Sarkar, "The highest aim of a Hindu in that age as even in our own times, was to

---

61. See letter of Dinkar in Chapter VIII.
62. Choksey, *A History of British Diplomacy at the Court of the Peshwas*. p. 387.
63. Sarkar, *Fall of the Mughal Empire*, Shivaji, p. 359

elevate his own family."[64] He further adds : "The leaders were actuated by an insane pride of birth, an all devouring jealousy about precedence, an ambition that blinded them to all consequences, an incapacity for self subordination to law and corporate loyalty that marks the lesser breeds, a lack of political vision and of practical realism. As for the masses, they were human sheep, worthy to be led by such shepherds; their horizon was bounded by the hard conditions of their daily toil, with a simple emotional faith as the only solace."[65]

Maratha leaders trusted too much to finesse. They did not realise that without a certain amount of manly openness and fidelity to promises, no society can hold together. While the Maratha spider was weaving his endless cobweb of hollow alliances and diplomatic counterplots, the mailed fist of Wellesley was thrust into his laboured but flimsy tissue of statecraft, and by a few swift and judicious strokes his defence and screen was torn away and his power left naked and helpless.[66]

The policy of leaving half crushed enemies free and to take recourse to arms again and again, as was the case with the Nizam and the Rajputs, proved disastrous to the Maratha empire, as it forced unnecessary wars without any permanent result. In the words of Sarkar, "Sunset overtook a state and society that was rotten to the core with official corruption and inefficiency, endless internal discord, the extinction of the breed of true leaders in war and councils, and utter financial exhaustion."[67]

64. Sarkar, *Fall of the Mughal Empire*, Shivaji, p. 362.

65. *Ibid.*, p. 363.

66. *Ibid.*, p.365.

67. Mr. B.D. Sanwal in his book Nepal and the East India Company laid stress on the contrast between the crude medieval diplomacy of the Indian world and the modern 19th century diplomacy of the East India Company, and the disparity between the old world Indian weapons and modern warfare and scientific military training, strategy and fire arms of the company, but concludes that Nepal's freedom was preserved due to the loyalty and patriotism of the Gorkha commanders. But Daulat Rao's commanders lacked these qualities and so he failed. Review by Dr. A.L. Srivastava, pp. 679-681 in Journal of Indian History Vol. XLIII, August 1965.

For details Raja Rao's vices, Khare Chapter XIV, 6710. Asaf Udaulla and Saadat Ali, Sarkar Vol. IV, p. 394, Tod, Bijai Singh and other Rajput Rajas and Jaipur and Jodhpur Ethil Raj Karnen by Parasnis, etc.

Daulat Rao Sindhia, like other Maratha chiefs of the day had no touch of genius. He was a child of his times. He had neither the personal magnetism of Shivaji nor the organising capacity of Baji Rao I, nor the diplomatic and political talents of Mahadji. He could not weld the scattered forces of the Maratha chiefs into an integrated unity. He naturally failed to come up to the needs of his times. We can give him only one credit, namely, that he realised the danger of the British power and resisted it with all his might. When he found the odds too heavy against him, he like a realist saved his state and ignored all else.

REVIEW

The reason why it has been felt necessary to discuss the causes of the fundamental weakness of the Maratha empire, consists in the fact that many writer have held that Daulat Rao Sindhia was responsible for its final destruction, but his real and only fault was that he could not check its precipitous fall because of his inability to unite others for a national cause, partly because of his own faults and mistakes and partly because of the stubborn factiousness of his contemporaries. While bowing down to the inevitable, he did carve out a place for himself and his dynasty, and his achievement lies in the fact that he could accomplish it against heavy odds. Percival Spear states "First came such states as Hyderabad and Sindhia which possessed an independent origin and claimed an independent states."[68]

His Role in the History of the Maratha Empire

Daulat Rao Sindhia was the last powerful Maratha chieftain and ranks among the highest of contemporary Maratha leaders. Raghoji Bhonsle II was an experienced person, but he stands now here in comparison to Daulat Rao Sindhia. Baji Rao II was a person of mediocre ability and fails to compare with him favourably. Sradesai praises Jaswant Rao Holkar. Sarkar does not subscribe to that view. He says : "I do not include Jaswant Rao Holkar, because after a short and fitful career, his genius crossed its limits and merged into madness."[69] It cannot be doubted that Jaswant Rao Holkar was greater general than

68. *Poona Residency Correspondence,* IV, p. 344.

69. *Oxford History of India,* p. 629 ed. by P. Spear, ed. 1958.

Daulat Rao Sindhia, but in statesmanship, in character, in diplomacy and in administrative ability, he was no match for Daulat Rao Sindhia.

Daulat Rao Sindhia fully understood the contemporary political situation and learnt things by experience as, in the words of J.B. Malleson, after the Second Maratha War he grew wise and did not rely the Pindaris openly, and signed the treaty on November 5, 1817. Similarly the Resident J. Stewart remarks : "The Peshwa, the Raja of Berar and Holkar have suffered infinitely more, power and influence being only relative terms, that of Sindhia may be said to have been raised by the depression or total extinction of that of all the other native states; and I really imagine that he does feel some pride in being the only chief, who has retained any thing like independence."[70]

It goes to his credit, however, that in his policy decisions he was never influenced by the nobles or petticoat influence. On all critical occasions, he always followed his own counsel. Hindu Rao Ghatge, Jaswant Rao Bhau, Gopal Bhau and other Sardars were in favour of helping the Pindaric[71], but Daulat Rao Sindhia refused to do so.

According to G.B. Malleson. Daulat Rao saw in the treaty of Bassein, "A threat against himself...and from this time he turned all his efforts to the welding together of the union...(for) the expulsion of the English from northern, central and western India.... But lack of co-operation of other rulers forced him to bow down to the inevitable."

Daulat Rao Sindhia was engaged in one of those undertakings in which success elevates a man to the rank of a hero, but failure denounces him as an obstinate and perverse adventurer. It is a risky undertaking to give any dogmatic verdict on a controversial personality, but perhaps it is permissible to say that he should be regarded in history as the last ruler, who desired to challenge the mighty sway of British imperialism

70. *Poona Residency Correspondence,* Vol. XIV, No. 409 J. Stewart Acting Resident with Sindhia to Adams, Secretary to Government from Gwalior to Governor General dated 24-4-1818.

71. *Ibid.*, Various letters and description of Pindaris in the Thesis Chapter VI.

and at least tried though unsuccessfully to award avert the general catastrophe that threatened the Marathas.

His diplomacy continued in the family of Sindhia. During First War of Independence of 1857, Daulat Rao's wife Baiza Bai symphethised with Maratha leaders and ruling Sindhian Prince of Gwalior with the Britishers.

After 1947, among ruling princely families, Sindhian family proved most successful. Maharani Vijay Raje Sindhia become leader of Bhartiya Janta Party along with her daughter Vasundhra Raje Sindhia, who became Chief minister of Rajasthan in December 2003 fulfilling old dream of Sindhia family to dominate Rajasthan. While her brother, Madhav Rao Sindhia became leader of Congress and as railway minister introduced many trains from Gwalior. Thus, even after fall of British empire in India, Sindhia family continued importance in Indian politics while British empire in India has disappeared. Thus, comparative study of Anglo-Maratha Relations is very important.

APPENDIX

Note on (Maratha) and Modern System of Law and Justice based on British System

There is a great controversy whether Law and justice system prevailing in India was better or modern judicial system based on English judicial system is better.

Writers of Maratha History, who knew Maratha judicial system have considered Maratha judicial system better than English system of Law and justice. These writers are of the opinion that Indian systems of which Maratha system was based, was for superior than British system of law and justice as it was based on the maxim that justice must be done, so even king used to roam about in disguise to find the true culprit and truth of the case, while British system of justice is confined to mere technicalities without being based on truth, thus justice is never done as it is based on evidence and not on truth. Moreover, British system of justice is dilatory and cases are decided after many decades, so 30 million cases are pending in India in 2004.

Lastly it is most expensive, and parties who, contest cases become pauper.

Thus, Historians differ with the modern elite class of judiciary, who are fortunate enough to become judges and adorn judicial offices and possess unlimited power as they can declare any law null and void.

With this even lawyers are dissatisfied and strikes of lawyers and lathi charge and firing over lawyers have become common feature in India which is not found anywhere in the world. As such it is given in appendix in this book. (as lot of persons contacted Author on this topic) Elphinstone, Kincaid and Parasnais writers of "History of Maratha People and Cambridge History of India Vol. V and Tone, writer of Institutions of Maratha People etc. have praised Maratha system of justice and criticised British system of justice. Lokmanya B.G. Tilak and other leaders of freedom movement were also critical British system of justice, so a brief note is attached in Appendix A.

Law and Justice

The Judicial administration of the Marathas was far superior to the British Judicial system as we shall presently see. Civil cases used to be compromised in the village through influential persons or matters were settled by arbitration or through Panchayats. In Panchayats both the parties used to select two persons each and fifth person was selected by these four persons or one person may be selected if both parties reposed their confidence in him. Justice was free, impartial and cheap. The greatest advantage of Maratha justice was that usually cases were decided in a very short time. Cases did not linger for scores of years as it had been under the British regime or as it is even now. Moreover, justice was not a costly affair depending on the capacity of the purse. Civil cases when man of ranks were the suitors, or which involved a large property were generally referred to the ministers and submitted to their arbitration, or tried by Panchayat. Small crimes and disputes were referred to Patel, who possessed the power of stripes but not of fine. Disputes of greater importance of different villages were referred to revenue officers, who either settled them themselves or constituted a panchayat for their disposal. Sardars adjusted disputes of servants and neighbours. Seths and Mahajan used to decide disputes in the trading centres. Punchayat was highly respected. "The Punchayats" writes Elphinstone "were more frequently named by the parties than the Judge. The members of the Punchayat received no fee but when they had much trouble, the winner of the suit made them openly a present of their pains.[1]

More emphasis was laid on justice than on technical language or legal complications. There were no lawyers to complicate matters. In both civil and criminal matters decisions were based upon customs and upon injunctions from Hindu Shastras and Muslim Shraiat. In civil cases, the main object aimed at was amicable settlement and usually cases were either

1. Kincaid and Parasnais, *History of Maratha People.* p. 243.

decided by arbitration or through punchayats. Most important cases used to go to the Maharaja himself in appeal. In justice, traditions of Vikramaditya and Jahangir were considered as ideal and it was believed if any one did injustice, he would be bound to get punishment before God. The current legal adage was "Raja Kare so Nayaya," meaning thereby 'Kings' decree was infallible. The king too always took care to follow the principles of justice except in political cases or in which he himself was interested. Daulat Rao Sindia punished even his maternal uncle Bobu Rao Angaria and removed him from Subedarship when complaint was made to him.

Torture was usually applied to elicit confession of guilt from the criminals. Flogging was usually the punishment for petty crimes, but theft and immorality were considered as great crimes and severe punishment was awarded in such crimes. Capital punishment could be given by the ruler of the state only, but this rigid rule was sometimes not followed.

Imprisonment was awarded comparatively in a few cases. Prisoners used to be kept in forts particularly dangerous, criminals like Kareem Khan were kept in dungeons. Sometimes relief was given to prisoners on the occasion of festivals and family Shradhs etc. Prisoners were also released on the occasion of the days of happiness to the ruler such as marriage or victory, amnesty was also granted on payment of heavy fines. It is refreshing to point out that Maratha justice has been praised by English writers and they have not failed to maximise the evils of British Justice. The following quotations will bring out the twin aspect of the problem. "The fact must be admitted that among themselves, within the confines of the self contained ancestral village, the peasantry did obtain a fair medicum of rude justice from the village punchayat.[2] Similarly a modern English writer states 'There were two innovations that Elephlstone especially dreaded the Establishment of English law courts, and the attempts to spread Christianity.[3]

He further adds, the English lawyers had evolved so intricate and unintelligible system that Bentham compared law of England to a poisonous parasite fastened to an oak, and asserted

2. *Cambridge History of India*, Vol. I p. 390, ed. 1929.
3. Kincaid, *History of the Maratha People*. p. 233.

that it was stifling the very life of country to which it clings. In the words of Kincaid and Parasnais "The Indian who was so unfortunate as to get entangled in a law suit might deem himself lucky, if escaped with a single rage to cover his nakedness or he lived long enough to see its conclusion. According to Colebroke's Elphistone Vol. II page 131 also quoted by C.A. Kincaid and Parasnais "a traveller riding through a village saw its population fleeing panic stricken into the Jungle. He assumed that they dreaded the expected arrival of Lake's forces. The peasants assured him that it was not so. It was something much worse. It was the 'Adalat' that was coming. They could have borne with stoic resignation the approach of British arms; but they were fleeing, sickling and unmannered at the rumoured advent of British justice.[4] The religious danger proved illusory...the legal peril proved more real."[5]

According to a modern writer British Government destroyed the most ancient institution of the country the village community the miniature republics of Munroe[6] and introduced new British system within the reach only of those who had the longest purse to pay for the stamp dues, the court processes and the unending principle of legal advice. It can be safely asserted that if the maxim 'Justice delayed is justice denied' is true and if cheapness is also a virtue of the system, Maratha Justice can be rated superior to the British Justice. Adoption of British System of justice in India has resulted in arrears of 3 crore cares pending from many years. Frequent strike of lawyers and lathi charge and firing of Police on lawyers is now common.

Police Arrangements

During the Maratha rule Patel was the unit of police force also. He was responsible for law and order in the village. He was helped by the Chaughula, the Kulkarni, and generally by the main body of the villagers. But his chief assistant was watchman or Mhar. It was the latter's duty to keep watch at night, scrutinize strangers, and report suspicious individuals to the Patel. When a theft was committed it was the Mhar's duty to detect the thief. And, as he was always moving about

4. *History of the Maratha People*, Oxford Press, p. 234.
5. *Ibid.*, ed. 1925, p. 234 Oxford Press.
6. Tone, *Institutions of the Maratha People*, p. 75.

the village either to collect his share of grain or his fees, there was little therein that escaped his observation. He was also a skilled tracker and could often follow the foot steps of the criminal to his home or hiding place. Over a head man, there was the Subadar who kept up a force of Sibandies, or irregular infantry and a small body of regular horse. They were, however, intended to oppose violence rather than to detect crime. There were also Tapasa Navises or C.I.D., whose duty was not only to detect crime but to prevent it by superior vigilance. "This system, rudimentary although it seems, worked admirably."[7] Thus, according to Historians, Indian Law and Justice system was more suitable to Indian society.

7. Kincaid and Parasnais, *History of the Maratha People*, p. 237.

BIBLIOGRAPHY

MANUSCRIPT

At the National Archives of India, *Queensway*, New Delhi.

Foreign Political Index and Papers, 1794-1799, 1806-1824.

Secret Foreign Political Index and Papers, 1801-1806, Poona particularly Sindhia and 1806-1815.

Foreign Secret Political Papers, 1818-1824.

Foreign Political Index and Papers, 1801-1806 transferred to Secret Department.

Foreign Secret Consultations (1794 A.D. to 1827).

Foreign Secret Political Consultations (1794 A.D. to 1826).

Foreign Department Miscellaneous, Vols. S.W., 168-A, B, C, D.

Central Agency Files List No. 23.

File Rahatgarh, 1818.

File 199/1818, Amjhera.

Gwalior Residency File No. 1361 and *Gwalior State Papers* (Selected Portions).

Parliamentary Papers (*Microfilm*), Vol., pages 9, 41, 49, Papers, 69-79 II, 1803-1804.

II

Gwalior State Records regarding Daulat Rao Sindhia.

Shivpuri District Records.

PRINTED DOCUMENTS

Poona Residency Correspondence, ed. by J.N. Sarkar and Sardesai — 15 Vols.

Dr. Sinha. H.N. : *Nagpur Residency Correspondence*, Vols. I and II.

Attichison Sir S.C. : *Collection of Treaties, Engagements and Sunnuds relating to India* — 10 Vols., Calcutta 1892.

Forrest G.W., *Selections from the Letters, Despatches and Other Papers* preserved in the Bombay Secretariat, Bombay 1885, Marathi Series.

Martin Montgomery : *The Despatches, Minutes and the Correspondence of Marquess Wellesley*, 5 Vols., London, 1837. *The Wellesley Papers*, 2 Vols.

Owen S.J. *A Selection from the Despatches, Treaties and other Papers of Marquess Wellesley*, Oxford, 1877.

Owen S.J. *A Selection from Wellington's Despatches*, 1880, Clarendon Press.

Papers Re, *Pindary and Maratha Wars.*

Gurwood Lt. Col. J., *The Despatches of Field Marshal the Duke of Wellington*, 13 Vols. 1799 to 1818 and Supplementary Despatches by his son.

Hastings Marquess of : *Private Diary*, 2 Vols., 1858.

Ross Charles : *Correspondence of Charles*, First Marquess Cornwallis, 3 Vols. London, 1858.

Basawan Lal : *Memoirs of Amir Khan*, Translated by H.T. Princep, Calcutta, 1832.

SECONDARY WORKS

Blacker V. *Memories of the Operations of the British Army in India during the Maratha War of 1817 and 1819*, 2 Vols., 1821.

Prinsep, Henary T. : *History of the Political and Military Transactions in India during the Administration of Marquess of Hastings*, 1813-1823, 2 Vols., 1825.

Crompton, H. *European Millitary Adventurers of Hindustan*, 1784-1803, ed. F. Unwine, 1892.

Pearse, Robert R., *Memories and Correspondence of Richard Marquess Wellesley*, 3 Vols., 1846.

Pearse; Col. Hugh : *Life and Military Service of Viscount Lake*, 1907.

Pester John : *War and Sport in India*, 1802-6.

C.P.C. *Calendar of Persian Correspondence* (Govt. of India Records Office).

Mannji and Parsnis Treaties, *Engagements and Sunnad.*

CONTEMPORARY WRITER'S BOOKS

Broughton Thomas D. : Letters written in a Maratha Camp during the year 1809. *Constable Edition* 1892 *Illustrated Edition*, Agra University Library and abridged (Nagpur University Library).

Malcolm Sir John : *The Political History of India* 1794-1823, 2 Vols., ed. 1826.

Ibid., A Memoir of Central India, Vols. I and II, ed. 1832 and 1970, reprinted by Sagar Publication, New Delhi.

Tod : *Annals and Antiquities of Rajasthan*, 3 Vols., ed. by Crooke, 1920, O.U.P.

Duff James Grant : *History of Marathas*, 3 Vols., ed. 1912 (National Library, Calcutta), ed. by Edwards Nagpur University Library) and one volume Agra University Library.

Warring : *A History of the Marathas,* 1810.

Tone W.H. *Illustration of some Institute of the Marathas People Cal.* (1818).

Wilks : *History of Mysore.*

Thornton : *History of British Empire in India*, 5 Vols.

Hope J. *The House of Sindhia.*

Skinnerg : *Military Memoir of James Skinner* by J.A. Fraser, 2 Vols., 1851.

Teighnmouth : *Memoir of Lord Teignmouth by his Son,* 2 Vols., 1843.

Maratha and Pindari War Compiled by the General Staff, Shimla, 1910.

Mill James : *History of British India* in fifth edition with notes continued by H.H. Wilson, 10 Vols., 1858.

UNPUBLISHED THESES

Dr. Mehta B.N. : *Sir George Barlow in India*, 1949.

Dr. Sharma E.G. : *Sir John Malcolm in Madhya Bharat.*

Dr. Mehta P.C. : *Relations between the Mewar and the Marathas.*

RECENT PUBLICATIONS IN ENGLISH

Sardesai G.S. : *New History of the Marathas,* 3 Vols. Phoenix Publications, Bombay.

Ibid., Main Currents of the Maratha History, II ed.

C.A. Kincaid and D.B. Parasnis : *History of the Maratha People*, 3 Vols., 1918-1925 (Agra University Library in one Vol., Central Lib. Gwalior, O.U.P.)

Sarkar J.N. : *Fall of the Mughal Empire*, 4 Vols. Pub. by M.C. Sarkar and Sons Ltd., Calcutta, ed. 1950.

Ibid., Shivaji.

Ibid., History of Aurangzeb, 5 Vols.

Ibid., Mughal Administration.

Ibid., India through The Ages.

Dr. Sen Surendra Nath : *Administrative System of Marathas*, 1923.

Ibid., The Military System of Marathas, 1928 and 1958 (Orient Longmans).

Dr. S.P. : *Diplomacy of the Marathas* (A Study in Maratha Diplomacy).

Ranade : *Rise of The Maratha Power.*

Roberts P.E. : *India Under Wellesley.*

Roberts P.E. : *History of British India*, ed. 1945, O.U.P.

Banerji R.D. : *History of Orissa*, Vols. I and II.

Keene : *Life of Mahadji Sindhia.*

Gupta Dr. Hari Ram : *History of the Sikhs* (Cis Sutlej) Vol. I and Vol. II, ed. 1944.

Basu B.D. : *Rise of Christian Power in India.*

Mehta, M.S. : *Lord Hastings and Indian States.*

Malleson Col. G.B. : *A Historical Sketch of The Native States of India* (Longman 1875).

P.C. Gupta : *Baji Rao II and the East India Company.*

Muir Ramsay : *Making of the British India.*

Dodwell : *Cambridge History of India*, Vol. V, ed. 1929.

Kaye J.W. : *Life and Correspondence of Major General Sir John Malcolm*, 2 Vols. London.

Colebrooke : *Life of Mountsturt Elphinstone*, 2 Vols., 1886.

Choksey R.D. : *History of British Diplomacy at the Court of the Peshwas*, 1786-1818, ed. 1951.

V.V. Joshi : *Clash of Three Empires.*

Auber Peter : *Rise and Progress of the British Power in India*, 2 Vols., London, 1837.

Bevridge Henry : *Comprehensive History of India — Civil, Military and Social,* 3 Vols., London 1867.

Banerji A.C. : *The Rajput States and East India Company.*

Ibid., Constitutional Documents, Vols. I, II and III.

Percival Spear and others : *The Oxford History of India,* edn. 1958.

Maratha Paramountcy, published by Vidya Bhawan ed. by R.C. Majumdar and Dighe — ed. 1977.

Lectures on Rajput History by A.C. Banerjee.

Studies in Indian History, ed. by Dr. V.D. Rao, ed. 1968, Kolhapur University.

H.C. Batra : *Relation of Jaipur States with East India Company,* S. Chand & Co., Delhi.

R.M. Sinha : *Bhonsales of Nagpur — The Last Phase,* 1818-54.

K.S. Gupta : *Mewar and Maratha Relations.*

Saxena : *Maratha Relations with the Major States of Rajputana.*

Karni Singh : *The Relations of the House of the Bikaner with the Central Powers,* Munshilal Manoharlal, Delhi.

Qanungo S.N. : *Jaswant Rao Holkar.*

JOURNALS, PERIODICALS, GAZETTEERS AND REVIEWS

The Asiatic Annual Register, 1799-1811.

The Journal of Indian History.

Proceedings of Indian Historical Records Commission.

Calcutta Review.

Imperial Gazetteer of India, Vol. II (Historical Clarendon Press, 1908).

Central India State Gazetteer by Luard Lt. Col. Calcutta and Lucknow, 1907-1908.

Gwalior State Gezetteer 1908 by C.E. Luard.

HINDI

Sunder Lal : *Bharat Men Angrezi Rajya,* 3 Vols., ed. 1938 and Vols. I and II, published by Government of India, 1960 and 1961.

Sindhey (Sindhia) *Ka Mool Udgam by Vidya Nand Swami* (Nagpur University Library).

Dr. Raghubir Singh : *Purva Adhunik Rajasthan*, ed. 1950 51.

Madhya Bharat Ka Itihas (V.T.P. Inter College Library, Shivpuri).

Chanderi Ka Itihas, Manuscript (By courtsey) of Pujari Jageshwari Temple Chanderi).

Ojha : *Rajasthan Ka Itihas.*

Sardesai G.S. : *Marathas Ka Navin Ithas*, Hindi Translation 3 Vols., published by Shivlal Agarwal, Agra, ed. 1964.

Gwalior Raja Ke Lekh.

Various books containing the poems of Padmakar.

Grant Duff : *Maratha Ka Itihas* translated by Kamlakar Tiwari, published by Itihas Praskahan Sansthan, Allahabad 1963.

Nana Phadnavis by Sriniwas Balaji Hardikar, published by National Publishing House, Delhi.

Gwalior Rajya Key Lekh.

MARATHI

Sardesai : *Historical Papers Relating to Mahadji Sindhia*, II ed., 1937.

Historical Papers of Sindhias of Gwalior published by Satara Historical Research Society, 2 Vols. (1934 and 1940).

Shinde : *Shahi Ithasanchi Sadhnen* ed. by A.B. Phalke Vol. I, 1742-67 (1929) II, 1738-1814 (1930) Vol. III, 1723-1802 (1937).

Selections From the Peshwa's Daftar, ed. by G.S. Sardesai 45 Vols (Relevant portions).

Thakur, Holkar : *Shahichaya Itihasanchi Sadhanen*, ed. B.B. Thakur, 2 Vols., 1944-45.

Marathi Riyasat by G.S. Sardesai, 8 Vols.

Khare : *Aitihasik Lekh Sangraha*, ed. by. V.V. Khare and Y.V. Khare 15 Vols., upto 1810.

Natu : *Mahadji Sindhia.*

Parasnis : *Life of Baiza Bai.*

Bhagwat : *Holkar-Shahi Patra-Byavhar*, ed. by A.N. Bhagwat, 3 Parts.

Dilli-Yethil Marathyanchi Raj Karnen ed. by D.V. Parasnis, Vols. I and II and supplement (1912-14).

K.N. Sane : *Holkaranchi Kaifyat* (1886).

Gulgule : *Records of Gulgule Family of Kotah.*

Hingane Daftar, Vols. I and II by Khare.

Aiti Patraviya : Atihasik Patra Ka Vyaihar, IInd ed. by Sardesai, Kale and Kulkarni.

Baroda Historical Selections from Baroda State Records, 10 Vols. and in English by Gensi and Banaji.

Rajwade V.K. *Marathancha Itihasanchi Sadhnen*, 22 Vols.

Ved and others : *Selection from Satara Raja and Peshwa's Diary* 15 Vols. (Including D.V. Parasnis supplement).

Atree M.M. *Malhar and Holkar Yanchi Charitra* (Poona 1813).

Nana Phadnavischi Charitra, Maharashtra Book Depot, Poona, 1902.

Khare Shastri Vasudev Vaman : *Itihasik Lekh Sangrah* 1-12, 1901-24.

Kara Shastri Vasudev Vaman : *Nana Phadnawis* Charitra III ed., 1967.

Dev Balkrishan Narain : *Nana Phadnavis*, 1904.

Dikhathar D.V. : *Sindheshahichi Raj Karnen Satara*, 1937.

Phadke Anad Rao Bhau : *Shindheshai Itihasihanchi Sandhan Gwalior*, 1929-34.

Rangreykar KM. : *Bhashan Bahadur Goeba Dada Karharyandhi Sanchipt Charitra*, 193.

(Marathi Material — a brief commentary)

A. Original Materials

Kavyaitahasa : *Sangraha* containing 501 detailed papers ed. by Kashinath Naryan Sane and Janardan Balaji Madhok and supported by Chiplonkar and Oak, Vol. VIII dealing with 1649 to 1817, compiled out of Gagan Varadekar Pant Amatiya's office and Vol. X, 1761-1817 A.D. was found invaluable.

Itihas Sangraha ed. by Duttareya Balwant Parasnais second part dealing with 1790-94 of Dilli Yethil — Marathyanchi Rajkarven and relating to 1784 Maheshwar Darbarchin Batani Patren — 1911 were useful.

Marathyanchya Itihansachi Sadhnen Patren Yadi, Wagre, published by Vishwanath Kashinath Rajiwade deals with early period 1750-1761 and gives glimpses of early background.

Atihasik Lokh Sangraha by Vasudeva Varman Shastri Khare deals particularly with South.

Adhikar Yoga deals with early period of the Maratha Politics in the South.

Atihasik Patra Vyauhar ed. by G.S. Sardesai, N.P. Kulkarni & Y.M. Kale 1933 are useful but deals with early period.

Atihasik Patren Yadi Wagre Lekh ed. by Sardesai Kale and Wahaskar IInd. ed. published in 1930 arranges paper in chronological order of scattered huge mass of Kayyati has a Sangraha and of Parsnais 246 papers Bharatwarsha 1898-1900 in collaboration of Harnarayan Apte supply valuable information of early period.

Sardesai : Selections from the Peshwa Daftar ed. by Sardesai and published by Bombay Government, 45 Vols. throw enough light on previous background.

Mahadaji Shindia Hyanchi Kagadpatren, ed. by G.S. Sardesai and published by Gwalior State December 1937, containing 608 Papers and deals with the period of 1774 to 1792 and are valuable for understanding the Maratha History and diplomacy of late 18th century.

Shindeshahi Itihasanchi Sadhnen ed. by Annand Rao Bhau Phalkon, 4 Vols., deal with an introduction by C.V. Vaidyas comprises of the true correspondence of the Shinde family preserved with the Gulgule, a Saraswat Brahmin family, originally belonging to South Konkan and placed by the Peshwas at Kotah as revenue collector under the order of Sindias. These Volumes contain 6000 to 10500 papers which deal with all details particularly with Mahadaji's relation with Rajputs. Vol. III, 1723-1802 published in 1937 and Vol. IV dealing with Balaji Lakshman Wakashar's correspondence is invaluable for early 19th century of the Maratha history. Introduction of all the four Volumes is illuminating.

Pethe Daftar by Bharat Itihasa Sansodhak Mandal Poona ed. by V.S. Chitale dealing letters of Trimback Rao Pethe, Vol. I & II is valuable for Poona Government of later 18th century.

Chandra Chuda Daftar ed. by Dattareys Vishu Apte published by Records Department Gwalior throws ample light on Holkar Sindia relations and Mahadaji's relations with the North.

Purandre Daftar ed. by Krishnaji Vasudeva Purandre, 3 Vols. by Bharat Itihas Sansodhak Mandal deals with early period.

Aithasik Samkirna Sahitya published by Bharat Itihas Sansodhak Mandal Poona, in a Magzine form, brings out useful documents, properly ed. by Potdar, Chandorkar, Kelkar, Oturkar and others is indispensible for all students of Maratha History.

PERSIAN

Delhi Chronicle : Sarkar Ms.

Mohan S. Waquai Holkar : Sarkar Ms.

Bhagwan Singh : *Life of Amir Khan*.

Munna Lal-Tarikh : *Shah Alam*, 1811, Bankipore Oriental Library M.N.S.J.M.S. copy. It is an account of Shah Alam II's reign from year to year 1760 to 1806.

Tarikh I Jagairdaran.

Tarikh I Maharajgan, 1. Gwalior.

Khair Uddin : *Ibarat Namah*, Vols. I, II and III, Bankipur Oriented Library M.S.J.N.S. copy. The work is voluminous. History written by influential officer of Shah Alam's son and an eye witness of many of the occurrences described by him.

FRENCH

De Boigne : *Memoire Sur La Carriere De D.V.* (Chanbery IInd ed. 1830) *B. Le General De Boigne Part V. St. Genis* (Poitiers, 1873).

Perron : *Le General Perron Para*, Martineau 1931.

Gentil M. : *Memories, Sur Plindoustan* (1822).

Martin F. : *Memories*, ed. by A. Martineau, 3 Vol. (Paris 1931-34).

Modave, Comte de : *Journal du Voyage du Bangala a Delhi*, (Paris ms.).

Anqueti du Perron : *Recheraches historiques et geographiques Sur 1 Inde*, Berlin.

Affairs de 1 Inde 1 Inde 2 torn Sondres, Paris, 1788.